Tobias Döring

Postcolonial Literatures in English

Klett Lernen und Wissen

Bildnachweis: S. 96: The British Library, London

Bibliographische Information der Deutschen Bibliothek
Die Deutsche Bibliothek verzeichnet diese Publikation in der Deutschen
Nationalbibliographie; detaillierte bibliographische Daten sind im Internet
über http://dnb.ddb.de abrufbar.

Auflage 4. 3. 2. 1. | 2011 2010 2009 2008
Die letzten Zahlen bezeichnen jeweils die Auflage und das Jahr des Druckes.
Dieses Werk folgt der reformierten Rechtschreibung und Zeichensetzung. Ausnahmen
bilden Texte, bei denen künstlerische, philologische oder lizenzrechtliche oder andere
Gründe einer Änderung entgegenstehen.
Internetadresse: www.klett.de/uniwissen
Satz: Kassler Grafik-Design, Leipzig
Druck: Druckerei Wirtz, Speyer
Printed in Germany.
ISBN: 978-3-12-939559-2

Table of Contents

1 Approaches _____ 5

    1 Why Postcolonialism? _____ 5
    2 Key Terms _____ 15
        1 "Postcolonial" _____ 16
        2 "Power" _____ 20
        3 "Resistance" _____ 24
        4 "Translation" _____ 27
        5 "Diaspora" _____ 30
        6 "Hybridity" _____ 34

2 Explorations _____ 38

    1 Historical _____ 38
        1 When did Postcolonial Studies begin? _____ 38
        2 When did Postcolonial Literatures begin? _____ 41
    2 Cultural _____ 45
        1 Writing Culture _____ 45
        2 Literacy vs. Orality _____ 48
    3 Critical _____ 51
        1 Frantz Fanon _____ 51
        2 Edward W. Said _____ 53
        3 Homi K. Bhabha _____ 55
        4 Gayatri C. Spivak _____ 58
        5 Stuart Hall _____ 61
    4 Textual _____ 63
        1 Life Writing _____ 65
        2 Place Writing _____ 70
        3 History Writing _____ 75
        4 Rewriting _____ 81
        5 Genre Writing _____ 88

3 Exemplifications _____ 93

    1 Focus on Irish Literature _____ 97
        1 Historical Survey _____ 99
            Chart: Some Dates in Irish History _____ 102
        2 Literary Paradigms _____ 103
            Chart: Some Irish Writers _____ 106
    2 Focus on African Literature _____ 108
        1 Historical Survey _____ 111
            Chart: Some Dates in African History _____ 114

2 Literary Paradigms ———————————————— 115
Chart: Some African Writers ———————————— 118
3 Focus on Indian Literature ———————————— 119
1 Historical Survey ———————————————— 123
Chart: Some Dates in Indian History ——————— 124
2 Literary Paradigms ———————————————— 128
Chart: Some Indian and South Asian Writers ——— 132
4 Focus on Australian Literature ————————— 134
1 Historical Survey ———————————————— 136
Chart: Some Dates in Australian History ———— 139
2 Literary Paradigms ———————————————— 140
Chart: Some Australian Writers ———————— 144
5 Focus on Caribbean Literature ————————— 145
1 Historical Survey ———————————————— 149
Chart: Some Dates in Caribbean History ———— 152
2 Literary Paradigms ———————————————— 153
Chart: Some Caribbean Writers ———————— 157
6 Focus on Black British Literature ————————— 158
1 Historical Survey ———————————————— 162
Chart: Some Dates in Black British History ——— 165
2 Literary Paradigms ———————————————— 166
Chart: Some Black British Writers ———————— 170

4 Differentiations ———————————————— 172

1 Sex and Gender: Transgressions ———————— 172
2 Text and Performance: Carnivalizations ———— 178
3 Books That Matter ———————————————— 183

Appendix ———————————————————— 188

Recommended Reading ———————————————— 188
Works Cited ———————————————————— 189
Index ————————————————————————— 194

1 Why Postcolonialism?

Students of literature often feel bothered by theory and the technicalities of academic reading. At one point, all of us decided to study literature because we were fascinated by the power of books and wanted to explore the ways their stories work and how they work on us. But in the course of studying, especially at an introductory level, students are often disappointed to find that "stories" seem to be the last thing that is of interest here. Instead, there are "structures" to be analysed, "contexts" to be dealt with, "figures" or "devices" to be learned and recognized; students are expected to apply "communication models", identify "discourses", "deconstruct" oppositions, pursue "intertextual traces", find "pretexts" or suspect "subtexts", i.e. to engage with so many different theoretical, sometimes rather abstract notions that the book they have been reading seems to disintegrate in the buzz of catchwords which surround it in the classroom and, even more so, in the critical studies about it. As a consequence, not just the pleasure but the interest in literature may well dwindle away. So to add yet another item to the critical vocabulary may well seem a dubious project. After trying to come to terms with complex concepts like "postmodernism" or "post-structuralism", why should we still bother with yet another term like this and now turn to "postcolonialism"?

The role of theory in literary studies: why bother?

As a matter of fact, this turn is not gratuitous. Postcolonialism does a great deal more than simply add something to an existing repertoire of theoretical notions or given critical procedures. It rather questions how such repertoires come about, how these procedures work and how they are worked with, in the classroom and beyond, thus urging us to reconsider our familiar ways of reading. Generally speaking, it is a serious misunderstanding (due perhaps to seriously unhelpful teachers) to think of theory as something outside or beyond the literary text. Such a view misjudges the complexity not just of literature but of all language. We surely need no expert knowledge of, say, syntactic theory to communicate or to produce syntactically well-formed sentences. But as researchers and students it is just this kind of knowledge that we seek. What we call "theory" is always already at work in language just as in literature, even if most speakers or readers are not usually aware of it. So our task in literary studies precisely lies in raising such an awareness and exploring what actually shapes or controls our usual methods

What theory does: relevant questions

to come to certain meanings: what are the ways in which we normally make sense of texts? What norm is involved here? What is it that a story means or does, under what conditions and to whom? Who are the authorities by whom the use of texts or the meaning of literature have historically been established? For what purpose? With what consequences? And how are such established meanings currently maintained?

The point of Postcolonial Studies

These are questioned raised and tackled, among others, in the field of postcolonialism just as in related fields of current critical theory. Etymologically, the word *theory* derives from the act of making visible, of bringing something to appearance. In this sense, literary theory in general is an enterprise to make us see and clearly formulate what otherwise goes without saying – and this means also: without seeing, thinking and reflecting – when dealing with texts and with literature. Postcolonial theory in particular sets out to make us see and think about the habits, notions, modes of meaning, ways of language and regimes of reading which have traditionally shaped the use of books especially in cross-cultural settings. As suggested by the word formation of the term, Post*colonial* Studies are centrally concerned with texts arising in some way from the social consequences or historical effects of colonialism, i. e. the powerful encounter between English and other cultures in the period of Empire, roughly between the late sixteenth and the twentieth century (see 2.1), still felt today in many cultural effects.

The field of postcolonial literatures in English

In fact, it is one of the strongest points of criticism raised against the term *postcolonial* that it takes colonialism as a point of reference and thus continues to imply imperial history even in present-day developments and cultures apparently long since moved beyond its grasp – a critique which must be carefully considered (see 1.2.1). But to speak of "postcolonial literatures in English", as in the title of this introduction, for most people generally means to speak about the global field of writing where literature is being produced and circulated in English, or some variety of English, but where a distinctly non-English cultural influence is at the same time at work in the text. In this sense, the field comprises the literatures of large parts of Africa, some parts of Asia, the Indian subcontinent, the New World of the Caribbean, just as of Australia, New Zealand, Canada and other countries formerly part of the British Empire.

Even this brief survey must at once suggest the enormously wide range of what we are looking at: a vast spectrum of texts and a great variety of authors, geographically as far apart as they are culturally diverse. Surely, the attempt to deal with them in any one consistent framework, let alone account for their specific backgrounds, their cultural agendas, their textual or literary strategies with a single set of critical terms, no matter how sophisticated, is ludicrous. Even with all optimism and good will, Postcolonial Studies could never answer this tall order – which is why, in recent decades, specialized disciplines like Canadian Studies, African Studies and Aboriginal Studies have established themselves to focus respectively on a particular country, geographical area or cultural context in greater detail. And yet, there is a case – indeed, a need – for Postcolonial Studies to take a broader view and address the fundamental issues raised above. For these questions concern not just the kind of writing produced in far-away and somehow ethnic and exotic places like Saskatchewan, Malawi or New South Wales. They are of central concern here and now, in English Studies and in all our engagements with any kind of literature, no matter where it comes from. This introductory book therefore sets out to show how postcolonial literatures explore the cultural use of meaning.

Is this field too large to study in a single framework?

Here is an example: what do we mean by an "African" writer and how do we understand "African" literature? The questions seem straightforward enough but are, in actual fact, quite difficult to answer. In the first place, centuries of slavery and plantation economy brought about large-scale violent displacements by which countless Africans were forcefully removed, mainly across the Atlantic to South and North America; later generations continued to live in the New World or possibly moved on to further places, often mixed with different people, local or themselves resettled, in some ways maintaining aspects of the cultural heritage once brought from African societies – for example, aspects of religious practice – in other ways adapting to the new locale and combining various strands from ancestral and adopted traditions. In the process they developed new and different cultural forms – for example, in the field of language – resulting from the history of these encounters and no longer necessarily resembling any of the elements that once went into their making. Should we then regard all writers of the African diaspora (as this socio-cultural setting is generally called, see 1.2.4), writers far removed from one another in space, in social circumstances and modes of expression, as part

A case in point: what is "African" literature?

of the same cultural field as writers who have always lived and worked in Africa? Is there anything they all share, by virtue of their ancestry or their experience, which might enable us to speak of "African" poetry with reference, say, to poets from Guyana, New York, London, Lagos, Dakar and Johannesburg?

Pan-Africanism: an answer from the early twentieth century

Since the twentieth century, this point has been vigorously debated. In 1900, the first Pan-African Conference was held in London, organized by Henry Sylvester Williams (1869–1911), a teacher and lawyer of African descent from Trinidad, a British colony in the West Indies, who went on to live in the US, in Britain and South Africa. And yet, Williams – like the activists he gathered – felt the need to assert Africanness as the defining element of contemporary identity. The point also arises with particular urgency whenever writing is collected for the purpose of anthologies. In 1948, the Senegalese poet (and later Senegalese president) Léopold Sédar Senghor (1906–2001), who had been studying and working in France since the early 1930s, edited the first African literary collection entitled *Anthologie de la nouvelle poésie nègre et malgache de langue français*, published in Paris with a preface by the French philosopher Jean-Paul Sartre. As the title indicates, the volume contains poems written in French and yet these are designated as *poésie nègre* on the basis of Senghor's view of pan-African connections that reach beyond any given place. More than half the texts included in his book are in fact by writers from the francophone Caribbean, such as his close associate Aimé Césaire (*1913) from Martinique. For him and Senghor and their intellectual circle set in Paris at the time, just as for Williams a generation earlier, the relevance of actual residence, cultural experience or even birth yielded to the relevance of African ancestry, even if many generations removed. So the issue of "African literature" is not easily resolved.

The colonial meaning of the adjective "African"

But there is a far more radical sense in which the term "African" writing has been challenged by postcolonial developments. Until the 1940s, i.e. the same decade in which the pioneering poetry collection first came out, it was common usage in English to construe the meaning of this adjective only on the basis of its object. An "African writer", in this traditional understanding, used to be a *European* writer who wrote *about* Africa, just as the phrase "African powers" used to refer to imperial powers like Britain or France with their long history of political control over large parts of Africa. In 1944, for instance, the novelist Joyce Cary, a very well-known and respected writer until the post-war period in England, published a historical tract in which he employed the adjective precisely in this sense (see Cary 1962: 120, 124). For him and his contemporaries it seems to have been inconceivable – strictly unspeakable – that any African could ever be the *subject* of literary production, let alone the agent of political power. Therefore, the phrase "African writer" functioned rather like "botanical writer", indicating an expert writing about some specimen of interest but clearly not expecting that this specimen could ever write back. This example serves to show what dramatic shifts in meaning have occurred, even to the point of dictionary definitions, with the historical shift from colonial to postcolonial perspectives. Postcolonial Studies are both a product of this shift and now an active agent to ensure its lasting force. They mean to question the semantics and change the uses of long familiar texts and terms.

The case just cited is particularly apt to illustrate how postcolonial perspectives turn a given view or attitude around and focus on the other side – the side of the other – that used to be positioned outside general attention. Joyce Cary (1888–1957) first made his reputation as a writer in the 1930s with a series of novels set in Western Africa and presenting a large cast of African protagonists. Some of these, like the titular hero of his novel *Mister Johnson* (1939), used to be singled out as remarkably sympathetic portraits of vivid and engaging human characters, in contrast to the clichéd views of an anonymous, black, faceless, savage crowd which pervades so much of previous colonial writing about Africans. As a basis for his fiction, Cary drew on personal observation from his time as an Assistant District Officer in the British administration of Northern Nigeria in the 1910s and, even in his later years in Oxford, he liked to think back to this early experience which, he felt, brought him close to many a native subject. And yet, the first generation of African writers – in the new, postcolonial meaning of this term – to emerge from Nigeria and come to international attention in the late 1950s were adamant that Cary's so-called "African" characters, sympathetic or not, mainly reveal his own colonial frame of mind, or rather, the framework of colonial culture in which he unquestionably lived and worked. The Nigerian writer Chinua Achebe (*1930), whose debut novel *Things Fall Apart* (1958) changed the course of African and world literature one year after Cary died, actually explained that he began to write in critical response to *Mister Johnson* so as to question the established English view and

Postcolonialism: a change of perspectives and semantics

look at African society "from the inside" (see Duerden/Pieterse 1972: 4).

Another case in point: English Romantic poetry

Postcolonial literatures, this goes to show, work to reverse common views, reposition our focus and perspective, revise established notions and redraw functional divisions between outsiders and insiders. Historically therefore they emerged most powerfully in the period after World War II, leading to the breaking-up of long established empires. However, important as this surely is, the foregoing examples refer to writing in or about Africa and so do not really show why or how any of these issues should concern us here and now, as claimed above, or affect our work in English literature and culture. Consider, then, another case: one of the best known and best loved English poems, William Wordsworth's "The Daffodils" (1807). A brief reading of its opening and closing stanza may suggest what postcolonial perspectives do to English Studies. The first stanza reads:

> I wandered lonely as a cloud
> That floats on high o'er vales and hills,
> When all at once I saw a crowd,
> A host of golden daffodils,
> Beside the lake, beneath the trees,
> Fluttering and dancing in the breeze.

Wordsworth's popular poem "The Daffodils"

A rightly celebrated piece of high Romantic writing, the poem goes on to highlight a harmonious relation between the poet-persona, i.e. the first person of the wanderer referred to in these lines, and the world of nature. Beholding this great "crowd" or "host" of wonderful spring flowers – "ten thousand saw I at a glance/ Tossing their heads in sprightly dance" – the poet-persona feels blissfully elated, his mood and spirits uplifted "in such a jocund company". With the fourth and final stanza, he reflects on this experience and draws some lasting comfort from it:

> For oft, when on my couch I lie
> In vacant or in pensive mood,
> They flash upon that inward eye
> Which is the bliss of solitude:
> And then my heart with pleasure fills,
> And dances with the daffodils.

This final focus on the "dance" of daffodils, vividly remembered and reviewed with the poet's "inward eye", emerges as the central image of the poem suggesting a sense of togetherness between the human and the natural spheres, a feeling of belonging and at-homeness, some meaningful correspondence expressed through the shared motion of dancing as if to the same tune. Over the course of the nineteenth century and beyond, Wordsworth's text has become one of the most popular and widely circulating poems in the language, the kind of text which generations of school children learned by heart and which is not just regarded as typifying the Romantic attitude to nature, but as indicating what is typically and quintessentially English.

As a result, the poem also featured prominently in the school curriculum of British colonies or dominions, aimed at training native subjects, from New Zealand via India or Africa to Canada, in the idioms and icons of their so-called mother country. In a 1993 collection of contemporary women's memories of their late-colonial education in the 1940s to '60s, the editors explain that "the narrative of Empire was constructed in terms of sameness" and specifically mention: "we could all recite Wordsworth's poem about daffodils and most of us celebrated Empire Day in our schools" (Chew/Rutherford 1993: v). But we need only ask what exactly Wordsworth's poem might have meant to school children, say, in India or Africa to understand where the fundamental problem lies with this imperial construction of "sameness". The Kenyan writer Ngũgĩ wa Thiong'o (*1938) once remarked how a schoolboy in colonial Kenya, who could impeccably recite the poem, actually thought that daffodils were little yellow animals that live at English lakesides. Such a misconception is entirely plausible, because the poem speaks of daffodils *as if* they were moving, dancing creatures. It is just our cultural knowledge telling us that daffodils are flowers, hence fixed in the ground, which transfers Wordsworth's description of them onto a metaphorical level. The central metaphor of the "dance" only works against a background of experience or knowledge, not necessarily shared in different cultural and natural settings where "daffodils" are as exotic as, for us, baobabs – a signifier without a signified in sight.

In such a context, instead of communicating a sense of home or homeliness, Wordsworth's poem clearly does the opposite: suggesting a sense of unbelonging, perhaps misrecognition or at least

"The Daffodils" in the British Empire: different readings

How and why this image of Englishness cannot be culturally translated

mismatch between the experiential and the literary level. The failing metaphor is interesting for several reasons. It shows that meaning has a local quality, because the construction of meaning differs in different localities, and that readings therefore change depending on the place of reading. Accordingly, if the Empire actually aimed to construct "sameness" by means of a curriculum that circulates the same literary repertoire far and wide throughout the world, this project is already undermined by the very circulation that was meant to implement it. The idioms and images of Englishness like the daffodils do not simply translate into foreign cultural contexts but are subjected to processes of re-interpretation – what we might call foreignization, as when daffodils are reinterpreted as animals – thus opening a field of cultural difference. But difference is productive whenever it is mobilized to question fixed constructions. It is this move that is crucial for a postcolonial perspective on established English literature because it prompts us to rethink what assumptions we hold and apply when trying to make sense of well-known texts, such as Wordsworth's poem.

Rereading Wordsworth's poem: how to control the crowd

We may, for instance, wonder how to understand the curious transition from the third to the fourth line of the poem (see the first stanza quoted on p. 10). "When all at once I saw a crowd,/A host of golden daffodils": in the context of a Romantic poem celebrating solitude, this observation of a crowd can hardly be good news. "Crowd" is a term with altogether ominous and threatening resonances in the early nineteenth century, the time of rising population numbers in the cities (especially in London), of revolutionary crowds (especially in Paris) or proletarian crowds in the industrial centres (especially Manchester). So it is interesting to note that the poem, with the fourth line, seems to revise this term and now speaks of "a host" of daffodils – an elevated, noble term with biblical echoes that might cover the unpleasant connotations of the first. Historically, crowds began to attract scientific thought in Britain at just this time. In 1798 Thomas Malthus published his *Essay on the Principles of Population* where he argued that the natural growth of populations always exceeds the growth of the natural resources they live by, so that their number must be checked through natural catastrophes or social engineering. This was later to become a key point for the theory of "natural selection" proposed by Darwin in his epoch-making *On the Origin of Species* (1859), introducing the disquieting notion of "the struggle for life". Darwin's notion can be seen as the reverse of the central metaphor in Wordsworth's poem: the "dance" imagines the relation between man and nature, not as antagonistic, but harmonious. But as we have seen, this understanding only works on a metaphorical basis. In actual fact, no one, not even the most Romantic reader, would believe that the poet-persona literally dances with the daffodils. Flowers are immobile, the crowd is under control. Yet this metaphor when read in foreign contexts fails, or rather does not cast its charm, so the central image of the poem turns into a moving, mobile crowd of animalistic creatures, swarming around the poet-persona – "ten thousand saw I at a glance" – threatening almost to overcrowd him. In this literal perspective, the "bliss of solitude" championed in the final stanza may rather arise from the acute anxiety of crowds, of the anonymous masses of modernity and urban life now taking over. In this changed view, Wordsworth's metaphorical image of the "dance" appears to be an effort at crowd control.

Surely this different reading of the poem suggested here is also rather questionable. But this is precisely the point. It serves to demonstrate the questionable nature of established readings, like the one summarized above, that assume stable and harmonious relations between, say, the Romantic figure of the poet and the natural world. It further serves to demonstrate the process of so-called "rereading" that is not just part of contemporary critical approaches broadly known as "deconstruction", but that specifically forms a central and a necessary strategy in Postcolonial Studies. We began by noting the essential difference arising from the understanding of the text in a different cultural place. But we went on – and this is crucial – to realize that this difference is not only something brought to this text from without; it is already at work in the text itself, as in the curious lexical revision of "crowd" to "host" between lines three and four of Wordsworth's poem. It is also at work in the central metaphor and so invites us to rethink what specific cultural meanings this "dance" draws on and what meanings it specifically resists. Metaphor is no ornamental device any text might do without, but a constitutive figure often linked to fundamental cultural structures in the way we understand the world. So to rethink the "metaphors we live by" – to cite the title of a relevant study (Lakoff/ Johnson 1980) – is a crucial way for postcolonialism to place the central texts a culture lives by into different perspectives. All this goes to illustrate the claim made earlier (p. 6) that Postcolonial Studies set out to make us see and think about the modes of

Questionable readings: the difference lies within

meaning, ways of language and regimes of reading which have traditionally shaped the use of texts.

A functional view: post-colonialism decentres and displaces the familiar

Trying to answer the main question raised in the chapter title, then, has led us to a different understanding of our central term. Post-colonialism does not simply refer to a historical period, nor to a geographical area, nor even to a set of given texts, a group of writers from a certain number of formerly colonized countries whose cultural products are all to be analysed by means of post-colonial theory. To be sure, postcolonialism is often used to do just this and widely taken to refer to the very things just listed. But in the *functional* understanding outlined here and explored further in the coming chapters, it is more helpful to define postcolonialism as a shift in critical perspective, resulting in decentred or displaced views of familiar texts and books. Not so much a set of clear-cut notions than a repertoire of practices and critical approaches, post-colonialism in this sense involves certain ways of reading, strategies and procedures by which the study of literature gains new relevance. As the examples discussed show, these strategies affect the meaning of individual words – such as the adjective "African" – they change the understanding of representative texts and their central metaphors – such as the Wordsworth poem – and they question the construction of cultural self-representations – such as the notion of Englishness and its dissemination in the world. This is why postcolonialism matters and why it should matter to us, whenever we engage in English literary and cultural studies.

SUMMARY

This chapter has

► raised questions about the use of critical theory
► argued for the need for postcolonial theory as a critical practice
► surveyed a geographical field for Postcolonial Studies, comprising the various countries once under colonial rule
► marked a historical period for Postcolonial Studies, beginning with literary projects in the late 1940s and 1950s that countered outside views and texts
► problematized this geographical and historical basis for defining the term
► offered a functional understanding of postcolonialism as a way of reading

2   Key Terms

Critical theory and practice generally begin by formulating a specific idiom and demonstrating how to engage its terms in arguments. To cite a prominent example, when Sigmund Freud began to formulate his psychoanalytic theory around 1900, his main work was to find conceptual means and linguistic terms to render the manifestations of the unconscious he set out to explore in some critical, conscious language. In central ways, then, any new theory constitutes both itself and the phenomena it wants to study by means of naming. The new critical language – or meta-language, as we should properly call it – is not necessarily new in the sense that all its lexical items are neologisms, i.e. words in the vocabulary coined especially for this one and only purpose; more often it develops in the process of using old words in different ways, often giving former meanings a particular twist and turn, sometimes even turning them around.

New theories define "new" terms

Postcolonialism follows this general pattern. Over recent decades, a set of terms and concepts have become more or less closely associated with postcolonial literature and criticism, familiarized through usage in professional contexts, books and journals, conferences and other academic ventures. To use a crude analogy, these terms are like the tools by which postcolonial readers, writers, critics, students do their work. Yet few items in their tool box are exclusive and even fewer are – we have to face it – uncontentious. In fact, most of the critical debates and vigorous discussions in and about the field concern precisely the question of what terms are appropriate – under what conditions? for whom? – when trying to address major postcolonial issues. Anyone who ever followed such debates, especially anyone not really part of them, may well feel they are fruitless quibbles over words, signifying nothing. But they are not. The terms we use, the words we work with and the concepts we apply are never innocent. They constitute not just the field under discussion, but determine the approaches taken to this field, the questions raised about it and the insights to be gained. If theories generally begin by naming, postcolonial theory begins with the awareness that names are never natural but always imposed, hence that naming is an act of power.

In postcolonial terms: naming is an act of power

This is why the key terms introduced and briefly discussed in this chapter would all require more consideration. We need them, but we need to be aware of their potentially contentious character. A simple glossary is therefore not enough. The following comments rather try, together with the word field and conceptual network introduced, to give an outline of the sort of issues each term is meant to address and of the sort of issues each term in the first place serves to raise. For this is where the crude analogy between "terms" and "tools" must end: tools, like a hammer or a saw, simply answer to a job which exists before them, like fixing or cutting, and which they are designed to do. Critical terms, by contrast, often actually create the job and must first define the work which they then set out to perform. Without them, we could not even start to think or talk about the issue which they bring up or bring about. This is the reason why debates about critical terminology are actually debates about the question of what should be at stake. With this in mind, let us look at some terminological fields in Postcolonial Studies.

1 "Postcolonial"

The Empire Writes Back: defining "post-colonial"

This defining and, one might assume, quite basic term has occasioned a great deal of criticism and is, in fact, quite often principally problematized if not downright rejected. The reasons for this become clearer when we look at its history. It came to prominence, much later than the field it now serves to describe, in 1989 with the publication of a little green book by three Australian critics, Bill Ashcroft, Gareth Griffiths and Helen Tiffin, entitled *The Empire Writes Back: Theory and Practice in Post-Colonial Literatures*. In this textbook, which has since gone through several editions and still serves as a recommended introduction, the authors offered a comprehensive critical approach to contemporary writing from countries once part of the British Empire, an approach *not* based primarily on regional characteristics nor on cultural features particular to each place and its local or indigenous traditions, but on the overarching political structures in which all such writing, they claimed, is positioned as a result of colonial history. It is this structure that they called "post-colonial" and that they thought manifested in the crucial relation between the metropolitan centre, i.e. the mother country and its capital London, and the so-called periphery, i.e. places like Australia which used to be seen, and used to see themselves, principally in relation to this centre, traditionally deriving all their standards, norms and values from it.

It is this way of seeing and the fundamental sense of being in some way derivative or secondary in relation to the "centre" that has been radically questioned with the move to "post-colonial" views, a determined turn against given authorities and their defining power. As Ashcroft, Griffiths and Tiffin argued in their seminal definition of the term: "We use the term 'post-colonial', however, to cover all the culture affected by the imperial process from the moment of colonization to the present day. This is because there is a continuity of preoccupations throughout the historical process initiated by European imperial aggression. [...] So the literatures of African countries, Australia, Bangladesh, Canada, Caribbean countries, India, Malaysia, Malta, New Zealand, Pakistan, Singapore, South Pacific Island countries, and Sri Lanka are all post-colonial literatures. [...] What each of these literatures has in common beyond their special and distinctive regional characteristics is that they emerged in their present form out of the experience of colonization and asserted themselves by foregrounding the tension with the imperial power, and by emphasizing their differences from the assumptions of the imperial centre. It is this which makes them distinctively post-colonial." (1989: 2) As these explanations show, their usage of the term (1) emphasizes the commonalities among the literatures from these different places, a common heritage of prominent concerns and strategies shared by virtue of their shared peripheral position. At the same time, their usage (2) emphasizes the antagonistic stance towards the centre whose dominance and communication privileges are acknowledged but no longer accepted.

This leads them to analyse the cultural development from colonial to postcolonial conditions as a movement in three stages: **assimilation, abrogation, appropriation**. In the first place, a settler colony derives all its ideas and standards from the imperial mother country whose cultural forms it tries to assimilate and reproduce (stage one). Nature poetry, for instance, by white eighteenth-century writers who lived on West Indian islands, emulates the neo-classical idiom of English writing of the time and depicts plantation life in bucolic terms, just like English rural poetry at that time. But historically there is a point when such an imitative attitude no longer works and cultural nationalists feel the need to define their own standards of expression, thus abrogating the continued influence of imported models (stage two). For instance, black Caribbean writers like Edward Kamau Brathwaite (*1930) have programmatically turned to Africa as a source of inspiration so as to develop entirely non-English forms and rhythms for their poetry. And yet, many of these texts continue to engage linguistically and culturally with aspects of the heritage that once derived from England and the Empire; the very fact, for instance, that African cultures have long established such a strong presence in the Caribbean islands along with European models is of course due to the history of slavery. To use such aspects from colonial history and heritage, but use them creatively and differently, subjecting them to new approaches and radical redefinitions – this is a strategy that appropriates the legacies of the past for present purposes (stage three). It is with such appropriations that Ashcroft, Griffiths and Tiffin see postcolonial literatures come into their own.

From striking back to writing back

This is what the title of their book expressed so tellingly with a quotation from the Indian writer Salman Rushdie: "The Empire writes back to the Center..." (epigraph). Rushdie's quip, wittily drawing on the 1982 Star Wars film *The Empire Strikes Back*, points to a change in the communication structures that corresponds precisely to the changed meaning of the phrase "African writer" discussed above (see 1.1): a reversal of the agency and direction of writing. Traditionally, the so-called periphery, i.e. colonial countries like India, Australia or Africa were only ever written *about* – in travelogues, administrative prose, fiction, letters and so on – sometimes in consequence of the simple fact that the cultural technique of writing was traditionally not practiced in many non-European, predominantly oral cultures, but more often in consequence of the fundamental attitude that the privilege of writing was to be shared only among those who had anything worthwhile to say, i.e. colonial masters. Writing "back" thus means to move against the dominant direction in this former one-way street of writing and to undermine its conceptual foundation – a process which Ashcroft, Griffiths and Tiffin described as "subversion" and saw as an "inevitable tendency" in postcolonial literatures (Ashcroft et al 1989: 33). All this, they emphasized (3), required an umbrella term to analyse the cultural traffic, not just in the 1960s period of political decolonization, but from the "moment of colonization to the present day".

Criticism of this definition: too broad, too biased, too unspecific

Criticism and rebuttals targeted against their term have been profuse and sometimes very harsh. They can be summarized with the following sceptical questions, most of which recur in some form or another in the relevant debates:

▶ should we risk such broad generalizations about the literatures from so many different places?

▶ what is it that these countries (alphabetically listed in the above quotation) actually have in common, beside their once imperial connection?

▶ what is it that their literatures might share, beside the fact that they are mainly (though not exclusively) produced in varieties of English?

▶ how can "subversion" be inevitable and ongoing in these literatures when the imperial structures which should be subverted are long dated?

▶ should postcolonial literatures, at some point in their history, not cease to "write back" to the centre, because this centre is no longer relevant? Should they then be renamed or repositioned in another theoretical framework?

▶ should we not seek more neutral, simply descriptive designations of the field, rather than employ a term already shaped by such a methodological approach?

▶ is it not ironic and deeply inappropriate when a theory so clearly critical of the imperial world order nevertheless perpetuates the basis of this order by virtue of its terminology?

This last question is revealing. It suggests that the notion of the "post-colonial" can never get beyond the defining power of the colonial "centre" which it otherwise spends so much time resisting and subverting. On the other hand, in our critical vocabulary we are long familiar with the equally puzzling case of other "post"-terms, such as "postmodern" or "post-structural", which have the same problem. The Canadian critic Linda Hutcheon once described it as "a contradictory dependence on and independence from that which temporarily preceded it and literally made it possible" (1988: 17-18). We could rather see it as a critical strength of "post"-terms that they signal their own history and constantly remind us of the acute tension between the different historical determinations that define them. With regard to our case, however, it is crucial to acknowledge that the temporal notion in "postcolonial" – as if referring to some recent period in history after the colonial period – is definitely superseded by the political emphasis on difference: the difference between normative and subversive, dominant and dominated, central and decentred modes of articulation. That is to say, in literary and cultural studies (though not, confusingly, in historical studies) the term "postcolonial" is not

The problem
and power
of the prefix
"post-"

19

used for chronology. It rather offers a particular take on literatures produced, received and circulated under some form of manifest political power, which it works on and works against by cultural means. In this functional understanding, the term is not limited nor limiting in time – although it also loses the clear boundaries it would have in the periodic sense.

Alternative names for the field

However wary we may be of "postcolonial", we cannot deny that the term has very widely been adopted, with no serious alternative in use. Almost twenty years after Ashcroft's definition, "postcolonial" now serves as a label for publishers, academic posts and classes, conferences, programmes and the like. Internationally it has fully supplanted the old term "Commonwealth literature", which had been used from the 1960s to '80s to talk about roughly the same corpus of writing, but which was equally under attack or suspicion for perpetuating outworn political structures. The only alternatives currently available are local. In French academia the phrase "littérature contemporaine d'expression anglaise", in German academia the phrases "New English Literatures" or "New Literatures in English" are often used and sometimes championed as alternatives to signify critical distance to the "writing back"-model and to suggest a more descriptive term. But none of these phrases are particularly catchy nor are they internationally understood. Besides, they have been seen as problematic for their emphasis on newness and contemporaneity which seems to ignore the fact that much of the writing supposedly covered by it is, by now, actually rather old (see 2.1.2). All this serves to show how the difficulties of naming the field, of finding appropriate cover terms that do not imply inappropriate histories or politics, at once lead us right into it.

2 "Power"

The framework of politics

As the foregoing comments have made clear, the terminological issue involves power issues, not only because naming is an act of power but also because power is at work in all the situations, texts and contexts that are to be named. In contrast to terms such as "Neo-Classic" or "Romantic" which derive, however mediated, from cultural and aesthetic spheres, "colonial" and "postcolonial" evidently derive from the sphere of politics and therefore challenge us to place our engagements with literary and aesthetic products in frameworks of power.

As a matter of fact, aesthetic principles or so-called purely literary arguments in view of postcolonial literatures have often been regarded with suspicion, because they often involve value judgements by whose standards these literatures were judged insufficient, lacking sophistication, artistry or simply taste. As long as, for example, the aesthetics of the modern novel were thought to be exclusively upheld and defined by Western European literature – or, to be precise, in a small élite segment of this literature – it was easy to dismiss any novel from the West Indies as inferior unless it conformed closely to this model (and even then, the imitation was more easily dismissed simply because it was judged imitative of the original). No doubt, such views can be dismantled as "eurocentric" – i.e. blind to alternative traditions of story-telling, different models and other aesthetic principles at work, for instance, in West Indian literature – and no doubt they have become rare in recent decades, due precisely to the recognition that aesthetic judgements also involve politics. As a consequence, however, should any novel by a writer suffering somewhere under some form of oppression, discrimination or social disadvantage be hailed as a significant achievement and therefore celebrated without attention to points of style, rhetoric, aesthetic and artistic features? Aesthetic rules, such questions show, are also rules of power. What, then, do we understand by this?

Aesthetic issues are also political issues

There are situations where power seems to be immediately, almost visibly, manifest. To cite a stark case, think of plantations in eighteenth-century Caribbean islands where a tiny population of white masters made enormous profits from keeping a vast population of black labourers under control. The whip of the slave driver here serves as an unambiguous image of power, concentrating physical violence, class oppression, colonial dominance and economic exploitation all in one. The case is highly relevant for postcolonial literatures and cultures, not only from the Caribbean, because many consequences of the plantation economy and its social confrontations are still at work today – for example, in many creole varieties of language and in many forms of creolized or hybrid modes of cultural expression (see 1.2.6). But other forms of power are just as relevant, even if they are not immediately visible or observable in direct ways. The example in the previous paragraph, referring to the question of aesthetic judgement, was to illustrate this point: there is power also in the ways of talking, thinking, judging; there is power in the concepts and norms used, power in

Beyond the whip: a broader understanding of power

their modes of circulation and enforcement; there is power in the choice of reading lists in university curriculums, power in their terms of inclusion and exclusion; there is power in the cultural notions about sex, sexuality and body functions; in short, power is at work in all acts of communication and representation.

Michel Foucault's analysis of power

This notion of power, crucial for contemporary critical studies in general and for Postcolonial Studies in particular, derives from the work of Michel Foucault (1926–1980), a French historian, philosopher and political thinker who was not at all concerned with developments in Third World countries – in fact, hardly with any developments outside France – yet whose arguments about the functional structures of modern societies have become invaluable. His view of power is helpfully summarized in the following comments by the socio-linguist Norman Fairclough: "The view of the nature of power in modern societies which Foucault develops [...] places discourse and language at the heart of social practices and processes. The character of power in modern societies is tied to problems of managing populations. Power is implicit within everyday social practices which are pervasively distributed at every level in all domains of social life, and are constantly engaged in" (1992: 49). This suggests that "power" should not be understood as a matter of physical violence only but of language, of everyday practices, routine business and habits we no longer think about – but which all bear serious thinking and reconsideration because none of them are historically unchanging nor without alternative.

Foucault's concept of discourse and of micro-politics

In Fairclough's summary as in Foucault's theory, the term "discourse" signifies this combination of the linguistic and pragmatic means of power by which social control is enacted. Most of the time, we may not be aware of it. Especially the so-called modern Western subject likes to think of itself to be fully in control or "autonomous", as the favourite term has it. It can be argued, though, that this notion of autonomy, typically formulated first in the aesthetic sphere and championed as a principle of artistic creation, is a form of either self-delusion or delusion. In the bourgeois attitude to art, autonomy is upheld to cover an uncontrollable reality, that is to say, to compensate or hide the fact that we are powerfully governed from outside precisely in the spheres we like to see as our most intimate, private, treasured, individual spheres of creativity. For as Foucault explained in his *History of Sexuality*, the power he identified in discourse "is tolerable only on condition that it mask a substantial part of itself. Its success is proportional to its ability to hide its own mechanisms." (1981: 86) This strategy of "masking" is crucial to understand the unobtrusive, unspectacular character of power that makes it all the more effective. It is not all to do with cracking whips and locking chains. As Fairclough continues in his summary, "power does not work negatively by forcefully dominating those who are subjects to it; it incorporates them, and is 'productive' in the sense that it shapes and 'retools' them to fit in with its needs. Modern power was not imposed from above by particular collective agents (e.g. classes) upon groups or individuals; it developed 'from below' in certain 'microtechniques'". (1992: 50) That is to say, we are not looking at some sort of conspiracy by which dark powers secretly place us under their rule, but at the process of regulation and regimentation by which social order comes to pass.

This understanding of power has prompted many analyses of what is called "**colonial discourse**" (see Barker/ Hulme/Iverson 1994) or the "**rhetoric of empire**" (see Spurr 1993), i.e. investigations into the figures of speech and structures of thought by which imperial world views were constructed as a basis for imperial projects. Since "discourse" is a pragmatic concept that combines language with action, its analysis reveals how specific ways of speaking, for example about plantation labourers, license specific acts to be committed to them. But since the power of discourse, as Foucault argues, usually "masks" its mechanisms, it must be identified also in unlikely contexts, apparently far removed from the actual field. The nineteenth-century English novel, for example, has been seen as helping to normalize an imperial world view, placing England at the centre of attention and using the colonial periphery as a kind of backstage area. Characters no longer needed for the plot may be removed there and made to reappear at crucial points, such as the convict Magwitch in Dickens's *Great Expectations* (1861); or entire settings like the English country estate may have their economic basis in this colonial backstage space, such as the West Indian plantations of the Bertram family in Jane Austen's *Mansfield Park* (1814), never focussed on but always drawn on in its social discourse. Thus, the notion of domestic space, dependent on this foreign outside space, is constructed and circulated with these novels precisely by keeping colonial issues in the background. It would be pointless to accuse novelists like Dickens or Austen of "having" or "showing" an imperial attitude, just as it is trivial to point out how common

Uses of Foucault's concepts in colonial discourse analysis

such an attitude historically was. The point is rather to acknowledge that even literary texts apparently quite unconcerned with Britain's colonial ventures can participate in colonial discourse, working to familiarize its power.

3   "Resistance"

Resistance and rebellion: historical examples

This is another key term used in Postcolonial Studies as the result of transfers from the field of politics. Usually we talk about "resistance", for example, in the context of the European dictatorships of the 1930s and '40s. In colonial history, too, acts of political resistance continuously accompanied and often countered the attempts to impose power onto a foreign place and to establish there some form of stable structure that would keep local populations at bay. Many of these acts may not have gained much attention and receive no mention in familiar history books, because it surely would be in the interest of the powerful to silence all resistance and keep it off the record. But some cases of anti-colonial rebellion came to spectacular prominence and caused tremendous outrage or, alternatively, admiration, like the Haitian revolution led by Touissant L'Ouverture in the 1790s, i.e. the first large-scale slave insurrection that led to the overthrow of French rule on Saint-Domingue, or the so-called "Indian Mutiny" of 1857 or many other violent confrontations in the colonial wars in Africa and elsewhere. Later these became important points of reference for the organized resistance movements against colonial power structures, such as the African National Congress in South Africa or the Congress Party in India, and helped define the political process in the twentieth century by which, eventually, independence has been "given" to most countries. But with regard to literary and cultural studies, we have to ask how "resistance" could potentially be identified in symbolic fields, i.e., how the term could be transferred from politics to textual and discursive strategies.

Discursive politics: resistance movements follow from the power they oppose

This is, indeed, a central claim made in the definition of "postcolonial" discussed above (see 1.2.1). To understand it, we should first acknowledge that many such political resistance movements made their case with recourse to the rhetoric of nationhood and nationalism, as formulated and propagated in nineteenth-century European discourse, even if this might seem to have no real basis for their case. That is to say, to counter their colonial masters they employed forms and terms partly taken from these masters. In Western Afri-

ca, for example, there surely was a long history of ancient kingdoms and political cultures (largely ignored by colonial explorers
and administrators), but the administrative structures established
in the course of Victorian colonial rule, the boundaries drawn on
the map and the borders imposed on the land were entirely for the
convenience and liking of the rulers, with no regard to local realities. The very name "Nigeria" was actually first suggested in the
London *Times*, as a convenient label to cover the amalgamation in
1914 of two British protectorates at the river Niger (this river, of
course, also bears a colonial name, derived from the Latin word for
'black'). And yet, with the rise of West African resistance movements in the 1930s, this name was turned into a badge for Nigerian
nationalism, a broad formation that increasingly identified its
cause with the administrative entity, literally a cartographic sign,
formerly created by colonial officials but now to be wrested from
their domination (see the comments on map-making in 3). The
example shows how acts of resistance actually follow from the
power they oppose.

The same scenario holds for earlier cases, such as missionary
projects in the ninenteenth century, targeted at introducing literacy
to the natives and teaching them the Bible. These missions began by
establishing a model of power – such as the holy books – to be
learned, adopted and internalized by the local population, in the
process often alienating people from their own culture, degrading
their traditions and disparaging indigenous religious practices. But
missionary power frequently ended with the former pupils taking
up the book and looking for themselves what it may have to say.
"Ethiopia shall soon strech out her hands unto God": this line from
Psalm 68, for instance, suggested to African readers trained in
missionary schools that they should strive to establish their own
Christian church, beyond European control, and so led in the
1870s to the formation of "Ethiopianism", a broad resistance
movement with strong political repercussions. This shows that
power, in the very process of establishing and propagating itself, at
the same time produces the conditions for resisting and, potentially,
overturning its effects. And this is where the term "resistance" can
be applied also in the symbolic spheres like literature.

**Another
example:
missionary
discourse and
resistance**

Such a process by which oppositional forces emerge from within
established power structures and begin to redefine or re-employ
their mechanisms, is usefully described as "**counter-discourse**": the

Counter-dicourse as resistance: manipulating the signs

term signals that not only the causes but also the means of resistance are provided by established powers. Yet to fight this cause, the means are taken up in different, unconventional, unexpected ways and so, instead of endorsing the discursive structures, are now used to manipulate their elements, appropriate their signs and ultimately change them. This concerns, above all, the means of language, including literacy and textuality, as in the case of missionary pupils eventually taking up the Bible to suggest their own interpretation. But since the concept of discourse, as introduced by Foucault (see 1.2.2), combines language and action, these linguistic or symbolic means directly bear on the political. To be sure, none of this is exclusive for colonial and postcolonial domains. In fact, a central study of this process, entitled *Discourse/Counter-Discourse*, is concerned with the symbolic strategies of resistance explored in nineteenth-century French fiction (Terdiman 1985) where upwardly mobile protagonists make their way into society by learning to take on the code of the élites while also learning to manipulate its signs. Such narratives of education also feature prominently in postcolonial writing where, in the same way, the socially established discourse is countered through the subjects it tries to incorporate but thereby endows them with the means to resist its power.

Masking, acting, camouflage: hidden resistance

In this view, the practice of domination looks rather more precarious than it might first appear. Indeed, colonial power constellations, like the Raj, i.e. British rule in India, principally appear as shaky, unlikely and extremely risky ventures: a tiny white élite of so-called Sahibs, unused to climate and local conditions, trying to govern a vast country with a huge population, whose languages, customs and habits are poorly understood, let alone mastered. Therefore, administrative structures could only be maintained with the help of local élites or so-called native functionaries, who mediated the commands and passed on orders and, by doing so, might also interfere with them. So, whereas in terms of colonial hierarchies, the Sahibs are of course on top, in terms of ground realities, subsistance and survival, power relations might be very different and oppositional strategies more wide-spread than often noticed. If power, as Foucault argued, hides and masks itself, so does resistance. It would even be the most effective form of resistance that takes place outside the master's view while it keeps up the appearance of submission, for instance by acting openly according to colonial preconceptions – such as the cliché of the child-like, lazy native – while at the same time acting elsewhere according to another script. Here the notion of theatrical performance is helpful: if practices of social dominance set up a stage, an area of observation and surveillance that regulates all interaction between the masters and their servants, the servants may well play this role for their masters' eyes and, in a backstage area outside the controlling gaze, still perform quite differently. J.D. Scott, a social anthropologist who studied such examples, speaks of "the arts of resistance" and "**hidden transcripts**" (Scott 1990), thus suggesting constitutive uses of aesthetic practices – like theatre and literature – in the political domain. As with the concept of counter-discourse, their point lies in the strategy to turn the instrument of domination against those who use it in the first place: the practice of resistance can shield its space by means of conformity.

The relationship between power and resistance, masters and slaves, colonizers and colonized thus turns out to be a lot more complex. As soon as we begin to focus on the intricate dynamics by which power manifests itself, the binaries begin to blur and the hierarchies to shake or crumble. This is not to deny the all-pervasive violence enacted with colonial rule and counter-acted in the often bloody wars of liberation and resistance. But it is to remind us that even here are other levels to consider, levels of discourse and social interaction, where things might look different. Postcolonial Studies, in this sense, ultimately aims to show that stable notions of colonial dominance are, fundamentally, groundless.

Domination is often unstable and mastery precarious

4 "Translation"

This term denotes, of course, one of the first and foremost operations in the field of literature. In the traditional, philological sense, translation is the key to what all students of foreign languages are meant to do. In the old tradition of scholarship in the humanities the relevant texts to translate were, of course, mainly Greek or Latin. Even when, roughly in the fourteenth century, European vernaculars had begun to establish themselves as languages of serious literature, Latin long remained the language of learning, providing the model and setting the terms for all kinds of high-prestige cultural projects. This situation where different cultural domains – formal vs. informal, elite vs. common, educated vs. popular domains – exist in a hierarchical relation and are maintained by means of different languages is known as diglossia, a situation prevalent in Western Europe well into the early modern period. As the philo-

Historical and traditional views of translation

logist E.R. Curtius once argued in a famous study (1948), the Latin models continued to exert their influence on vernacular writing, especially through rhetorical devices such as topoi, i.e. the formulas and images of literary expression, which Latin provided and which were taken up and translated into the various European literatures. By means of such translation processes, the different vernaculars remained connected through a shared literary repertoire, evident in their rhetorical structure, which testified to the lasting cultural impact of Latin literature even though the Roman Empire, whence this repertoire derived, was no longer extant. In this model, translation is the cultural means to manifest connectedness and continuity.

From the Roman to the British Empire

This historical model suggests intriguing analogies to the twentieth-century situation where, with the break-up of the British Empire, many new fields of literary activity have come about world-wide, fields which continue to use elements of English literature, translating some of them into indigenous languages and confronting all of them with alternative vernacular traditions. Such analogies between the cultural after-lives of the British with the Roman Empire have, at any rate, been pursued by some critics or writers like Edward Kamau Brathwaite (1984). And indeed, most would agree that postcolonial writing, in whatever place, engages in many ways with issues of translation simply because the cultural contexts where it operates are rarely monolingual and often characterized by diglossic structures. But, general reservations against historical analogies aside, we need not see translation processes as enacting and confirming only continuity. This was the particular view taken by humanists and philologists like Curtius eager to emphasize, or reconstruct, the classical heritage to be shared, upheld and perpetuated in times of threatening diversity. Translation may well help to do so – and yet it also works, on the contrary, to emphasize diversity and to enforce cultural difference. It all depends on the particular strategies enacted in translation processes, often difficult to control. This suggests why and how translation also denotes one of the foremost operations in Postcolonial Studies.

A different view: foreignizing translation

Principally, it has been argued, a translator can pursue two opposing strategies (see Venuti 1995): he or she can either try to domesticate the foreign text, making it look and sound as if it had been written in the target language (i.e. in the language of the translation), thus aiming to erase all traces of the very process of translation; or, conversely, he or she can try to highlight this process and point up the cultural difference which it mediates, i.e. show in the vocabulary and structure of the translated text that we are actually dealing with a piece of foreign writing – whose meaning has partially been reconstructed, partially perhaps been lost, but which has partially also changed the modes of meaning *within* the target language. This latter point is crucial: translation can help to "foreignize" the language into which it leads. By reaching out into another linguistic field, transferring elements from other cultural grounds and transforming categorically different concepts, translation does not just enrich or enlarge the frame of reference in the target language, but can also confront it radically with alternatives, reframe its lexical and, possibly, syntactic repertoires, thus generally defamiliarizing old and established ways of speaking. In this view, translation works as an act of exposure and destabilization, an act from which neither of the codes involved comes out unchanged. Its relevance for postcolonial literatures in English is clear: even if many writers work with a cultural and often linguistic background that is not English, their writing uses a variety of English as its main code. But precisely because this code here serves as the target language of some cultural translation, it cannot remain the same, unscathed or unaffected by the foreignizing process. Instead, it is displaced and dispossessed of former dominance.

In translation theory, the strategies of domestication versus foreignization stand for a major opposition. In practice, however, the two are sometimes difficult to tell apart and often difficult to be quite sure about. Any given case would have to be carefully considered in these terms: does a given translation foreignize or domesticate the source text and the target language? And who is in a position to decide this? Surely someone who must have specific competence in both languages, i.e. another translator and go-between who mediates the various sides and codes and could negotiate or judge their difference and potential changes. Yet go-betweens are often seen as doubtful figures, uncertain in their loyalties, suspected of double-dealing and even treachery. In this sense a famous quip, based on the Italian pun *traduttore/traditore*, ironically declares that "translators are traitors". Such a notion simply follows from their intermediary position between given languages and parties, a position of strategic power but also of political ambivalence, a position situated in a precarious, interstitial space of in-between-ness, belonging neither to the one side nor the other. And yet this space can only be defined with reference to the

Contact zones: the working space of go-betweens

tension between the two spaces bordering on either side which are not really part of it. In concrete terms, such borderlands have very prominent and powerful referents, usually highly policed, in international politics, for instance at the Mexican–U.S. border. In postcolonial theory, meanwhile, such notions have developed into central terms like "**third space**" (Bhabha 1994, see 2.3.3) – in the more abstract, discursive sense of a space beyond the given binaries – or "**contact zones**" (Pratt 1992) – in the more immediate sense of cross-cultural encounters and transactions in the field.

Uses of the prefix "trans-"

While these postcolonial terms are rather versatile and often puzzling in their theoretical potentials, it is important to remember that they strictly derive from the dynamics of translation, as sketched above, and thus from age-old principles and practices of cultural work. Translation thus emerges as a centrally operative concept. It could account for the constitutive tension, noted earlier (1.2.1), between the two parts of the term "post/colonial". Just as it accounts for the prevalence of other terms in the field with the prefix "trans-", like "**transnational**" and "**transcultural**", used to describe the same kind of foreignizing dynamics. This is where they differ from the previously established terms "international" and "intercultural": they do not focus on the links between two given entities – nations, cultures – assuming that these entities essentially remain the same; they rather presuppose border transgressions and constitutive transformations to take place all along and they explore the productive instabilities, fluidities and conflicts *within* such entities – nations, cultures – which render all political attempts to draw a rigid boundary around them questionable. In this way, the cultural politics of translation engage with **transculturation** and respond critically to so-called identity politics that maintain, for whatever valid reason, rigorously defined markers of identification.

5   "Diaspora"

The Jewish history of scattering and cultural memory

This term, which literally means 'scattering' or 'dispersal', is traditionally used with reference to Jewish history where it describes the experience, predominant at least since the destruction of the temple in Jerusalem in 133 A.D., of living outside the Holy Land: in foreign countries, with sometimes hostile host societies and often under acute forms of oppression. In such diverse conditions, to keep up elements which define a distinctly Jewish way of life – through rituals, prayers, language, dietary rules or clothing – requires extraordinary determination and the strong awareness that the current place of residence is just a stage in transit, a provisional abode before returning to the true homeland. And yet it is just such an attitude that has maintained Jewish communities through centuries of migration, wandering and violent persecution, by keeping alive cultural memories of their real place, beyond present predicaments, and by cultivating practices to mediate these memories to coming generations. In this wider sense, the term "diaspora" has proved extremely useful also in Postcolonial Studies where, as in the case of Jews historically spread around the world, we often look at situations of displacement, of people forced or attracted to leave their homes, now trying to cope under adverse circumstances. Especially in view of African experience, diaspora has become a central notion when defining black identity.

There is more than one way in which the language of black self-description has drawn on Jewish history. For example, the period of Babylonian captivity or exile, as recounted in the Bible in the books of Jeremiah, Isaiah and Ezekiehl, when the first temple was destroyed and Jewish people forcefully subjected to a foreign king, serves also as a vehicle to speak of Africans and their subjection to the yoke of slavery and colonialism. In the philosophy and idiom of Rastafaris, i.e. black communities in the New World, particularly in 1930s Jamaica, "Babel" signifies all powers of oppression, which they strive to overturn through relocating to their Promised Land, their real home, in Africa (see 3.5.1). In general terms, the history of colonialism, with centuries of slavery, violent dislocation, enforced migration and actual genocides, has radically shaken up, if not eliminated, the traditional structures of belonging. As a result, people of African descent now find themselves in North or South America, in the Caribbean, Europe or wherever, in a diasporic situation where the only way to counter their condition and cultivate a feeling of togetherness is by means of cultural memory, as in the Jewish case – hence also the conceptual transfers. In principle, though not in the specific circumstances, the situation is not really different for people from Asia and the Indian subcontinent, many of whom must equally confront and come to terms with diasporic life-styles in the aftermath of empire.

From Jewish to Black diasporas: historical transfers

The diagnosis is significant, not least because it has been taken to suggest that identity formation principally proceeds from such conditions where the sense of self is challenged, and perhaps produced,

How identities are formed and formulated

by the experience of otherness. Simply put, we find out who we are or who we like to be under pressure of the realization who the others are and how the others have positioned us. In a postcolonial perspective, "**identity**", even ethnic identity, is less a fixed, inherited and given point of reference, which may subsequently be tested, confronted or disturbed in social interaction; it is rather the result of such disturbances, confrontations and ongoing interactions, possibly changing in their course and constantly transforming itself in response to them. Diaspora would thus be the prime site for notions of identity to be defined and defended. In literary terms, therefore, diaspora is often a precondition to establish a fixed repertoire of narratives or texts, a so-called canon, by which the missing homeland can be culturally compensated for and people find a basis of belonging – as, again, the Jewish case might illustrate, with its emphasis on studying the holy texts. Yet here the analogy reaches a limit. Quite apart from the fact that most African societies entertain oral traditions where canons are less easy to maintain, the great diversity of cultural experience and expression that has always existed in Africa makes it unlikely, perhaps impossible, to set up any one of them as the identifying mark of all. By and large, the same holds true for Asian and other diasporas.

"Imaginary Homelands": the case of négritude

This is why postcolonial diasporic subjects have made rather greater imaginative investments in constructing a sense of cultural belonging, across linguistic, geographical and other divides which have historically shaped them and which, in retrospect, turn out to have been productive factors in determining new identities. These are grounded, not in actual nor in textual, but in "imaginary homelands", as Salman Rushdie put it once (1991), often through a process of translation (see 1.2.4) and in transgression of existing boundaries. Thus, there is a sense in which the notion of "India" or "Africa" or, of course, "Europe" has only emerged from without, through a crisis of belonging and a desire to return, i.e. from the experience of alienation. Historically, one of the prime and most productive concepts of postcolonial identity, prevalent in the middle decades of the twentieth century, bears this out: the notion of "**négritude**". A neologism that first entered the French language in 1939, it was formulated in a poem by Aimé Césaire, a diasporic African resident in Paris, and propagated mainly in the works of Léopold Senghor, another diasporic African also resident in Paris. It derives from the declared urge to end colonial oppression and foreign cultural determination by seeking out ancestral Africa –

Césaire's poem is entitled *Cahier d'un retour au pays natal*, i.e. *Notebook of a Return to My Native Land* – a place, not of birth, yet of imaginary origin for all who see their history rooted there. It would be trivial to suggest that Césaire's "native land" was, strictly speaking, Martinique, i.e. a Caribbean island and French départe-ment. But it is not trivial to ask what exactly all the diasporic Africans included in this broad term are supposed to share. What is the essence of their "négritude"?

Senghor was eloquent on this issue, but he tended to phrase it in terms that other African intellectuals, especially from anglophone countries who came to prominence a generation later, found deeply troubling. To him, the essence of négritude was everything the European was not: emotional, vibrant, rhythmical, dedicated to the powers of the heart and soul and so on. Even this inadequate summary makes clear where the problem lies with négritude: it wanted to shed European dominance and reaffirm alternative "African" values long suppressed by colonialism, and yet in doing so it reinforced the set of binary oppositions – between "European ratio" versus "African emotion", for example – defined by colonial thinking in the first place. Négritude revalued the pattern, giving the formerly neglected side new emphasis while downgrading the other, but it kept the pattern otherwise intact, rather than question-ing its oppositional structure. As a notion forged from diasporic situations, négritude collected and transmitted considerable cultu-ral energies across a broad pan-African spectrum. But it soon lost the radical momentum it might once have had. As the anglophone Nigerian writer Wole Soyinka (*1934) cannily remarked in the 1960s, "a tiger does not proclaim its tigritude; it jumps" (Ashcroft et al 1989: 124), thus suggesting that the verbal celebration of supposed identities is feeble, self-conscious and spurious. (And to avoid all impressions of nativism, Soyinka chose the tiger as his image, i.e. a predatory cat that, contrary to popular assumption, does not live anywhere in Africa.)

Criticism of the négritude concept

As a consequence of such debates, and of ongoing political devel-opments in migration, refugee experience and global displacements, diaspora is nowadays not just noted as a cultural condition ever more widespread but also changing in its nature, with fewer people still convinced of how cultural memories of any home-land, imaginary or otherwise, should be maintained. Even though in recent years the rise of fundamentalism has become a pressing

Patchwork patterns of change and belonging

issue, this only offers proof, if proof were needed, that patchwork patterns – evident in literature, culture, society – are everywhere increasing in the multiple modernities of our times. Cultural homogeneity, let alone ethnic homogeneity, should it ever have existed, is clearly an exception, not the rule – even though ruling élites often like to champion it. Thus, the terminological issues arising with transferring "diaspora" into domains beyond Jewish history has led Postcolonial Studies to question fixed notions of home as well as given categories of belonging. In the words of the Caribbean writer Derek Walcott (*1930), "I carry my home within me".

6 "Hybridity"

The racist background of this term: breeding and miscegenation

This term, the last to be considered in this chapter, is perhaps the most notorious in the vocabulary of postcolonial theory. The reasons for the widespread reservations against it become clearer when we consider its background. In a plain sense, "hybrid" denotes the outcome of cross-breeding, as in gardening or livestock farming where certain plant or animal varieties, such as the mule, can be produced from mixed parentage, i.e. a donkey and a horse. The animal analogy is apt because it was exactly this kind of biological language and bluntly naturalist thinking by which nineteenth-century discourse, in the newly coined Darwinian argument, specified human "races" such as "Caucasian", identified their features such as skull measurements, and categorized their supposed merits such as intelligence. Especially in the colonial contact zones overseas, whether in Asia, Africa or the New World, there were many specimen to be studied and accounted for in these terms by the rising science of anthropology – which often proclaimed, for instance, the strikingly simian, i.e. ape-like, features of colonial subjects. In this context, any mixing of their "blood" with that of Europeans, as a result of sexual contact, was officially regarded with concern, sometimes outright horror – even though, unofficially, sex across the colour line has surely been a common form of age-old cultural encounters. In the language of racism, the practice of black-white sexual affairs is known as "miscegenation" and beset with cultural anxieties of loss and degeneration; its products are commonly called "half-breeds" or "hybrids". So how can Postcolonial Studies, critically poised against this legacy, make use of such a crudely racist term?

In contemporary critical discourse, "hybridity" is employed in a cultural sense. It serves to talk about phenomena that elude the given structure of familiar oppositions or to describe processes which transgress central boundaries like the one between colonizer and colonized. As such, the term is closely allied to notions like transculturation and, even more, that of "third space" (see 1.2.4) – notions that acknowledge the essential heterogeneity of all cultural determinations and try to address the work of difference *within*, not just the difference between, operative concepts like "identity". Consider, for example, the missionary scenario once more (mentioned earlier, 1.2.3) where a superior, colonizing power manifests itself by teaching the Bible to the natives, thus trying to deliver them from ignorance and to remedy their pagan ways. To begin with, the hierarchy seems quite intact, with the European dominance secured by literacy, religion, knowledge, power. Yet in the very process of rendering this power effective through biblical teaching, the position of dominance puts its own securities at risk, exposing itself to radically resistant notions and alternative interpretations – as when, for instance, missionary pupils find out that people in the Bible frequently eat meat – quite unacceptable to proper vegetarians like Hindus – or find out about King Solomon and his many wives – rather welcomed perhaps by African patriarchs who used to be harangued by missionary preaching against polygamy. As a consequence, colonial teachers would now find themselves explaining crucial differences within their Bible, like the difference between the Old and the New Testament, in the process subtly undermining its supposed superior status as the one and only cultural model to adopt. With a cross-cultural debate, the biblical text no longer issues a coherent, uncontentious meaning but becomes contingent on conflicting interpretations which change crucial identifications not only of native pupils but also of their missionary masters. The force of hybridity affects all.

Still, it can be argued that, given its racist background, "hybridity" is altogether the wrong word to describe such subtleties and cultural cross-overs. An alternative often suggested, especially with reference to religious notions, is "**syncretism**". Not an exact cognate, this term nevertheless refers to a mixing or merging of opposing principles or different practices into a newly defined form, without recalling anything so troubling as nineteenth-century biological legacies, ill-suited to be perpetuated in postcolonial theory. And yet, there is a case to make for the term "hybrid" precisely because

Critical uses of the term: in-between positions and their force

Postcolonial uses of hybridity both recall and redraw racist legacies

it keeps such poignant or offensive legacies alive while arguing to redefine their premises. If "hybrid" products long used to be denigrated in racist discourse elevating the idea of – racial or cultural – purity, this may be all the more reason to own up to this term and show that, principally, purity is a chimera: an ideologically powerful but strictly groundless notion to which no actual case in history or culture ever corresponds (outside, perhaps, of pigeon breeding there is no such thing as a "pure" heritage). Rather than condemn the term "hybridity" we might therefore embrace it and acknowledge the essential heterogeneity of *all* culture, always constituting itself in varying constellations made of impure, mixed and crossbred elements. In this way, the term may be radically shifted from its once defining context, with its previous connotations turned around. Incidentally, this is the process which several other terms, like "queer", have undergone: wrested from their hostile usage and twisted in their meaning.

Problematic over-uses of the term in the consumer market

Even in this redefined understanding, however, "hybrid" has proved a problematic term to work with. In contemporary postcolonial conversations, it runs the danger of inflationary, over-enthusiastic uses – sometimes to the point of calling any product made of more than one cultural component a "hybrid", like a "sushi burger" or "tandoori chicken pizza" or perhaps a "mango chutney vodka cocktail" or the like. Especially in the consumer market, typified by culinary items, such "fusion food" offers easily assimilated products, which may be successful sellers but which have nothing whatsoever to do with the notion of "hybridity". For this notion to work productively, the point is not that anything emerges from a cocktail shaker or some other cultural blender. The point is that the tension in the difference is kept sharp and the power relations between opposing sides are not miraculously transcended but strategically transformed. In the words of Homi K. Bhabha, its most prominent propounder, hybridity "is the name for the strategic reversal of the process of domination through disavowal" (1994: 112), i.e. a term that works towards reversing and repudiating the one-way streets of power by drawing our attention to the ways in which the dominated interfere with power processes. Thus, like the word "postcolonial" with its internal tension, the figure of the hybrid is a constant challenge to all notions of seamlessness, unity and coherence.

SUMMARY

This chapter has

▶ introduced six salient terms and their terminological networks in Post-colonial Studies
▶ argued for the need to acknowledge the specific and often shifting history of each term so as to understand its critical potential, often arising from central ambiguities within it
▶ surveyed the various uses and, sometimes, misuses to which these terms have been put
▶ discussed cases of especially contentious concepts
▶ offered a functional understanding of each term as not simply addressing a given issue but, by means of naming, actually defining the issue to be addressed

1   Historical

1   When did Postcolonial Studies begin?

"Always
historicize!"

When trying to get started in a field of research, it clearly is a good idea to ask when – under what conditions? for whose purpose? with what kind of aims? – research in this field itself got under way. Just as the terminological issues introduced in 1.2 can best be understood in view of their historical background, the larger project which they serve should also be addressed in view of the developments and changes it has undergone. In fact, a central lesson learned from critical approaches since the 1970s in the wake of Foucault's work (see 1.2.2) has been precisely this: never to take anything for granted across time and never to suppose that the concepts we employ, especially notions of the normative – such as "the subject", "the human", "justice", "sanity" or "culture" – are fixed and unproblematically given. "Always historicize!" is the imperative to warn us against generalizations and remind us how important the specific contexts are, i.e. the historical, cultural and other local circumstances in which meaning is principally made and maintained. So it is not just a useful but a necessary point to think about the circumstances in which Postcolonial Studies first began.

A point of
beginning:
Said's study
Orientalism
of 1978

Given the debates about the term "postcolonial" and the terminological alternatives that are considerably older (see 1.2.1), it will not come as a surprise that no straightforward answer to this question is available. Yet pressed to give a date for the foundation of the field, we could do worse than saying 1978, the year when Edward W. Said published *Orientalism*, his wide-ranging historical, political and literary study that soon became a hotly-discussed reference text (see also 2.3.2). Its title, in the first place, simply refers to an academic discipline, grounded in the great tradition of European philology, that deals with all things "Eastern": the languages, literatures, cultures just as the history, politics and religions of the East from Egypt to Japan. In this sense, "orientalism" is an eminent scholarly pursuit, including for example Sanskrit, Persian or Arabic studies, that emerged in the eighteenth and early nineteenth century from the European fascination with ancient languages and scripts, an interest especially pursued by German scholars such as Wilhelm v. Humboldt and Max Müller or translators such as Josef v. Hammer, whose work inspired Goethe to write his *West-Östlicher*

Divan (1819). But there is more to it than poetry. In the sense Said defines the term, "orientalism" effectively signifies a colonial project: the Western desire for domination. How can we understand this shift from the philological to the political, a shift which indicates the issues broached in Postcolonial Studies?

Orientalism is a long and somewhat convoluted book, yet its argument is clear and quickly grasped. It rests on the connection between knowledge and power – i.e. the insight famously formulated by the early modern English statesmen and philosopher Francis Bacon: *scientia potentia est* – and it draws critical attention to the fact that the geographical area, for which orientalist scholars claim authority, is not just congruent with the sphere of imperial interests, but actually a product of such interests. Why is it possible, Said asks, that such a large, varied and heterogeneous continent like Asia, plus various parts of Arabic Northern Africa (plus even parts of Southeast Europe, especially the Balkan), comprising countless different peoples, languages, religions, cultures – why has all this been conceived and positioned simply as "Eastern", i.e. subsumed, studied, administrated and, potentially, controlled under one such term as "the Orient"? Why has there never been a reciprocal discipline called "Occidentalism"? (see Buruma/Margalit 2004) Is this asymmetrical relation not indicative of the fundamental and long-standing conceptual hierarchy that puts "the West" in a powerful position of knowledge, production, intelligence and enlightenment, and "the rest" in the contrasting position of ignorance, submission and darkness? Once constructed in this way, the Orient has consequently "helped to define Europe (or the West) as its contrasting image, idea, personality, experience" (Said 1985: 1–2), not just in any fanciful or imaginative manner, but in the material dimension of political structures. These structures determine, Said argues, philological, literary and poetic projects like the ones mentioned above, just as military or imperial campaigns such as the Napoleonic invasion of Egypt in 1798, which was "in many ways the very model of a truly scientific appropriation of one culture by another" (1985: 42) or any such enterprise before or since, right up to present-day world politics. *Orientalism*, in short, wants to reveal the power at work in all Western engagements with the East, or rather, the notion of "the East" set up to serve self-gratifying purposes.

The two epigraphs of the book highlight this point and make clear how it could give momentum to the rise of Postcolonial Studies.

Key points of Said's foundational argument

Representing and inventing "the East"

The first is by Karl Marx, from *The Eighteenth Brumaire of Louis Bonaparte* (1852), where he famously wrote with reference to French peasants: "They cannot represent themselves; they must be represented." In the context of Marx's argument, *representation* refers to participation in the political process of power and decision-making, in the sense that we now speak of MPs as "representatives" of their constituency. In the context of Said's argument, however, *representation* is also used in the sense of aesthetic practice, what Aristotle called "mimesis": the act of recreating or imitating, constructing or representing something in a cultural medium like literature, thus to make present what is absent and, potentially, control, contain or subjugate it in this way. The central claim of *Orientalism* has been to conjoin these two meanings of *representation* and, consequently, to insist on a conjunction of aesthetic with political engagements. In concrete terms, to represent someone in literature means to exert a form of discursive power over him or her, by which orientalist writers construct and perpetuate the Western dominant position and perspective. Said's second epigraph bears this out and gives it cultural specificity: "The East is a career." This quip is from *Tancred* (1847), a Victorian novel written just before the heyday of the British Empire and, in fact, written by one of its most splendid representatives, Benjamin Disraeli (1804–1881), later the Tory Prime Minister who made Queen Victoria "Empress of India". The citation exemplifies the fashionable attitude of English gentlemen intent on rising in society who, as a means to this end, use "the East" as their field of social training and upward mobility. Taken together, Said's two epigraphs suggest how Westerners have represented or, indeed, invented Eastern others as a way to stage themselves as their superiors and so serve purposes of self-invention.

The world in 1978: "East" and "West" in transition

To understand why and how Said's book made such an impact that it led to the foundation of a new academic field, it is helpful to consider the context of its publication. When *Orientalism* came out, the general understanding of the terms "East" and "West", for decades dominated by the frontlines of the Cold War, was undergoing fundamental change. In 1978, a terrible late-imperial war in Vietnam and a bloody civil war in Lebanon had recently come to some kind of ending; Soviet leader Breshnyev died; an Iranian revolution overthrew the Shah of Persia, long supported by the West, before a tough Islamic regime installed itself there in the following year, while the Soviet Union invaded neighbouring Afghanistan.

Complex as these various events clearly were, they all contributed to shifting the semantics of "East" and "West" away from the exclusive sense of signifying the two superpowers and towards new theatres of war and cultural confrontation, notably in the Middle East where legacies of century-long colonial involvements came back on the agenda of world politics. In academia, political approaches to literature and cultural analysis were at the time widely influenced by Marxist views regarding the Third World as a contemporary site of class struggle (as Said's repeated references and credits to the work of Noam Chomsky illustrate) or, in a more recent move, by feminist views trying to establish Women's Studies as a new field, dedicated to those areas in literary and cultural history which had long be excluded from male-dominated research. Especially in the US where Said mainly lived and worked, this combined with the move towards African-American Studies dedicated to what had been ignored in white research. *Orientalism* tapped on these various critical energies while also redirecting them to other areas. The book was, in effect, a large-scale application of Foucault's concept of discourse to a broader spectrum of cultural manifestations than he had done himself. Without once using the term *postcolonial*, Said diagnosed the predicament and raised the question that was to become central: how can the power structures of representation be appropriated and reversed?

2   When did Postcolonial Literatures begin?

As we have seen, questions of beginning, just as issues of naming, are so important and contentious because they exemplify the very power of representation that is at stake in Postcolonial Studies. Wherever we say anything begins, we draw a line against all sorts of earlier developments and so arrogate the right to say these played no role. Ironically, Said wrote an earlier study on just this problem, entitled *Beginnings: Intention and Method* (1975). Published three years before *Orientalism*, it is entirely concerned with European fiction and philosophy in the canonical tradition of Comparative Literature (in which Said was trained and which he made his life-long project, see 2.3.2) and yet it engages in precisely the discussion that concerns the rise of non-European literatures, too. The key question is how the cultural authority manifest in literary authorship can ground itself, short of a divinely authorized origin, on a validated basis, i.e. how speaking positions are socially defined and critically defended. In historical terms this translates into the crucial

Why beginnings matter

question of when – under what conditions? for whose purpose? with what kind of aims? – postcolonial writing first began.

"Postcolonial" does not mean "post-independence"

It would, of course, not be a problem to address this question if we understood the term *postcolonial* in a purely chronological sense, i.e. referring to the period after the formal independence of a previous colony; in this sense, any writing produced in post-1947 India or post-1960 Nigeria could be classified as such and give a clear point of beginning. Indeed, for many practical purposes, the 1960s seem to be the general consensus by which the emergence of new literatures in English from former colonies can be dated. But as indicated earlier (1.2.1), as a point on which to base a theoretical perspective, this notion of chronology is too limited. The long-standing dynamics of cross-cultural transactions, the interplay of domination with the arts of resistance and the manifold involvements of colonial subjects in cultural and literary projects long before political decolonization – projects which are of prime interest for Postcolonial Studies – make the use of independence dates as a defining mark unhelpful. In fact, some of the most interesting texts, like Sol Plaatje's novel *Mhudi* from South Africa (1930) or Raja Rao's *Kanthapura* (1938) from India, were written and published well before that date. With reference to the leading role that many African, Asian or West Indian writers, as so-called Third World intellectuals emerging from colonial education systems, played in the momentous political developments of their countries, it could more plausibly be argued that postcolonial literatures *preceded* and actively *prepared* decolonization, rather than the other way round.

An eighteenth-century example: Equiano's life writing

So, given the functional understanding of the term "postcolonial" outlined above (1.1), we should widen the historical frame even more, going back in our studies at least to the eighteenth century. In 1789, for instance, an English book was published, paid for by private subscriptions, that soon became a bestseller and remained so after the author's death in 1797. Under the title *The Interesting Narrative of the Life of Olaudah Equiano, or Gustavus Vassa, the African, Written by Himself*, it offers the adventurous account of a diasporic life across three continents and many cultural frontlines. The writer, who defines himself so impressively in the title, tells us that he was born in West Africa, sold into slavery and shipped to North America, renamed, baptized, resold to an English master, fighting on the continent, travelling the circum-Atlantic world while educating himself all the time, before in 1766 he could buy his freedom; eventually he settles down in London and becomes an activist for abolitionism. His memoir thus offers an intriguing narrative of liberation, conversion and self-determination, against the odds of power systems established to exclude the likes of him from articulating their position but which are here, with the act of writing, wrested from the control by others and used to reinvent himself. As he claims participation in public literary discourse, he is turning himself from an illiterate slave who used to marvel at the powers of the English book (as told in a moving scene in Chapter III) into a learned gentleman who is author of an English book. In just the sense of *postcolonial* suggested in the introduction (1.1), Equiano can therefore be seen as the first African writer – even though, as recent research has suggested, he was probably not even born in Africa (Caretta 1999). Yet it is precisely because his English text shows crucial contradictions, multiple allegiances and shifting acts of self-positioning (see 2.4.1), that it offers such a strong example of the strategies at work also in the more recent postcolonial literatures since the 1960s.

Nor is the question of postcolonial beginnings simply a black and white affair. As another example of this point we may briefly consider the case for Scottish literature championed in the second half of the eighteenth century in a clear effort to install – or to invent – literary catalysts and conduits for nationalist sentiments. Following a crushing defeat under the English army in 1749 that led to a policy of Highland clearances including the suppression of the Gaelic language, Edinburgh intellectuals soon began to seek remnants of an old local tradition, untainted by the culture of Anglicization which they themselves partly represented and yet partly resented because it robbed them of their sense of self. Instead of fully surrendering to English models, they needed some alternative to endow Scottish landscape, history and culture with new value and significance. This is what they found in the *Works of Ossian* (1765), a series of epics full of passion and heroic downfalls, allegedly coming from an ancient Celtic bard, newly discovered, transcribed and translated into English by a schoolteacher called James Macpherson. These Ossianic songs, appearing in great numbers for an enthusiastic, ever growing readership, soon stirred into veritable Celtomania, were seen as founding narratives on a par with the Homeric epics and so helped to claim and maintain a sense of Scottish cultural identity held up against the English – even though, ironically, the texts were published and read only in English. As a

A Scottish example: Macpherson's fiction of a Celtic bard

matter of fact, it turned out in the following three decades that no Gaelic original exists. "Ossian", should this bard ever have lived, certainly left no heroic epics: their alleged author and point of beginning is a mere fiction. Macpherson, posing as a translator and editor, had craftily constructed these texts from whatever fragments he might have gathered in the Highlands combined with his own creative talents and some pertinent phrases from writers like Homer, Shakespeare and Milton. But instead of calling him a forger, we should better see his work as a clear case of the "invention of tradition" (Hobsbawm/ Ranger 1983) by which many people, especially people living under colonial conditions, have taken the decisive step towards redefining their position. This is exactly what, two centuries after Macpherson, postcolonial writers in Africa and elsewhere have attempted: to present or produce texts whose effects in the world help to change the discourse of this world.

The need for historical perspectives

In view of such examples we can see how the question of historical beginnings immediately leads us to explore the conditions by which history is made. This is the reason why a presentist perspective, i.e. an exclusive focus on recent developments in the field, is so unsatisfactory. For an adequate response to the challenges posed here, we need to include what has been called "postcolonialism in the past" (Fuchs/Barker 2004), i.e. to turn to contact zones where cultural and political divides have long been defined and defied.

SUMMARY

This chapter has

▶ raised the question of beginnings
▶ introduced Said's study *Orientalism* (1978) as a foundational text for Postcolonial Studies
▶ looked at some eighteenth-century examples of postcolonial writing
▶ argued for the need to include such historical material so as to work towards functional, not simply chronological, uses of postcolonial terms and concepts

2 Cultural

1 Writing Culture

Readers of the previous chapters will have noticed frequent references to "culture", to "cross-cultural" realities, or "transcultural" developments, i.e. to a specific field of experience with bearings on the texts under discussion, even if this field is not traditionally part of philology. The point has come to discuss briefly what it may involve. As a matter of fact, it is hard to imagine any productive engagement with postcolonial literatures that would not, in some way or other, situate them in the wider framework of the specific cultural forces which have shaped them and which, in the course of writing, may in turn be reshaped. Such an approach is crucial, though not exclusive to Postcolonial Studies. In recent decades, there has been a parallel development in many literature departments, closely related in several theoretical and critical concerns, towards an academic project known as Cultural Studies, which merits full discussion in its own right. At this point we can just consider what its interfaces are with postcolonial issues and what these imply (see Klein/Kramer 2001).

Cultural Studies and their relevance for postcolonial issues

A particularly influential – and, for the purposes of textual analysis, very useful – definition of *culture* was offered in 1973 by the American anthropologist Clifford Geertz. He argued for an essentially semiotic concept, claiming "that man is an animal suspended in webs of significance he himself has spun"; in this sense, we should take "culture to be those webs, and the analysis of it to be therefore not an experimental science in search of law but an interpretive one in search of meaning" (2000: 5). What this means can be explained with a strikingly helpful example on which Geertz draws: the difference between twitching and winking. As physical movements of the eye-lid, these two are quite indistinguishable. However, twitching is an involuntary tick provoked perhaps by nervousness, whereas winking is a speech act, a deliberate signal with a message addressed to someone who is meant to receive and interpret it. Unlike the twitch, the wink is part of culture, an element of meaning intentionally produced and communicated, so it is part of the "webs of significance" that we have "spun". Anyone interested in the textures of these webs should therefore take an "interpretive" or, we might say, a "hermeneutic" approach. Cultures

Geertz defines "culture" as a text and cultural analysis as interpretation

are matters to be thus carefully described and understood, not explained in general terms, which is why the search for "laws" as in the world of physics, leads us nowhere.

Cultural webs and acts of reading

Geertz consciously elaborated this analogy between cultural and textual interpretation. To him, an anthropologist in the field trying to come to terms with certain practices in, say, Balinese society is doing just the same as a philologist trying to decipher a foreign script. So we see why this semiotic concept of culture is favourable to literary critics who, by virtue of their own professional training, are particularly apt for an interpretive approach. Everything becomes an act of reading: "The culture of a people is an ensemble of texts, themselves ensembles, which the anthropologist strains to read over the shoulders of those to whom they properly belong." (Geertz 2000: 452) Note that plural terms ("ensembles", "webs") are stressed throughout. This serves to distinguish such a descriptive concept of culture from older, especially nineteenth-century uses of the term in a normative sense: "Culture" (with a capital C) which used to be opposed to "anarchy" or "barbarism". The work of recent social anthropology has gone a long way to dismantle this old, exclusive, evaluative and authoritarian concept of "Culture", which was also a central part of colonial practices. And yet it is clear that, as a discipline, anthropology emerged from these very practices. For it was in view of governing, controlling and subjecting natives that historically a more detailed knowledge of their culture was required.

The colonial heritage of modern social anthropology

Before professional anthropology took over in the later nineteenth century, this kind of knowledge used to be provided by colonial travellers, explorers, traders, missionaries and the like, who often answered general demand and published the considerable field expertise they gathered about remote places – including the cultural or, more often, natural points of interest – in print. Such books, like travelogues, adventure tales, accounts of missionary or administrative work among the natives, were highly popular, their authors sometimes turned into celebrities. They still make fascinating reading and have since become the subject of a rich and productive area in Postcolonial Studies. Even though we should clearly be wary of the information they provide on the Asian, African or New World cultures allegedly described in such texts, they are certainly informative about the English or European notions that shaped the perception of these cultures just as their subsequent representation in writing. It has therefore been argued that such literature, especially travelogues, can tell us more about the place from which the traveller set out and where his or her readership is located than anything about the cultures travelled to.

This is the sort of argument Said develops at great length in *Orientalism* (see 2.1.1) and, significantly, its legacies are still with us. They can even be traced in Geertz's statement quoted above (see p. 46). When he speaks of the anthropologist reading "over the shoulders" of the people to whom the cultural texts "belong", he seems to be at pains to avoid all colonial gestures of taking possession – but his scenario of cultural encounters clearly shows who does the reading, the looking and, eventually, the writing: the anthropologist and participant observer whose authority over the cultures looked at is thus established. All his acts of interpretation require and reinforce just the kind of power long exercised in Western attitudes towards non-Western people because to read "over the shoulder" still sets up a position of control. In a more recent move in anthropology, therefore, this scenario has been critically revised and extended: "If the ethnographer reads culture over the native's shoulder, the native also reads over the ethnographer's shoulder as he or she writes each cultural description." (Clifford 1986: 119) The second part of this statement is crucial: "natives", whoever they may be, have neither remained unaffected nor unaware of the various attempts at observation or description they have undergone; they return the gaze that is directed at them and their culture. The very fact that they are subject to interpretation has thus transformed what is to be interpreted.

Ethnograph and cultural authority: recent revisions

This re-examination of the practices of anthropological work on culture was part of an important movement in the 1980s towards self-critically reconsidering the premises on which it rests and the conditions which place ethnographers and their informants into precarious double binds: "Much of our knowledge about other cultures must now be seen as contingent, the problematic outcome of intersubjective dialogue, translation and projection." (Clifford 1986: 109) This is how James Clifford, a central figure in this movement, puts it. Instead of the one-way street of observation implied in Geertz, he emphasizes the significance of two-way interaction, mutual interpretation, multiple authorities and shifting interfaces which, taken together, all in some way contribute to what gets written down as "culture": a relational, multi-centred,

Clifford emphasises mutual cultural entanglements

open-ended network that does not "properly belong" to any one side. The moment which Clifford in his statement designates as "now" is the postcolonial moment, the point when hierarchies of representation, formerly taken for granted, crumble and give way to the awareness of complex entanglements. These include the emerge of so-called "indigenous ethnographers", i.e. interpreters and writers of a cultural text they would claim as their own. These indigenous interpreters are not necessarily more qualified by virtue of their inside status, but they offer evidence that cultural techniques of representation like writing, in postcolonial contexts, are no longer exclusively used by the West over the rest.

The *Writing Culture*-debate

Writing, in fact, is crucial here – so much so that the critical debate exemplified by Clifford is known as the *Writing Culture*-debate (the title of a book he co-edited in 1986). With obvious implications for the works of postcolonial literature, this phrase suggests a double meaning: stressed on the second word, "writing *culture*" designates the technology of writing that takes culture as its object; stressed on the first part, "*writing* culture" indicates that writing is itself contingent, the product of particular cultural developments, not without alternatives. These are what we should next consider.

2   Literacy vs. Orality

Oral cultures and their features

Postcolonial literatures are often seen to be affected in fundamental ways by the differences between literate and oral cultures. Many postcolonial societies have, or used to have, comparatively lower literacy rates than First World countries and consequently have long developed very complex modes of oral story telling, knowledge codification and social interaction. This is certainly not an exclusive feature and it relates to postcolonial literatures in English in varying degrees, depending on the cultural realities constructed or conveyed in any given text. But with regard to works by, for example, Maori writers from New Zealand or by West African writers who use English as a medium to represent local communities also speaking some indigenous language, the difference between literacy and orality is highly relevant – just as for Caribbean writers whose work frequently includes the Creole languages locally spoken on the islands and increasingly used also in literary domains. In such cases we see that the issue is not simply a choice of convenience, but involves key cultural traditions regulated and perpetuated in written or in oral modes.

However, "choice" is clearly the wrong word here: first of all, because we are principally concerned with literature in printed books, hence with products of literate cultures; secondly, because the condition of pristine orality, i.e. of cultures with no knowledge of writing, can no longer be found in any part of our contemporary world. Even if only a certain – still growing – percentage of today's languages are widely and intensely used in writing, there are no extant language communities without contact whith some form of literacy. Conversely, with the spread of new communication technologies like radio, telephone, email and text messaging, new oral domains have opened up in literate societies, registered also in literary production. We are not talking, therefore, about a fixed opposition but a spectrum of cultural possibilities realized through orality and literacy, as matters of degree and emphasis.

Orality and literacy form a spectrum of cultural expression

These possibilities, however, have far-reaching consequences when we look at them in functional perspectives: what does an intensive use of writing, for example, indicate about a society? "Literacy", it has been said, "made the Roman Empire possible" (Ong 1984: 6). Indeed, it is intuitively plausible that cultures with a strong emphasis on literacy would hold specific views on authorship and authority, would organize questions of memory, identity and power in very different ways from cultures engaging in predominantly oral modes (see Assmann 1997: 87–129). Writing, as a sign system of graphical marks on a durable surface, loosens or even overrides any palpable link between the sign and its sender. In this way, writing widens the communicative range across space and time, but therefore demands greater efforts and techniques of interpretation. These are to guard the message from corruption through temporal and spatial transfers and, consequently, work towards reifying institutions of control. In Western philosophy (exemplified by Plato's dialogue *Phaidros*) just as in linguistic theory (exemplified by early twentieth-century structuralism), writing was indeed long viewed with suspicion, as a debasement of speech and a derivative form of language. It was only with the rise of post-structuralist theories in the 1960s, especially with the work of Jacques Derrida, that such "phonocentric" attitudes resenting written signs have come to be scrutinized and critically questioned. Derrida's *Of Grammatology* argued in 1967 that the emphasis on spoken over written language indicates an ideology that champions the use of personal "presence" – like a speaker who is always present in a communicative situation – over the impersonal play of signs.

Political and ideological uses of the spoken as opposed to the written word

Postcolonial combinations: diglossia in African literature

At just this time, postcolonial literatures, especially from Africa, gained prominence in experimenting with these cultural possibilities in other ways. Given colonial language policies, the writer's choice of language – e.g. whether to use English or, say, Igbo, Yoruba or Gikuyu or any other African language which used to be predominantly oral but which, as a result of colonial encounters, now also have writing systems – has long been a contested issue with strong political repercussions. Yet again, "choice" was and is no question here of either/or. The linguistic situation in postcolonial African societies is diglossic (cf. 1.2.4) where English (or French or Portuguese) represents just one, albeit powerful, medium of expression. In fact, its power is three-fold: "(1) it is a written language and therefore a modern language since, in the popular consciousness at least, writing is associated with modernity; (2) it has a literary tradition articulated around the concept of authorship; and (3) it is a 'textualized' or chirographically controlled language, that is a language tied to the text", as Chantal Zabus helpfully sums up the situation (1991: 15, see also Ong 1984). But in her detailed study of linguistic strategies in West African novels, she also shows how anglophone writing involves other layers, too, signifying the indigenous African languages and their cultural impact on the given text. She highlights and exemplifies concrete linguistic strategies – such as code-switching, relexification, calquing and others – which all, by syntactic and lexical devices, help to indigenize the English language used and so transform the anglophone into an African text. As a cover term to describe such strategies Zabus draws on the term for medieval documents containing more than one layer of script, and speaks of "the African **palimpsest**". Many novels like Amos Tutuola's *The Palm-Wine Drinkard* (1952) or Gabriel Okara's *The Voice* (1964) thus achieve highly fascinating ways of 'oralizing' their written text.

Orality works in and on writing

Taken together, all such examples can suggest (in the sense argued earlier, 1.2.4) how postcolonial literatures draw on the cultural possibilities of both literacy and orality, while also redrawing this cultural difference in the process, so as to wield the foreignizing power of translation.

SUMMARY

This chapter has

▶ looked at the meaning and uses of "culture" in postcolonial domains
▶ introduced ethnographic accounts and the Writing Culture-debate
▶ noted the prevalence of oral communication in many indigenous societies
▶ argued that orality and literacy frequently work in combination in post-colonial texts and contexts
▶ explained the concepts of "diglossia" and "palimpsest" which are used to describe such linguistic interactions

3 Critical

Like many disciplines and academic projects, Postcolonial Studies has mapped its field with a number of critical concepts and approaches associated with the names of critics who defined them. It goes without saying that such name associations are simply short-hand for complex processes of dialogue and interaction that cannot easily be narrowed down to any single person. Nevertheless, these critics have come to stand for particular issues when studying postcolonial literatures. A survey of five critical writers, widely noted in the field of theory, will help to outline why or how their work has been of special interest and in what circumstances – historical, cultural, biographical – it emerged.

Prominent names in postcolonial theory

1 Frantz Fanon

A francophone pioneer for all work in the field, decades before the term *postcolonial* came up, Fanon exemplifies and examines many central issues – issues of power, violence and identification – at the heart of colonial predicaments, which he theorized in both political and psychological terms. His first book *Black Skin, White Masks (Peau Noire, Masques Blancs)*, published in 1952 in Paris, sharply responds to attempts at the time to diagnose some sort of colonial "inferiority" or "dependence" complex among blacks by which previous writers (and, not surprisingly, white writers) had sought to explain continued patterns of subjection. The opposition set up in Fanon's title, by contrast, highlights that these patterns are products of particular modes of perception and interaction; rather than given facts of black psychology, they are constructed by the

A pioneer for analysing black predicaments in the 1950s

colonizers like masks and then imposed upon the colonized. In a chapter entitled "The Fact of Blackness", Fanon offers a detailed account of the social genesis of this "fact" as a drama staged with looks and gestures of control and directed by racist attitudes: "Look, a Negro!" goes the cry heard everywhere in the colonial world, interpellating blacks in such a mask and arresting all efforts of self-recognition in the colour of their skin: "And then the occasion arose when I had to meet the white man's eyes. An unfamiliar weight burdened me. The real world challenged my claims. In the white world the man of color encounters difficulties in the development of his bodily schema." (Fanon 1986: 110) As this brief quotation from Fanon illustrates, his is a powerful, emphatic, personalized and passionate account of oppression, using the language of existentialism and psychoanalysis available at the time.

Fanon's political argument: a manifesto for decolonization

A decade later, his political analysis was extended in *The Wretched of the Earth (Les damnés de la terre*, 1961). Written during Algeria's armed struggle for liberation, in which he was himself involved, Fanon finds strong words to describe the rigid structures set up by colonialism: "The colonial world is a world divided into compartments. […] The colonial world is a world cut in two. The dividing line, the frontiers are shown by barracks and police stations. […] The zone where the natives live is not complementary to the zone inhabited by the settlers. The two zones are opposed, but not in the service of a higher unity. […] No conciliation is possible, for of the two terms, one is superfluous." (Fanon 1965: 31–2) The relentless focus on such binary oppositions – what he calls the "Manichean" character of the colonial world, as in dualistic religions pitting darkness against light – is meant to reveal the violence which is manifest in them and which, to be overcome, demands that violence is also used in anti-colonial revolutionary movements. In this way, Fanon's work became a manifesto throughout the Third World and the contemporary moves towards decolonization.

Fanon's background and critical legacy

Frantz Fanon (1926–1961) came from the Caribbean island of Martinique, a French département; he studied psychiatry in France and worked in an Algerian hospital in the 1950s when the conflicts with French domination reached a climax. His concerns were entirely dedicated to this struggle, and he never commented on literature. But in subsequent decades, his concepts came to be applied in cultural and literary analysis, too, especially when studying colonial writing and its so-called "Manichean aesthetics" (see Jan-

Mohamed 1983), i.e. for fiction whose symbolic order seems to be constructed by mutually excluding binaries. However, recent critical interest has shifted to the space Fanon seemed to rule out in this analysis, the grey area between "the two zones" and the moves that transgress given frontlines. In an effort to re-examine Fanon's pioneering studies, we can indeed find passages of productive irritation, for instance when he writes: "decolonization unifies that people [living under oppression] by the radical decision to remove its heterogeneity, and by unifying on a national, sometimes a racial, basis." (1965: 37) Here the categories violently imposed on the colonized are turned into key instruments of self-redefinition and the sense of national unity that they help to define rests on recognizing its contigent, colonially constructed nature. Similarly, the central term in his first book, masks, can also be regarded as a trope for all sorts of masquerade, mimicry and camouflage, political techniques that question, rather than affirm, the effects of colonial authority. By way of such rereadings and re-evaluations, prominent for instance in the work by Homi Bhabha (2.3.3), Fanon's foundational texts continue to serve as a stimulus for postcolonial debates.

2 Edward W. Said

The seminal importance of Said's work for Postcolonial Studies has already been established (2.1.1), with *Orientalism* marking a point of beginning. What he analysed in this book, placing his main focus on Western attitudes towards the Middle East, was a repertoire of "style, figures of speech, setting, narrative devices" (Said 1985: 21) and other textual stereotypes by which, he alleged, the West has consistently represented – and, indeed, invented – the East with astonishing persistence and consistence across time, from early Greek tragedy like Aeschylus's *The Persians* to Professor Bernard Lewis's scholarly writings on Islam in the 1970s. What emerged from Said's analysis and was soon extended to other areas such as the invention of Africa or the New World, is the notion of "colonial discourse" or "the rhetoric of empire" (Spurr 1993). This refers to the fixed rhetorical routines manifest in travelogues, journalism, literature etc., which purport to describe various places under Western eyes and power but which are unspecific, hence unable to capture any of the particular conditions in these places, instead revealing and repeating only the colonial mindsets that define the rhetoric (see also 2.2.1).

The rhetoric of orientalism

Criticism of Said's argument: too general, too categorical

Critiques of this notion have been profuse. Their main point is the charge that *Orientalism*, in the process of its argument, reproduces the very problem that it sets out to reveal: far too sweeping and boldly generalizing in his whole approach, Said subsumes so many different things and cultural circumstances under the same heading that his insights are themselves too unspecific to be helpful or convincing. Especially his constant emphasis on the two opposing zones, "the East" versus "the West" – what we, in Fanon's term, might call the Manichean structure – is seen as problematic because it disregards the space and scope for cultural entanglements, historical entwinements and differentiations that are not just manifest in literary transactions between Eastern and Western traditions but that have also shaped many scholarly and political engagements. As a result, the positional superiority claimed in Western discourse is actually far more precarious than Said assumed because the agency of others, i.e. the counter-claims and reassertions of the colonized, should never be ignored. In addition, Marxist critics like Aijaz Ahmad from India (1992) have pointed out that the discourses of Third World élites often repeat the arrogant gestures identified as "orientalist" when they champion exlusivist notions of nationhood.

Said's revised argument: "contrapuntal readings"

In another major book, *Culture and Imperialism* (1993), Said responds at length to several of these charges, calling his first chapter "Overlapping Territories, Intertwined Histories" so as to revise all Manichean notions. In a central passage he describes the anti-imperialist imagination which is articulated by many postcolonial writers as follows: "our space at home in the peripheries has been usurped and put to use by outsiders for their purpose. It is therefore necessary to seek out, to map, to invent, or to discover a *third* nature, not pristine and pre-historical [...] but deriving from the deprivations of the present." (1993: 272) With this emphasis on a "third" space, beyond present predicaments and between the old colonial frontlines, he suggests that an imaginative return to pre-colonial situations, some paradise untainted by any outside influence, is not really an option (see 2.4.2). Instead, imperial legacies should widely be acknowledged to have "consolidated the mixture of cultures and identities on a global scale", so much so that "no one today is purely *one* thing" (1993: 407). In this sense, his major project in this book is to initiate new ways to approach cultural productions, such as novels, operas or other works which used to be employed for purposes of Western self-identification, but which also often involve other histories and covert realities not usually seen. This is what he calls "contrapuntal reading" (see also 2.4.4), a changed review of our cultural archive "with a simultaneous awareness both of the metropolitan history that is narrated and of those other histories against which (and together with which) the dominating discourse acts" (1993: 59).

A highly controversial figure all his life, Edward Said (1935–2003) managed to pursue several careers at once, including his much noted political commitment to the Palestinian cause as well as his forceful critique of Palestinian leaders. Born in Jerusalem to a Protestant Palestinian business family who also lived in Cairo and soon had to leave their Jerusalem home with the foundation of Israel, he came to the US at the age of sixteen. Eventually he made New York the place for his activities in academia, media criticism, public speaking and campaigning. But basically, as he often argued, his own territorial displacement mirrored the larger, and clearly more severe plight of Palestinians forced into diasporic lives as refugees. His memoir is entitled *Out of Place* (1999) to indicate the condition which he saw as the general predicament of his people but which, at the same time, he suggested may provide special advantages for intellectual work: the position of an outsider or exile, at the margins of the mainstream, gives him a changed perspective on the world and so opens different views on long-held notions. However we may judge his work, Said clearly made productive uses of this special position. His legacy for Postcolonial Studies (a term he never used) can be summed up in his concept of the "worldly text", i.e. the argument that texts are "events and, even when they appear to deny it, they are nevertheless a part of the social world, human life, and of course the historical moments in which they are located and interpreted." (Said 1983: 4) This argument gives relevance to all our engagements with literature and texts, making every act of reading a way to relocate positions in the social world.

Said's background and critical legacy: "worldly texts"

3   Homi K. Bhabha

Even though claims of genealogy are often doubtful, it can be said that Homi Bhabha's contributions to postcolonial theory set in where Said's argument had taken the debates and, by insistent probing and often dazzling formulations, continue to explore the contradictions and ambivalences that emerge when critically thinking through the issues of colonial discourse. Unlike Said's works, how-

The challenge of ambivalence

ever, Bhabha's texts are densely written, highly allusive and termi-
nologically so sophisticated that they at times appear almost
obscure. This impression also comes from their engagement with
the strategies of post-structuralist criticism, especially by Derrida,
as well as psychoanalytic notions as formulated by Freud and
Lacan, which all combine to formidable challenges when trying to
come to terms with Bhabha's work. But it surely is a challenge well
worth taking. A more extensive reading of his essays published
since the mid-1980s and collected in his best-known book entitled
The Location of Culture (1994) quickly shows how they all work
through a number of key points that keep recurring and that form
a network of closely related arguments.

Bhabha's critical attention to forms and spaces in-between

The main insight they offer, if such a generalization can be risked,
lies in the recognition that the oppositional structure – "us" versus
"them", "colonizer" versus "colonized", "white" versus "black",
"West" versus "East" – set up in imperial practice and analysed by
critics like Said can never fully capture the intricacies of power nor
contain the fundamental insecurities on which this power rests.
Instead of binary oppositions, Bhabha always highlights the inter-
stices, the cracks or fissures in the system, the spaces in between the
assumed opposites, where he identifies all sorts of subtle transactions whose subversive effects he describes with a number of critical terms (some of which are introduced above in 1.2.4 and 1.2.6)
like "mimicry", "hybridity", or "sly civility".

An example: education, assimilation and dissimulation in English India

Take for instance the scenario of colonial education in India. As
British nineteenth-century administrators like Macaulay famously
argued (see 3.3), schooling natives in the literary and cultural
canon of the West should serve to educate an élite of local interpreters who were to act as go-betweens for the remote imperial
authority trying to govern the uncultured local masses. That is to
say, some specially selected Indians were to be singled out as cultural agents, trained in the symbolic codes of their colonial masters
which they came to imitate, assimilate and so help to perpetuate.
On one level, such a project simply installs power structures to
confirm, once more, the general assumption of European superiority by subjecting Indians to foreign cultural norms. But Bhabha's
analysis goes further. Crucially, he argues, these norms are now
themselves becoming foreignized, as they are divided from Europe,
transferred elsewhere and made into a subject of training, i.e. of
cultural replication. The replica, however, robs the original of its

once singular status and, with its act of reproduction, introduces difference. In the context of colonial education, to be *anglicized* thus means emphatically: *not* to be English, but to have taken on merely the semblance and the guise of Englishness. Therefore, in the very process meant to reconfirm their powerful positions, colonial educators actually displace it and, with eventual success, disown themselves of their authority. This effect is described as "**mimicry**": the constant slippage and internal splitting of a cultural model by means of its own replication. In Bhabha's words, "colonial mimicry is the desire for a reformed, recognizable Other, *as a subject of a difference that is almost the same, but not quite*" (1994: 86, emphasis in the original).

Drawing mainly on examples from the Indian context, Bhabha has variously modified this argument, always emphasizing (1) that colonial power is a shared transaction in a cross-cultural arena, never a secure means to assert oneself, (2) that the racist stereotypes by which the colonized used to be seen, such as "the bimbo", "the coolie" or "the paki", always effect distortions – in the sense of a Freudian *Entstellung* – of the regular authority who first imposed them but cannot ultimately keep control, (3) that all such partial and partializing ways of identification are "strategies of subversion that turn the gaze of the discriminated back upon the eye of power" (1994: 112). This is rather like the way, we may add, that postcolonial subjects frequently turn against the ethnographic gaze that formerly observed them (see 2.2.1). However, critics of Bhabha's arguments – again, a large and a resounding chorus – have not been inclined to endorse his approach. In an important early article, Benita Parry (1987) opened a materialist critique that attacks what she regards as undue privileged attention paid in Bhabha's work to modes of discourse and to fine semantic shifts whose subtleties obscure the fundamental pragmatics of power that continue to shape colonial realities and legacies in our world. Along these lines, many further critics doubted any claims of postcolonial empowerment that are suggested in his theory and insisted that a rhetoric of "subversion", "masquerades" and setting up "third spaces" should not distract us from the larger frame of domination in which all these take place.

Key points and criticism of Bhabha's analysis

Born in 1949 in Bombay where his father was a very well-known scientist, Bhabha belongs to the same generation as Salman Rushdie, born into the turmoils of recently independent India in the after-

Bhabha's
background
and continuing
relevance

math of its bloody partition from Pakistan. Like Rushdie, whose works are central concerns in his writing, he has moved on to live and work in England and, more recently, in the US. His 1990 essay collection *Nation and Narration* responded to the growing need to question and examine the cultural strategies by which forms of nationhood have been defined and defended in modernity – an important line of inquiry begun in the 1980s with Benedict Anderson's much-cited study *Imagined Communities* (1983/1991). Both books revisit nineteenth-century discussions, such as Ernest Renan's famous speech "Qu'est-ce qu'une nation?" ("What is a nation?", 1882), and explore how their ideas have been reformulated, transformed and, at times, reclaimed in postcolonial debates on national affiliations in a transnational world. Bhabha's latest work continues these debates in view of global migrations, trying to stake out what he calls minoritarian cosmopolitanism.

4   Gayatri C. Spivak

The so-called
"Holy Trinity"
of postcolonial
critics

With Spivak's work we are looking at another theorist in post-colonial debates whose prominence was established in the mid-1980s and who has since become one of the most often cited and discussed critics. Like Bhabha, she has her theoretical background in post-structuralist concepts of language and psychoanalytic concepts of the subject (and, as many readers quickly note, she shares the complexity of academic prose, rich in allusions and dense with sophisticated formulations). Together with Said and Bhabha, Spivak has at times been seen as forming something like the core or canon of postcolonial theory, ironically referred to as the 'holy trinity' of Postcolonial Studies. Apart from sheer polemics, the point that such a designation might suggest is well worth some reflection. It indicates the central status that these three writers hold – or held especially in the 1990s – even though their work is all concerned with theorizing marginal positions. But this status, we must say, was actually thrust upon them in the US-based university life where they mainly operate and where celebrities are quickly made with the rising fortunes of new academic trends. If anything, the 'holy trinity'-idea therefore says more about their readers, students, colleagues, publishers and followers, all perhaps inclined to 'worship' certain figures, rather than anything about these theorists themselves.

Regarding Spivak's contribution to postcolonial theory, the most important point is the relation to the field of gender theories and gender difference she has made her project to explore (see also 4.1). Women in colonized societies, she argues, live under conditions of double oppression, because they are dominated both by patriarchal and by imperial institutions. Even if political liberation movements, in India and elsewhere, have historically lifted the strictures of colonial rule, the situation of women continues to be strictly ruled by others as long as they are under forms of male authority continued in the new regime. The question is about the primacy of race, gender or class: which of these three categories captures the main productive tension? In classic Marxist analysis, it used to be thought that matters of class were the basis for all social conflicts, so that matters of race and gender were only secondary in their relevance. While reconsidering Marxist ideas as well as the idealist philosophy on which they rested, Spivak offers far more subtle and productive arguments about these interrelations, above all responding to the complications that arise when considering colonial society in India.

Feminist thinking in Postcolonial Studies

Her best-known essay, whose title has become proverbial, addresses just this point: "Can the Subaltern Speak?" (1988) As the question raised here indicates, it is concerned with issues of speaking positions, of having, giving, claiming or recovering voice. In particular it asks whether female voices from the hidden layers of colonial society can still convey a message, make their presence felt, mark a sense of subjectivity and be acknowledged for it. Spivak's answer is negative, categorically ruling out any such possibility: "There is no space from which the sexed subaltern subject can speak." (1993: 103) To begin to understand this tough – and, for a feminist critic, perhaps surprising – stance we might think about the meaning of the English phrase "she is spoken for": this is a way of saying that a woman is engaged to get married. The analogy to Spivak's Indian examples is loose, but it indicates the general ways in which gender positions are defined by male speech acts relegating women to a prescribed place. Yet the main point for us to understand is the term and figure of "the subaltern".

Spivak: the "subaltern" cannot speak

Frequently just used in the sense of any oppressed person, this term is in fact quite specific. In the first place "subaltern" denotes a low-ranking officer in the military hierarchy, i.e. someone in a subordinate position but himself part of the system that controls him. The

Who or what "the subaltern" signifies

term was influentially redefined in writings by the Italian communist Antonio Gramsci in the early 1930s who used it as an alternative to "proletarian", i.e. to the economically given class identity, because he recognized that ideological formations are not always congruent with class formations: workers are defined as such not only 'from below' by their material basis but also 'from above' by the ideology they make their own, even if this has been imposed on them. More specifically still, "subaltern" was the key term for a group of India-based historians in the 1980s searching for new ways to write Indian history. Known as "the Subaltern Studies group" around Ranajit Guha, their project was to rethink colonial historiography from the point of view of Indian peasants and their insurgency movements. It is this group and their focus on 'the people' that Spivak targets in her critical analysis.

The case of *sati*: she is spoken for

Forcefully questioning the historians' honourable idea to 'retrieve' the voices of the oppressed, she points out that whatever 'voice' may be recovered in this well-meaning process is always already spoken for: by the historian or critic or whoever now makes it articulate and thereby necessarily makes it silent again. Spivak's main example is the complex case of *sati*, i.e. of Indian widows burned on their husband's pyre. Discussing the cross-cultural misunderstandings through which colonial administrators named this practice and tried to suppress it in the name of modernity while anti-colonial activists resisted all such moves in the name of cultural identity and tradition, she notes that the women around whom the *sati* debate turned principally remained excluded from it: "Between patriarchy and imperialism, subject-constitution and object-formation, the figure of the woman disappears, not into a pristine nothingness but into a violent shuttling which is the displaced figuration of the 'third-world woman' caught between tradition and modernization." (1993: 102) In this context, Spivak also reflects on ways to reconsider widow-sacrifice politically, as martyrdom or motivated suicide – in the sense of Ghandi's *satyagraha*, i.e. hunger-strike as resistance, the term sharing its etymological root with *sati* – but comes to the same conclusion. The female subaltern, she argues, cannot speak.

Spivak's background and continuing challenge

It does not come as a surprise that such an argument has encountered very severe criticism – again, Parry (1987) is the most relevant source – to which Spivak has responded with vigour and alacrity, especially in her book *A Critique of Postcolonial Reason*

(1999). Born in Calcutta in 1942 and academically based in the US, Spivak is also an important translator, having produced English versions of Derrida's theoretical works and Mahasweta Devi's Bengali stories, and generally refuses to be pigeon-holed by labels readily at hand. Her critical interventions continue to challenge facile notions of authentic voices to be romanticised or salvaged in the work of postcolonial writing.

5   Stuart Hall

The final critic to be introduced in our incomplete chapter on post-colonial theorists, Stuart Hall, exemplifies the productive interrelations between Postcolonial Studies and the field of Cultural Studies (noted earlier, 2.2.1), in the specific sense in which this field was founded in 1960s Britain. Many of the academic interests Hall pursues are grounded, as he frequently points out himself, in the circumstances of his own life as a Caribbean and Black British intellectual between the New World and the Old. Born in 1932 in Kingston, Jamaica, he came to Britain in 1951 among the first large group of Caribbean immigrants, the so-called "Windrush"-generation so named after the *SS Empire Windrush*, the boat that brought the first large group of West Indians to post-war England in 1948 (see 3.6.1). Unlike most of these migrants, however, Hall did not come to seek employment; he came as a Rhodes scholar to Oxford. In 1964 he joined Richard Hoggart at the new Centre for Contemporary Cultural Studies, Birmingham University, and soon was at the forefront of research into media discourse, social mechanisms of representation, TV and film culture, or labour conditions. Since his move to London in the 1980s, Hall's work has become increasingly concerned with questions of race, ethnicity and diaspora, offering important contributions especially to debates about Black British identities.

A pioneer of Cultural Studies and Black British Studies

His 1990 essay "Cultural Identity and Diaspora", for instance, looks at two of the most often employed concepts in our context and critically re-examines the assumptions on which they are based. "Cultural Identity", he notes, has generally been regarded and constructed with reference to a shared heritage, something given in the past, withheld or not accessible under present circumstances but now to be reconstituted by reclaiming the essence of some original sameness. In just this way, for instance, the sense of 'Africanness' on which Césaire's and Senghor's notion of négritude

Identities in histories: differences within

rested (see 1.2.5) was formulated and received. Hall questions these assumptions because they disregard the processes of mediation and representation which are crucially at stake here; instead, he argues, we need to acknowledge not just the difference *between* identities, but the difference *within* identity so as to see it, permanently, as a process of becoming: "Cultural identities come from somewhere, have histories. But, like everything which is historical, they undergo constant transformation. Far from being eternally fixed in some essentialized past, they are subject to the continuous 'play' of history, culture and power. Far from being grounded in mere 'recovery' of the past, which is waiting to be found, and which when found, will secure our sense of self into eternity, identities are the names we give to the different ways we are positioned by, and position ourselves within, the narratives of the past." (1993: 394) Along the same lines, Hall also redefines "diaspora", not as the fixed relation to some sacred homeland, but in terms of continuous heterogeneity, transformation and difference.

The sugar at the bottom of the English cup of tea

The consequences of such a revised view are far-reaching; they do not only concern Black British identity but questions of English identity as well, in their mutual transformations and material re-constitutions (see 4.3). What this should mean was explained when he addressed a 1989 conference on "Culture, Globalization and the World-System." For Hall, the crucial contrast between what he terms "old" and "new" identities lies in their relation to historical narratives. The "new" discourses of identity establish common ground with historical antagonists, i.e. they recognize the legacies shared among colonizers and colonized as a material bond of connection: "The notion that identity [...] could be told as two histories, one over here, one over there, never having spoken to one another, never having anything to do with one another [...] is simply not tenable any longer in an increasingly globalized world." By way of illustration, Hall gives a personal example: "People like me who came to England in the 1950s have been there for centuries; symbolically, we have been there for centuries. I was coming home. I am the sugar at the bottom of the English cup of tea." (1991: 48) This statement is still a profoundly challenging remark: the narratives of English identification, Hall insist, include the unacknowledged agency of others. Slavery and the sugar trade have long established a Caribbean presence within the so-called mother country. The cup of tea, nationally celebrated as a daily ritual and globally recognized as an icon of civilized Englishness, contains a product, which materially connects it to the Caribbean and so redefines its meaning.

In just this way, we might conclude, postcolonial literatures have redefined the English canon in the increasingly globalized world, insisting that it is no longer tenable to read its narratives without engaging with the presence and productions of, in Hall's sense, new identities and constant cultural transformations.

Ongoing cultural transformations

> **SUMMARY**
>
> This chapter has
>
> ▶ introduced five well-known names in postcolonial theory
> ▶ given a brief outline of their careers and some of their most prominent critical preoccupations, such as:
> ▶ Fanon: the predicament and politics of blackness
> ▶ Said: the invention of the East and intertwined histories of rereading
> ▶ Bhabha: the problem and promise of locating in-betweenness
> ▶ Spivak: feminist politics and the difficulties of subaltern voices
> ▶ Hall: shared and changed identities in post-imperial Britain

4 Textual

This chapter sets out to consider some of the central concerns and textual strategies to be found in postcolonial literature, i.e. concerns and strategies by which the critical issues identified and initially discussed in previous chapters actually become manifest in given texts. However, the distinction between "critical" and "textual" that is implied in our chapter sequence is quite problematic and itself in need of critical consideration. It suggests a basic division between two kinds of writing, "theoretical" as opposed to "creative", which might be a convenient shorthand but is not really tenable. It disregards the fact that critical writing by any of the authors introduced above (see 2.3) is also in some central ways 'creative' and in this respect no different from literary texts – just as, conversely, the novels, plays or poems we shall now discuss are just as 'critical' and hold as much 'theoretical' potential as other texts. The issue rather lies in the specific ways by which this potential has been realized and brought to bear on concrete circumstances.

Critical and textual always work together

Rushdie, Bhabha and hybridity: shared concerns

A case in point is *The Satanic Verses* (1988), Salman Rushdie's much debated – yet, unfortunately, little read – novel which has become an icon or flag of world politics and so-called East-West confrontations. One of the reasons why this novel of migration and transformation, whose critical edge, incidentally, is more directed against Thatcher's Britain than against Islamic faith, merits reading and attention is its powerful engagement with the meanings and uses of hybridity, a term we otherwise associate with Homi Bhabha's work (see 1.2.6). Yet Rushdie's narrative is so constructed – with its tropicalized London cityscape reversing Orientalist fantasies, with its characters and their metamorphoses and, above all, with its inventiveness of language – that it manages not just to illustrate hybridity but to explore and question this theoretical concept, thus offering clear contributions to the critical debate. We should not see this as a case of borrowing or application, as if *The Satanic Verses* merely exemplified what Bhabha's theory had previously and independently worked out. Rather, both the critical and the creative texts can be seen as working through the same issues, closely related and mutually inspired, each drawing on the other's strategies and formulations. In fact, the case of these two writers – both coming from Bombay, born in the late 1940s, and both pursuing highly visible careers in Britain and the United States – also includes personal connections and shared backgrounds, which might partly account for their shared concerns. But even where no such biographical entanglements are evident – as with the Caribbean novelist Jean Rhys and the American feminist critics Gilbert and Gubar, for instance, who have all famously explored *Jane Eyre* (see 2.4.4) – it is just as important for us to acknowledge the constant entanglement of critical with creative writing and of theoretical and textual strategies.

How post-colonial literature is intertwined with theory

As argued at the outset (see 1.1), whatever we may understand by it, "theory" is never absent, outside or beyond a given text but provides the flesh and bones of textual meanings, uses and effects. This holds true even for the works of writers who, as they well might, declare themselves to be altogether unconcerned with theoretical or academic discourse and take no interest in what "the critics" have to say. Especially in view of postcolonial writing, we should be wary of such notions. They often go along with the notion of an international division of labour by which third-world texts are processed and packaged in Western academia, as if the raw material mined in African or Asian literature should then proceed to be refined and prepared for the consumer market in Northern Europe or America. This, surely, is not just a gross misreading of cultural transfers and cross-currents but also a serious misjudgement of the critical processes always at work in literary texts. The following points of this chapter should therefore suggest, with reference to some prominent examples, how such cross-currents and key processes might be mapped and to what cultural use they have been put.

1 Life Writing

The term "life writing" refers to various forms of autobiographical texts, such as memoirs, diaries, journals, testimonials or letters. Especially in postcolonial literature, this is a highly productive field of major interest, and it is not difficult to see why. If postcolonialism begins, as we have seen (2.1.1), by reversing the familiar points of view and by providing insights into hitherto unrecognized or unrecorded fields of experience, the best way to do so may indeed be to set down personal memories, sufferings, trials, tribulations, triumphs, travels or adventures in some written form. No doubt, autobiographical literature abounds in many cultural fields and is a central part of the Western canon (see Wagner-Egelhaaf 2000). Still, it is in postcolonial contexts where it becomes most pertinent and prominent for its function to formulate the life stories of the oppressed and to present alternative perspectives on the world, i.e. to manifest views and voices previously not acknowledged.

The scope and relevance of autobiographical writing

Many examples bear this out. In 1953 the Caribbean writer George Lamming (*1927), who had come to England from Barbados three years earlier, published his first book, *In the Castle of My Skin*, written, as he put it in his later introduction, "in the desolate, frozen heart of London, at the age of twenty-three" (1991: ix), as he was trying to reconstruct the world of his childhood and adolescence. Yet for all the sense of isolation, loss and alienation that gripped the young black migrant in his first English winters, the world of his Barbadian background, as represented here, turns out to have been no less oppressive. He speaks of the colonial experience at that time as a "kind of subjugation", a "terror of the mind" and "daily exercise in self-mutilation" (1991: xxxix). In fact, he opens his narrative with memories of his ninth birthday, calling it "my ninth celebration of the gift of life, my ninth celebration of the consistent lack of an occasion for celebration" (1991: 9). Like him,

A Caribbean-English example: George Lamming

several other postcolonial writers in many different places, but especially in diasporic situations have built their literary careers – often actually *begun* their literary careers – with some such autobiographical project.

Key strategies of life writing as self-positioning

Several points typical of life writing, and for the strategies of postcolonial writing in particular, can be seen in Lamming's book. First, autobiographies are means of self-orientation, of trying to come to terms with unfamiliar or bewildering circumstances. Twenty-three may seem an early age for anyone to write his life, but for an immigrant who seeks to find his bearings and to reconstruct himself in a hostile host society, writing may well offer ways to do so, when the order of his narrative confers order on the life narrated, too. Second, it is the distance from home that makes this home available for imaginative reconstitution, for describing and for criticizing it, even for naming it as such. Life writing can only be about a life already lived, hence lost, a time and place long left behind and now accessible, if not recoverable, through acts of memory. Distance and loss are therefore constitutive for such texts, setting out to find not just some meaning but often also causation, rationale and motivation for the present in the past. Third, this has important consequences for the narrative procedure and the forms of language used. Above all, it is clear that autobiographical texts use the first person singular in two ways: the "I" marks the speaking voice of the adult persona – the homodiegetic narrator, as we can more technically put it – as well as the young persona who undergoes the earlier experience; the narrating I provides the language and interpretation for the lived events of the narrated I. It is unlikely, for example, that a nine year-old would call his birthday the "celebration of the consistent lack of an occasion for celebration": this bitter irony is part of a much later frame of mind and comes from the harsh voice of the twenty-three year-old narrator who thus articulates what he now recognizes as the misery of a colonial existence.

Political effects: claiming authorship and authority

If colonial experience, as Lamming says, consists in subjugation, mental terror and daily routines of self-mutilation, we can indeed understand why life writing offers such a powerful medium for postcolonial projects: it is a way to move from self-mutilation to self-mending, perhaps self-creation or -recreation and, at any rate, to self-assertion. In the words of Julia Swindells, autobiography provides powerful means for marginalized or subjugated people to turn from "subjects *of* discourse" to "subjects *in* discourse" (1995: 5), i.e., for people to claim their own speaking positions and thereby claim their social power. Swindells in fact includes women, blacks and working-class people in her analysis – so the complete series of gender, race and class – because all these have traditionally been excluded from official discourse (in Foucault's sense, combining linguistic and pragmatic means of power by which social control is enacted, see 1.2.2). But in the case of black writers this turn involves a special challenge. As Frantz Fanon argued in *Black Skin, White Masks* (see 2.3.1), his analysis of black predicaments published the year before Lamming's debut, "in the white world the man of color encounters difficulties in the development of his bodily schema. Consciousness of the body is solely a negating activity. It is a third-person-consciousness" (1986: 110). That is to say, as long as "blacks" are defined solely from without and with reference to skin colour they may easily internalise such racist designations and perceive of themselves in such terms. As argued earlier, "Look, a Negro!" is the constant cry by which, according to Fanon, blacks have been sealed in "crushing objecthood" (1986: 109). This situation may be remedied, we can now see, by engaging with life writing, i.e. by asserting a first-person consciousness and subjecthood.

It is no coincidence that many such projects culminated in the 1950s, the decade of decolonization, large-scale migration and postcolonial emergence. But the political uses and effects of life writing are of course much older. Think for instance of slave narratives, i.e. the stark accounts of oppression, escape, rescue and/or liberation, by which in nineteenth-century America the plight of slavery became known. These first-person narratives, based on oral modes and often the first public articulations by black people widely noted, were used in abolitionist campaigns and marketed in contexts where their individual life story could be interpreted as representative of larger social ills. *The Interesting Narrative of the Life of Olaudah Equiano, or Gustavus Vassa, the African, Written by Himself* (1789), too, belongs to this genre (as mentioned above, 2.1.2) and has been taken up in several versions or revisions by later postcolonial authors. But we should also think of white settlers, planters, travellers and explorers, who frequently have tried to cope with their encounters through forms of life writing, i.e., by recording their observations and impressions of an unfamiliar place in some familiar mode of bookkeeping. The Caribbean writer

Equiano and the uses of first-person narratives

Caryl Phillips has constructed an entire novel, *Cambridge* (1991), by juxtaposing two autobiographical accounts providing two different versions of the same events: the narrative of a white English woman visiting a West Indian plantation, and the narrative of a black slave whom she encounters there. The mode is fictional but the textual strategies employed here clearly come from classic documentary forms of life writing.

Equiano's textual transfers from Defoe's *Robinson Crusoe*

This leads us to the vexed question about the truth value and authenticity of autobiographical texts. As historical records, we usually understand them to refer to some empirical reality existing 'outside' the text, unlike novels which we read as fiction and understand in terms of their 'intrinsic' properties. But these neat distinctions rarely hold. The critical debate about Equiano's famous book, for instance, has suggested that he must have consulted not just existing travelogues on Western Africa so as to describe an African childhood he might never actually have had, but also adventure novels like Defoe's *Robinson Crusoe* (1719) so as to make his own narrative more "interesting". Yet such textual borrowings or transfers should not be misjudged as invalidating the entire life story he tells us. Rather, they are characteristic of the fundamental strategy that all life writing must pursue: the voice it seeks to raise and the identity it tries to claim are always already inhabited by other voices and framed in pre-existing categories because the language used for even the most personal experience can never be a truly personal language, but is an established public medium whose forms and modes can just be cited. The point lies in the *usage* of these given forms. In this sense, patterns of story telling, too, for instance the Aristotelian convention that stories have a beginning, a middle and an ending, are generally transferred, used and cited for the purposes of life writing – even if, as in the question of the ending, their relevance may well be doubtful here.

Beyond the fact/ fiction-divide: what memoirs do

Instead of the fact/fiction divide, therefore, it is more helpful to think of autobiographies as performative texts (in the sense of J.L. Austin's 1955 pragmatic analysis of so-called speech acts): they are not just descriptive, but productive; they *do* things with words and change the way things are. What they are doing can be characterised as self-formation by self-formulation. On the basis of existing strictures and in the framework of given power structures, the autobiographer turns into the author of his or her own life and thus of his or her own self. A celebrated case of this is Harriet Jacobs's

Incidents in the Life of a Slave Girl (1861), an American slave narrative which recounts how the young black woman eventually responds to her seduction by a white man, commenting that "it seems less degrading to give one's self, than to submit to compulsion" (1987: 55). Note that the text does not say "give oneself", i.e. the fact of the "self" that the slave girl gives away with her own body actually resists the patriarchal and economic system of slavery in which blacks were denied all selfhood, ownership and self-determination. As Ulla Haselstein has argued (2000: 137), her "gift of self" thus produces a remarkable act of self-appropriation: by telling how she gave her self she transforms herself from slave woman, i.e. from a victim owned by others, into a self to be given and gained.

In the history of the emerging postcolonial nations, such acts of life writing have often received strong political and nationalistic interpretations, sometimes openly championed by the autobiographers themselves. Kwame Nkrumah (1909–1972), for instance, first president of independent Ghana and one of the father figures of Pan-Africanism, published his autobiography on March 6, 1957, to mark the exact day of his country's liberation from colonialism, and he first entitled the book *Ghana* (in accordance with the new name for what was formerly known as Gold Coast), so as to emphasize the convergence of personal and political ambitions on this triumphant day. By contrast, Jawaharlal Nehru (1889–1964), first prime minister of independent India in 1947, emphasized that his *Autobiography* (1936) was just an account of personal developments, not a historical survey. But then, he already wrote it in the mid-1930s, while he spent two solitary years in a colonial prison. Indeed, he ends with rather melancholic reflections on his own position: "I have become a queer mixture of the East and West, out of place everywhere, at home nowhere" (1989: 596), as if the personal uncertainties reflected the political anxieties of India's future at the crossroads. The ongoing quest for a "place" or "home" which he might finally come to inhabit is thus implicitly parallelled to the ongoing nationalist struggle for his country's independence.

Two postcolonial nation builders and their memoirs

All this is to show that postcolonial life writing is a threshold genre. It traces and crosses boundaries between fact and fiction, memory and history, selves and others, home and exile – sometimes drawing these distinctions but more often blurring them.

Life writing is threshold writing

SUMMARY

This chapter has

▶ established the significance of first-person narratives in formulating and thus forming notions of the self
▶ pointed to the uses of such narratives in the postcolonial field
▶ looked at a range of examples, from the eighteenth to the twentieth century, all moving along the threshold between borrowing authority and bringing it to bear in new social contexts
▶ argued that it is less productive to ask what is fictional or factual in life writing than to ask what difference it makes and how to do things with life writing in the world

2 Place Writing

The problematic sense of place and home in postcolonial writing

This term refers to forms and modes of writing which aim to give as rich as possible a description of a particular locale. This occurs when postcolonial writers set out, in poetry, narrative or drama, to capture or create a sense of place, i.e. to give to local feelings and impressions a literary habitation and a name. There are other contexts, too, in which place writing has been prominent, but these are often treated with suspicion or even denigration, critically referred to as *Heimatliteratur*. It is not difficult to see why this kind of writing, in German for example, may seem a rather doubtful and parochial affair (although it is inappropriate to generalize about it in such terms), whereas in postcolonial contexts it is a powerful, productive and even consciousness-raising strategy. The point lies in its engagement with a place whose nature, culture, history and even name have not been rendered in literary language, at least not in the English language and not as properly and fully as the writer feels it has deserved. In many cases the particular view and version of the place that is constructed in a postcolonial text is also set against competing versions and colonial perceptions of it that have hitherto been dominant. That is to say, if place writing in general attempts to build a sense of "home", for postcolonial literatures this is not easily given or unproblematically available, but often involves complex histories of conquest, settlement, reclamation and reinvention.

A Victorian South African example: Schreiner's paint-work

The first novel, for instance, to have been written in South Africa is *The Story of an African Farm* (1883) by Olive Schreiner (1855–1920), daughter of a missionary, born in Cape Town and later resident in England. Her remarkable text describes the lonely, Bible-dominated life on a mid-nineteenth-century farm in the mountains, with stark evocations of the bleak landscape of the South African veld. As her preface points out, the writer saw her greatest challenge in finding an appropriate language for this place, familiar to herself but quite unfamiliar to the English readership she had in mind: "should one sit down to paint the scenes among which he has grown", she writes in the voice of her male alias, "he will find that the facts creep in upon him. Those brilliant phases and shapes which the imagination sees in far-off lands are not for him to portray. Sadly he must squeeze the colour from his brush, and dip it into the grey pigments around him." (1987: 28) What Schreiner refers to as the "brilliant phases and shapes" are the exotic notions which Victorian readers entertained about distant places, clichés of some rich and colourful life far away. But in fact, she notes, the place is fundamentally different, so that her attempt to render it in writing is compared to dipping her paint-brush always into grey. Yet even this comparison suggests a discrepancy between the aesthetic categories available and the experience of place, a farming settler colony, far removed from any established artistic creativity.

Just like postcolonial life writing, as we have seen (2.4.1), can best be understood as a production of the self under adverse circumstances, so postcolonial place writing cannot take its object for granted but must try to produce it by whatever means available, often also trying to construct these very means along with it. In fact, the two projects frequently go together, since narratives of self and place often proceed by defining one in terms of the other. This connection is central, for example, in Sally Morgan's much-debated *My Place* (1987), an Australian autobiography that seeks a fuller understanding of personal identity through a fuller understanding of the place in which it is located. For this purpose, the narrator and central persona goes on a quest into her family's as well as her country's hidden layers and moves from alienation to identification, as she discovers that, beneath the surface structure of a white world, there are Aboriginal presences. The narrative presents these indigenous realities, part of a more intimate involvement with the land, its natural topography and life-cycles, as an available alternative for the autobiographer to embrace: she recognizes her Aboriginal belonging and is, in turn, recognized for it by the tribe. Identity, then, is not seen as a result of blood lines or genetic coding but of

An Australian example: Sally Morgan's place

cultural framing and personal acts. The "place" mentioned in the title as her own is thus the product, not the starting point of her discovery. Unlike Schreiner, in whose text all non-white figures occupy just marginal positions, Morgan finds a way to redefine herself by reclaiming this place.

Colonial place names evoke memories of elsewhere

The Australian example is especially instructive for place writing because the history of the country, since its eighteenth-century foundation as a British penal colony, has added many layers of significance. These are explored in detail in Paul Carter's ground-breaking study *The Road to Botany Bay* (1987), an "essay in spatial history" (as the subtitle has it), which examines the ways in which European sailors, settlers and colonizers once took possession of the place through acts of naming and mapping. Most current place names in this country – as in most other colonial territories – are foreign transfers, the results of conquest and cultural inscription by which political authority seeks to found itself through symbolic power. In the decades following the first white settlement in 1788, Carter shows, the "Australian interior was explored, its map-made emptiness written over, criss-crossed with explorer's tracks, gradually inhabited with a network of names" (1987: xx-xxi). The same holds true for other continents and countries in the Empire, like the New World or like Africa, where many of the given or invented names – such as San Salvador, New York, New Caledonia, Leopoldville, Rhodesia or Lüderitz – refer to colonial people, values, memories or places from elsewhere or, as in the case of Gold Coast and Ivory Coast, to central economic goods. Since Columbus and the early modern conquest of America, to which Tzvetan Todorov has dedicated an important discourse study (1982), colonial power has thus been manifest in acts of toponymic dispossession.

Aboriginal topographies: along different lines

As a consequence, postcolonial place writing may try, wherever possible, to trace older tracks and retrieve different names so as to suggest alternative constructions of locality. With regard to Australia, this has been demonstrated by Bruce Chatwin, an English writer, whose travelogue *The Songlines* (1987), published the same year as Carter's monograph, tries to follow in the footsteps of Aboriginal travels and their musical topographies. As one character explains, each "ancestor, while travelling through the country, was thought to have scattered a trail of words and musical notes along the lines of his footprints" so that "these Dreaming-tracks lay over the land as 'ways' of communication between the most far-flung tribes" (Chatwin 2005: 13). While Chatwin's text explores this fascinating field in the consciously performed role of an outsider, there have been several Australian writers, poets in particular, whose work sets out to re-map the settler version of their country and to provide a different vision of its ground realities, like Judith Wright (1915-2000) or Les Murray (*1938) or, even more urgently, poets writing from Aboriginal perspectives like Oodgeroo Noonuccal (1920-1993), Kevin Gilbert (1933-1993) or Mudrooroo (formerly known as Colin Johnson, *1938). For Caribbean poets, by contrast, no such alternative access to space and place is possible, because few remnants from indigenous languages or cultures, i.e. Arawaks and Caribs, and only few indigenous names have survived early modern European conquests. As a result of genocide, migration and large-scale resettlements, their Caribbean locality is largely without ancient local memory (see 3.4). Poets like Derek Walcott and Edward Kamau Brathwaite have therefore stressed the need, on the basis of transferring languages and names – whether from Africa, Asia or Europe – to produce new versions of home.

For all postcolonial place writing, however, it is crucial to acknowledge that it can never actually reconstitute its place in pure and pristine form, whatever it may have been like under precolonial conditions. This is a central point which Said makes, as mentioned earlier (see 2.3.2), in *Culture and Imperialism*. First, he notes the "primacy of the geographical element" in anti-imperial writing; for "the native, the history of colonial servitude is inaugurated by loss of the locality to the outsider", a loss of land that is recoverable "only through the imagination" (1993: 271). Then he describes the literary strategy of such recoveries, as quoted above, with reference to an Irish example: "To the anti-imperialist imagination, our space at home in the peripheries has been usurped and put to use by outsiders for their purpose. It is therefore necessary to seek out, to map, to invent, or to discover a *third* nature, not pristine and pre-historical ('Romantic Ireland's dead and gone', says Yeats) but deriving from the deprivations of the present. The impulse is cartographic, and among its most striking examples are Yeats's early poems collected in 'The Rose'." (1993: 272) That is to say, the project of such a literary remapping is not to seek idylls or utopias outside historical determinations, but to construct a space beyond colonial confines and yet based on their premise, a space

No return to a pre-colonial paradise: literary remapping

that Said characterizes as "a *third* nature". It could be argued, therefore, that this nature corresponds to what Bhabha has repeatedly referred to as "third space" (see 2.3.3).

An Irish example: double space in Joyce's *Ulysses*

The example mentioned here, the early poetry of W.B. Yeats in the context of Irish nationalist movements around 1900, is highly interesting and merits more discussion (see 3.1). More should also be said about the issue that postcolonial *place* writing is not necessarily *nature* writing, as in the texts briefly considered in this chapter, but also involves *urban* places, especially the metropolis London, whose cultural construction and social structures have been transformed in Black British literature (see 3.6). The same point about transforming a colonial city through literary remapping has, in fact, been made about Dublin in the early twentieth century and its detailed reconstruction in the text of Joyce's *Ulysses* (1922). In Chapter 10 of this novel, the colonial cityscape, dominated by the English viceroy's cavalcade, is both underwritten and undercut by a multitude of local presences with their different authorities, voices, views and stories (see Jameson 1988). Setting up such spatial double structures, Joyce's famous city text, written in a situation of diaspora, redescribes the place by reintepreting its name – *Dublin* turns into *doubling* – so as to produce a counter-version of it, just as in postcolonial place writing. All these are cases therefore where, in Salman Rushdie's words, "description is itself a political act" because "redescribing a world" becomes "the necessary first step towards changing it" (1991: 14).

SUMMARY

This chapter has

▶ established the importance of place, of home and landscape in post-colonial literatures
▶ shown that this derives from the colonial history of mapping and subjecting territories through imperial conquest and renaming
▶ looked at a number of examples, from South Africa via Australia to Ireland, which suggest some ways in which the outlines of alternative topographies can be traced
▶ argued that, instead of a recovery of pre-colonial places, we are looking at historical landscapes and their remapping in contemporary writing

3   History Writing

Since the beginning of literary criticism, i.e. since Aristotle's *Poetics*, the relationship between history and literature has been a fundamental issue of debate. Aristotle said that, principally, historians write about "actual events" whereas poets write about "the kind of things that might occur", and he assigned a higher value and greater philosophical significance to literature because it "relates more of the universal, while history relates particulars" (chapter 9, Aristotle 1995: 59). But such distinctions have proved hard to hold. How do we know what actually happened and when can we ever be sure of the particulars that historians write down? Generally speaking, the past is not accessible or observable for us except through certain traces and remains – artefacts or texts – which we must read as documentary evidence. Therefore, like the notion of culture discussed earlier (see 2.2.1), what we call "history" is actually a textual product, in Western cultures most often a written one, assembled and collated from various sources and the particular interpretations they receive. Nevertheless, the interpretations given to them are often claimed to express "universal" values or truths. Whether or not such claims about the past are accepted and successful often comes down to questions of mastery and domination, that is to say, the real question is who succeeds in imposing his (or, less often, her) version on others. This suggests why this general problem of historiography, frequently discussed and dismantled in postmodernist critical works such as Hayden White's *Metahistory* (1973), has special relevance to postcolonial writing.

As all chapters of this introduction illustrate, postcolonial literatures have gained much of their urgency and substance from the critical engagement with the use of history and its involvement in the ruse of power. When Paul Carter, for example, at the outset to his study *The Road to Botany Bay* (see 2.4.2), examines some of the established text-book histories of Australia, he finds that their "primary object is not to understand or to interpret: it is to legitimate", and shows that a larger historiographical project is at the centre of colonial discourse and imperial politics: "This is why this history is associated with imperialism – for who are more liable to charges of unlawful usurpation and constitutional illegitimacy than the founders of colonies? Hence, imperial history's *defensive* appeal to the logic of cause and effect: by its nature, such a logic demonstrates the emergence of order from chaos." (1987: xvi) In the same way that Said argues in *Orientalism* (see 2.1.1 and 2.3.2), the demonstration of this order is really a self-demonstration of power; by means of such a logic, then, the act of *writing* history has actual, worldly consequences. And here is where the strategies of literature come in: through making cause and effect cohere in a full story – i.e. by turning random or coincidental events into a plot with a beginning, a middle and an ending, according to Aristotle's precept – narrative is instrumental for such a project and politically effective.

Making History:
an example from
postcolonial
theatre

This point is made, for instance, in an Irish play by Brian Friel, entitled *Making History* (1989). Set around the battle of Kinsale in 1601, i.e. the decisive military defeat of Irish insurrectionists led by the Earl of Tyrone against the imperial English power, it examines the crucial strategies by which such power is defined and used. The final act shows the defeated Earl in exile, where he discovers that the bishop who is writing his personal history takes extraordinary liberties with what Tyrone considers to be the plain facts. But the churchman and historian remains unperturbed: "I'm simply talking about making a pattern", he explains to the disenchanted hero. "That's what I'm doing with all this stuff – offering a cohesion to that random catalogue of deliberate achievement and sheer accident that constitutes your life. And that cohesion will be a narrative that people will read and be satisfied by." (1989: 67) So the title "making history" emerges to have several meanings: first of all, it emphasises that history is something made, i.e. produced and fabricated, not anything that simply happens. Yet what is more, the title does not just refer to the historical protagonists like Tyrone whose heroic deeds have tried to change the world, but rather to their *textual* making, i.e. the representation and production of heroism in historiographical writing. History drama has long been used to highlight and explore such ambiguities. Friel's play can be seen to stage the hidden Irish plot behind the Shakespearean history plays, especially *Henry V*, which contains topical allusions to English campaigns in Ireland in 1599. *Making History* thus follows previous theatrical engagements with the Irish past on the stage of the Irish National Theatre around 1900 (see 3.1.), which have, in turn, inspired Caribbean writers like Walcott, whose early history play *Henri Christophe* (1949) deals with the Haitian revolution around 1800.

Postcolonial novels, too, frequently set out to offer narratives of some historical event or figure in order to disrupt the patterns by which these have been represented and so reclaim or reassess their relevance in the historiographical record. Thomas Mofolo's *Chaka* (1925, new English translation by Daniel Kunene in 1981) is a case in point. The first novel written by an African in an African language, Sesotho, this text from South Africa is centred on a major warrior figure in the history of the country, Shaka Zulu (1787–1828), sometimes referred to as "the Black Napoleon", who in the early nineteenth century gathered large territories and populations under his military leadership. This mighty figure of black power, to whom Mofolo drew attention shortly after the white-dominated South African Union had been founded in 1910, also features in a lot of other writing, such as Léopold Senghor's francophone poem "Chaka" from *Ethiopiques* (1956), Wole Soyinka's poem "SHAKA!" from *Ogun Abibimañ* (1976) or Mazisi Kunene's epic *Emperor Shaka the Great* (1979). But even though these various examples all engage with the same historical protagonist, they construct him and his legacy in very different ways: Kunene, drawing on traditions of Zulu praise songs, openly celebrates him as a shining model of personal and political strength; Senghor casts him as hero in an allegorical morality drama to propound his vision of négritude (see 1.2.5); Soyinka fuses him with Ogun, a god from Yoruba mythology, and uses him to explore possibilities of committed writing, especially in view of the 1976 Soweto uprising in South Africa; and Mofolo narrates an emblematic life story, tightly balancing sympathy with scepticism, thus presenting the titular hero as admirable and terrifying, ambitious and tyrannous at the same time. In fact, the Basotho people, Mofolo's ancestors, historically used to be subdued by the Zulu nation Shaka founded. So the different versions of this historical figure are all part of complex contemporary agendas.

Shaka: a historical hero in contemporary African writing

The example serves to show how uses of the past in history writing – whether in novels, plays or poems – generally respond to present needs. Shaka, as a historical protagonist, is not just portrayed differently in these different texts but actually invented by them, in accordance with contemporary purposes and interests (see Golan 1994). This suggests that the present is not just shaped by the past but also actively shapes and begets its own past through continuous acts of interpretation and invention. Therefore, we should analyse history writing always on two levels: the level of what is

Two levels of analysis for historical fiction: *Things Fall Apart*

historically represented (e.g. the Zulu wars in the 1820s) and the historical level of representation (e.g. in Mofolo's case, South African politics in the 1920s). The more complex and subtle post-colonial texts already involve reflections on this double issue. *Things Fall Apart* (1958), for instance, Chinua Achebe's first novel and a founding text for African literature (see 3.2), is set in Igbo-land, Nigeria, in the early 1900s. The narrative closes with a colonial perspective: the district commissioner thinks about how to include the events narrated by the novel into a book he plans to write himself. As he concludes that "a reasonable paragraph", rather than an entire chapter, will be quite enough for them, Achebe's text highlights the conventional pattern long dominant in English administrative prose about "native" affairs. In this way, the postcolonial historical novel offers a critical engagement with colonial historiography. But in the double way just mentioned, its title suggests two different readings: on the level of what is historically represented, it might refer to the falling apart of indigenous social structures under the impact of English missionaries and colonialists; on the historical level of representation, however, it rather signifies the falling apart of the British Empire and its discursive structures, a process rapidly under way in the late 1950s when Achebe's novel first came out and, indeed, much facilitated by this publication.

Eurocentric views: history as an exclusive property

In the case of African writing, such an emphasis on history is all the more significant because, for centuries in European literature, philosophy and science, it used to be received opinion that Africans had no proper history anyway, or, if so, then only through outside contacts or colonial intervention. This preconception rested on related assumptions like the notion that only written documents or architectural monuments, such as the pyramids in Egypt, could truly constitute historical manifestations whereas oral traditions, as prevalent in sub-saharan societies, were not recognized as such. Prominent thinkers like Hegel therefore held that the rest of the continent was frozen in some timeless, primary state of nature, barbarous and primitive, without development, dynamics or participation in the wider movements of world history. So colonial ventures could long be justified and morally vindicated with the claim to 'open' Africa 'at last' to progress, civilization and enlightenment. In *Europe and the People Without History* (1982), Eric Wolf has studied the remarkable career of this idea and noted the glaring contradiction that, with the seventeenth-century rise of the slave trade, Europeans conducted large-scale business transactions with the

African élites co-operating in the trade but never once considered the social developments that must have gone along with economic ventures.

Since the mid-nineteenth century, especially with the rise of Darwinism and evolutionary thinking, the notion of timeless, primitive and prehistoric forms of life preserved in Africa – and indeed in many other places at the margins of the imperial world – became increasingly associated with the figure of the "missing link", i.e. the putative connection between animals and humans. Central texts of European modernism, like Joseph Conrad's *Heart of Darkness* (1899, see 2.4.4), draw on these problematic notions, as do popular adventure novels like Arthur Conan Doyle's *The Lost World* (1912), where an English expedition to South America discovers a prehistoric Jurassic world fully preserved on a remote plateau in the interior. The examples show that, for imperial world views, history and temporality were posited as properties exclusive to the colonizing power while the colonized were thought to be arrested in the primitive conditions which cultured people had long left behind: 'they' still are what 'we' once used to be. As a consequence, travellers to the colonial peripheries could stage themselves as descending into prehistorical layers of human existence, confronting early, child-like or savage versions of themselves. The other in colonial encounters was thus taken as a discarded double of the self.

Time travels through the imperial world: the colonized as earlier versions of the self

Against this background, we can understand the central role of history writing in postcolonial literatures, not just in Africa. Especially in the decades of decolonization, i.e., beginning with India's independence in 1947 and culminating in the 1960s, one of the principal projects was to assert historical realities and to manifest historical consciousness in writing, as books like Nkrumah's autobiography (see 2.4.1) and many others demonstrate. In more recent postcolonial texts, however, such assertions, often steeped in nationalist rhetoric, have themselves been subject to critical scrutiny, sceptical reconsideration or downright parodistic treatment. The prime example of such moves is *Midnight's Children* (1981), Salman Rushdie's highly acclaimed novel. It presents the "birth" of the Indian nation on midnight, August 15, 1947, to have happened concurrently with the birth of Saleem Sinai, its narrator, and of a thousand other Indian children precisely at this moment. By virtue of this historic coincidence, these children are not just said to be endowed with magic qualities and supernatural powers, they are

Postcolonial writing reclaims history: the case of Midnight's Children

also, as Saleem puts it, "handcuffed to history": in response to Prime Minister Nehru's letter of congratulation, the narrator remarks: "I was linked to history both literally and metaphorically, both actively and passively" (1981: 238), thus parodying the pervasive rhetoric of national destiny and its fulfilment at this midnight hour. In this way, the novel critically examines the myths of postcolonial nationhood and reviews the historical tropes on which imagined communities are founded. But in fact, Rushdie's central trope is transferred from a Victorian English classic, *David Copperfield* (1850) by Charles Dickens, whose narrator and hero, too, tells us at the beginning that he was born at midnight – "It was remarked that the clock began to strike, and I began to cry, simultaneously" – thus raising the question of how our personal histories relate to the simultaneous, communal or national history in which we always find ourselves embedded.

Postmodern engagements in postcolonial fiction

In *Midnight's Children*, this question is tackled on the level of narrative discourse by foregrounding the situation in which Saleem is trying to tell his story to an inquisitive, but often unsympathetic listener, a woman named Padma, who interrupts, corrects, chastises or rebukes him all the time. To her, he also has to admit so many shortcomings, errors and mixed up identities that his entire narrative, allegedly celebrating Indian history, is rendered more and more doubtful. Rushdie's novel therefore suggests a fundamental critique of historiography and its narrative conventions that we also find in several postmodern novels, just as in theoretical analyses like Hayden White's (1973). The Canadian critic Linda Hutcheon (1988) has characterized the strategy of contemporary novels which engage in such a project, among them many postcolonial texts, as **"historiographic metafiction"**; that is to say, they construct fictions about the construction of fictional worlds in order to reveal and question how history is being written, made, perpetuated and interpreted. Among this larger field, history writing with a postcolonial provenance stands out, as our brief discussion shows, through rejecting or reworking the specific narratives by which colonial history long used to be made.

SUMMARY

This chapter has

▶ established why and how issues of history and historiography are crucial for postcolonial literatures

▶ suggested the literary and the political realities of historical narratives in their patterns of constructing stories and their impact on the world

▶ shown that exclusive views of history were central in colonial discourse and its notion of the advanced European self

▶ looked at literary examples from postcolonial Ireland, Africa and India to argue that their strategies of "making history" should be analysed on two levels: the level of what is historically represented and the historical level of representation

4 Rewriting

This is a broad and quite inclusive concept which is often – and often controversially – employed to describe in general terms the strategies at work in postcolonial texts (see Döring 1996). It is used to emphasize that many writers from formerly colonized countries have placed their books in programmatic opposition to the English books they were brought up with as part of a colonial education, i.e. the novels, plays or poems by English and colonial writers who clearly construct or perpetuate such eurocentric world views in their fictions that non-European characters or settings are represented in stereotypical and degrading ways. As a consequence, many postcolonial writers have felt the challenge to respond to fictions of this sort, trying to reverse the narrative perspective, to reconsider the plot, to reposition marginalized characters, to redress the symbolic structures – in short, to "rewrite" the given texts. As such, the practice of rewriting is long established and widely employed (see Childs 1999). The controversies in Postcolonial Studies that nevertheless surround it as a theoretical concept arise because of its connection to the so-called "writing back"-model, first introduced by three Australian critics in 1989 (see 1.2.1). This model has been taken to suggest that *all* postcolonial writing, no matter when and where produced, is principally engaged in nothing but responding to "metropolitan" texts (i.e. texts from England, the former imperial mother country) and correcting their distortions. Such a view, however, is itself quite a distortion of what the three authors argued in *The Empire Writes Back* and, at any rate, it is not adequate to understand the concept of rewriting.

Rewriting and "writing back": common critical confusions

**Textual passages
and cross-cultural
connections:
a more complex
view**

To be sure, cross-cultural connections in the wake of Empire are far
more complex and varied than to be always and only defined by
the relation between "centre" and "periphery", i.e. England and
the former colony. So any *exclusive* focus on the ways in which
anglophone writers from Africa, Asia, Australia or wherever "write
back" to the English canon and so respond to the colonial classics
they used to read in school, must surely miss a lot. And yet, it
would be equally problematic to deny that such literary responses
have been going on, some of them very prominent and powerful
indeed, and that they are, if a prediction may be risked, likely to
continue. The prediction rests, firstly, on the observation that younger writers, too, who have not actually themselves gone through
colonial education still show a marked interest in drawing such
connections to colonial classics in their works, e.g. the Asian-
British writer Hari Kunzru and his much-noted novel *The Impressionist* (2002, see Griem 2007). Secondly, it rests on the fundamental point that all literature engages with previous literature –
critically, creatively, constructively, deconstructively – because *all*
writers draw on the traditions in which they find themselves even
while redrawing them. So the concept of rewriting involves a great
deal more than a narrow view of response and correction would
suggest. The complexities suggested by it begin to emerge when we
consider once again the writing strategies discussed in the previous
sections, i.e. postcolonial history writing, place writing and life
writing. In each case, we have seen that the relevance of these
stategies emerges from the textual situation in which authors begin
to work. For example, for African writers to discover that their
history has consistently been denied, or for Australian writers to
realize that their place has historically been misnamed, may indeed
motivate their own work in history writing (2.4.3) and place writing (2.4.2). Even for life writing (2.4.1) we have noted how often
it engages with some previous text which is taken up and, at the
same time, taken on, so that we could actually speak of life rewriting.

In this way, our three preceding sections also suggest that the
notion of rewriting captures the fundamental sense in which all
literature partly continues and partly contests previous writing:
continues because the very forms of language are inherited and
taken over; *contests* because these forms are now used in a different
context to establish different meanings. This is what literary theory
since the 1970s describes as **intertextuality**, i.e. the view that texts

are never closed, contained and clearly bounded by their authors, but principally open, limitless, accessible from many sides and for diverse influences. In short, that texts are always entangled with all sorts of other texts. Rewriting should be seen as a special case of intertextuality. It differs from the general concept in that it is best understood as a concrete strategy pointed at an explicit target, i.e. an identifiable previous text to which it responds and against which it proceeds. It repeats some aspects of this previous text so as to resist it and to redraw its premises. Rather like the prefix *post-* in the term *postcolonial*, the prefix *re-* in *rewriting* thus designates a double function: repetition and resistance, or reliance on and reversal of the given structures. The following examples will not just help to illustrate but also to problematize this fundamental pattern.

There are a number of major English classics which have repeatedly and pointedly been subject to postcolonial rewriting (see Childs 1999). Above all, these are William Shakespeare's play *The Tempest* (ca. 1610), Daniel Defoe's novel *Robinson Crusoe* (1719), Charlotte Brontë's novel *Jane Eyre* (1847) and Joseph Conrad's novella *Heart of Darkness* (1899). These texts are so relevant for postcolonial projects because all of them, on the level of their plot, deal with the history and culture of the Empire and all involve some figure of the "native other", i.e. of the colonized, as part of their fictional construction. So all these works can and have been analysed at greater length in terms of their colonial discourse, to which postcolonial writing then provides a counter-discourse (for these terms, see 1.2.2 and 1.2.3). Typically, this pattern is manifest in a central couple of white master and black slave, and most famously this has been realized in *Robinson Crusoe*. Often seen as the first true novel in a modern sense, Defoe's narrative presents the account of an English castaway, who after many years of solitude on a tropical island rescues an indigenous young man from so-called cannibals; he names him "Man Friday" and makes him his eternally grateful servant. At the same time, Friday becomes a willing figure of learning and cultural inscription, who constantly gratifies and reconfirms his master's civilized, superior position. Caribbean writers like Walcott, in his comedy *Pantomine* (1978), have revisited this archetypal couple and given their roles different interpretations, while the South African writer J.M. Coetzee, in his novel *Foe* (1987), has rewritten the literary tradition by which these roles are defined, suggesting that Friday's personal story can never be retrieved. But Walcott, importantly, has also drawn on the

Some prominent examples: Defoe's *Robinson Crusoe*

Crusoe figure and explored the castaway, cut off from his familiar background and forced to remake his entire world, as an ancestor of contemporary Caribbean culture. This shows that the project of rewriting is not simply a black and white role reversal but involves far more complex and nuanced engagements with the formative texts.

Conrad's *Heart of Darkness* and the post-colonial debate

The same holds true for postcolonial engagements with Conrad's *Heart of Darkness*, a tale of travel and adventure into an unnamed African country and, at the same time, a disillusioned review of the old rhetoric by which colonial ventures used to be hailed as "light-bringing" and glorious. For this reason, Conrad's powerful novella has often been read and praised as a strong indictment of imperial attitudes and colonial practice. And yet, its own symbolic structures are steeped in just such attitudes. The text proceeds on a fundamental pattern that sets up the dark African interior as a place for European travellers to reach into their own dark selves, so that all sense of historical development or social realities has been extinguished from this psychologized mindscape. In a much-noted attack on Conrad and his Western readers, Chinua Achebe has therefore called the author a "thoroughgoing racist" and demanded to recognize his use of Africa for Europe's unacknowledged double as a blatant degradation of the African as "human factor" (in Conrad 1988: 251-62). Other responses in postcolonial rewritings, such as Wilson Harris's enigmatic Caribbean novel *Palace of the Peacock* (1960), however, have stressed the cultural anxieties that Conrad's narrator must fight, while writers like Abdulrazak Gurnah in *Paradise* (1994) or David Dabydeen in *The Intended* (1991) have rewritten the journey into the interior as a central trope of cultural encounters.

More examples of rewritings, especially on the stage

Besides, there are many other texts which have also functioned as the template and target of postcolonial rewritings: Joyce Cary's novel *Mister Johnson* (1939) for Chinua Achebe (see 1.1), Charles Dickens's novel *Great Expectations* (1861) for Peter Carey (*Jack Maggs*, 1997) or, to cite a particularly interesting case, J.M. Synge's Irish comedy *The Playboy of the Western World* (1907) for Mustapha Matura and his Trinidadian rewriting *Playboy of the West Indies* (1984). This last example is so interesting because Synge's play, first produced in Dublin in the context of the Irish nationalist movement (see 3.1), can itself be seen as a critical engagement with prevailing stereotypes and colonial mindsets, so that Matura's Caribbean version in a sense continues as much as complements this critique. Nor are examples limited to rewriting English texts. Matura has also written a play entitled *Trinidad Sisters* (1988), a cultural translation of a modern Russian classic, Anton Chekhov's *Three Sisters* (1901); Derek Walcott's *The Joker of Seville* (1974) is a Caribbean version of Tirso de Molina's early modern Spanish play about Don Juan, *Il Burlador* (ca. 1630); and the Australian Aboriginal writer Mudrooroo is author of a complex stage play, in which an Aboriginal theatre company performs Heiner Müller's *Der Auftrag* (1980) entitled *The Aboriginal Protesters Confront the Declaration of the Australian Republic on 26 January 2001 with the Production of the Commission by Heiner Müller* (1996).

It is no coincidence that plays are paradigmatic for the concept and strategy of rewriting. After all, every theatrical production is an opportunity and challenge to rethink an old text in new terms, to recast given characters, reinvent a setting and thus, in the process of performance, explore to what contemporary uses cultural traditions may be put (see 4.2). In just this way, contemporary writers are often challenged to revisit and reuse old forms and texts anew. The most important case concerns Shakespeare's *The Tempest*, not only because this play is also set on a solitary island and thus recalls long-standing colonial fantasies of conquest and settlement, but because it centres on the dominating figure of a patriarch named Prospero whose authority and benign power, surely evident for Renaissance spectators, have been called into doubt. Three figures are shown to be under his command, and all three have become central in postcolonial rewritings: his young daughter Miranda, the airy spirit Ariel who serves as his attendant and assistance, and a half-beastly figure called Caliban who is introduced as a "savage" and "deformed slave". Since the dialogue suggests that Caliban was born on the island (although his mother Sycorax came there, like Prospero, as an exile) and that he has strong claims of belonging to the place, it is this figure in particular that has become a major focus for rewritings.

Especially in the Caribbean, the generation of writers who came of age in the period of decolonization have seen their own struggle against domination prefigured in Caliban and recognized themselves in the angry curses against his master: "You taught me language, and my profit on't/ Is I know how to curse" (*The Tempest*, 1.2.366-7). But as this very curse makes clear, Caliban's verbal expression of resentment and resistance still relies on what he gained

Shakespeare's The Tempest: a key text in postcolonial debates

Caliban, Ariel, Miranda and their postcolonial counterparts

from the experience of domination, i.e. the English language – just as writers from the Caribbean used this very medium to contest English cultural power. Central for this project are: *Tempest*-rewritings by George Lamming in his essay collection *The Pleasure of Exile* (1960) and his novel *Water With Berries* (1972), the francophone stage play *Une Tempête* (1969) by Aimé Césaire and J.-M. Serreau, poems by Nkem Nwankwo (1968) from Nigeria, Lemuel Johnson (1973) from Sierra Leone and David Dabydeen from Guyana (1988) or the novel *A Grain of Wheat* (1967) by the Kenyan Ngũgĩ wa Thiong'o. Likewise, Shakespeare's Ariel, an intermediary and go-between figure, has become central in Latin American explorations of the "mestizo" condition, for instance by J.E. Rodo (1900), and the figure of Miranda, who is placed under paternal power but belongs to the side of settlers, has been focussed on especially in Canadian rewritings, such as in Margaret Laurence's novel *The Diviners* (1974). More recently, the English writer Marina Warner has produced a complex interweaving of feminist and postcolonial responses to *The Tempest* in her novel *Indigo* (1992), revisiting Britain's imperial past from a post-imperial point of view (see Zabus 2002).

Feminist readings and a Victorian narrative of female emancipation

These last examples suggest an important parallel between postcolonial and feminist concerns. Before questions of colonialism and race relations became a major issue in literary studies, the 1970s and '80s were much concerned with questions of gender and the retrieval or reconstruction of women's views and voices from the cultural tradition. This project has a lot in common with postcolonial rewritings, because in either case the effort to gain access to alternative articulations, from beyond or below the established mainstream, involves very similar challenges: it must begin with a rereading of the literary canon, i.e. with a critical reconsideration of the books that have been central instruments of social control and self-definition. With regard to the feminist project, a key book to initiate such rereadings has been *The Mad Woman in the Attic* (1979) by two American critics, Sandra Gilbert and Susan Gubar. Their title derives from Brontë's *Jane Eyre,* where Mr Rochester's first wife, Bertha, whose disturbing presence long prevents the happy union between the heroine and her love, is secretly kept in the attic room of his country house, imprisoned like an animal and declared mad. Gilbert and Gubar see this imprisonment as symptomatic of the position of women writers in patriarchal society, such as Brontë's in Victorian England, relegated to marginal spaces and demonized as threatening the social order. "Madness", for them, figures as a strategy of resistance by which women can transgress the boundaries set up to contain them and break through the systems of male rationality and control. In this way, Gilbert and Gubar offer a rereading of the novel that sees Bertha as the heroine's double because she "not only acts *for* Jane, she also acts *like* Jane" (1979: 361), i.e. the madwoman enacts all the transgressive moves that Jane first hesitates to perform.

Significantly, however, such a view of Jane and Bertha and their relation as doubles is already implied in an earlier postcolonial rewriting of Brontë's novel, *Wide Sargasso Sea* (1966) by Jean Rhys. Here, in a subtle modernist response to the Victorian female classic, the story is changed by providing it with a different beginning: Rhys's fiction is a so-called "prequel", setting a new premise on which the later and familiar plot proceeds. In *Jane Eyre* we learn that Bertha is a creole, member of a run-down planter's family in the West Indies. Jean Rhys (1890-1979), who was born in Domenica and later lived in London, Paris and Cornwall, does not just provide her with a fuller story and narrative presence but also suggests to see her identity as twinned or doubled, not just contrasted or juxtaposed, with that of Brontë's Jane. Two larger points, then, become clear from this example. First, the significance of the imperial world for domestic English fictions, especially of the Victorian age: *Jane Eyre* is in no obvious way "about" colonial projects (such as *Robinson Crusoe* certainly is); set entirely in England, the plot and its symbolic structures nevertheless presuppose the marginal world of the colonies like an off-stage space, whence disturbing characters (like Bertha) are derived or where restless characters (like Jane's frustrated cousin) can depart. Second, the significance of postcolonial rewritings for our view of English literature: *Wide Sargasso Sea* holds a critical potential which has only later been brought out in Gilbert and Gubar's feminist study and has, even later, been incisively analysed by Gayatri Spivak (1985). This suggests a kind of intertextuality which sees the postcolonial novel not simply as a "derivative" text trying to gain all its meaning from some canonical English work, but as a vanguard text suggesting different meanings and giving renewed critical force to English Studies.

An earlier Caribbean rewriting of this female narrative

SUMMARY

This chapter has

▶ introduced the term "rewriting" as a double strategy of literary repetition and resistance, pursued in several postcolonial texts
▶ argued that this strategy is part of the wider field of intertextuality, yet with a more evident political agenda
▶ looked at some central texts from the colonial canon – by Shakespeare, Defoe, Brontë, Conrad and others – and sketched their transformations in postcolonial perspectives
▶ emphasized the critical potential in postcolonial rewritings, urging us to reconsider familiar texts and readings

5   Genre Writing

Two ways to understand the term *genre*

The term *genre* is used in literary studies in two ways: first to designate the basic modes of literary production, second to refer to certain types of narrative that follow rather strict conventions of story telling and draw on predefined, hence often quite predictable, patterns of construction. In the first sense, *genre* applies to the three modes first set out by the Greeks, i.e. lyric, drama, epic. In the second sense, we speak of *genre writing* with reference, for instance, to mystery and crime fiction, spy thrillers, fantasy novels or science fiction, all controlled by a given set of narrative formulas and standards. It is because of this formulaic nature that genre writing is sometimes looked down upon and regarded as a lesser, or trivial, form of literature. But in fact there is no need for condescension nor prejudice against it. Principally, value judgements should not predetermine any choices and approaches taken in serious critical study (unlike practical criticism, on the level of reviewing, we are not really concerned with questions of 'good' or 'bad' writing). Besides, it should be emphasized that all the genres mentioned can be handled in very intricate ways and have been realized in highly significant and challenging texts. These are relevant in our context because in recent years postcolonial writing, too, has become ever more interested in exploring such conventions.

The sonnet as a genre of wooing

Understanding *genre* in the first and broad sense, of course, all writing – including postcolonial literatures – is genre-derived. But there have also been some very interesting and far-reaching experiments by postcolonial writers to make use of specific genre writing for their purpose, sometimes suggesting significant creative tensions which result from their transfer or translation into a different cultural context. The sonnet form provides a case in point. One of the most tightly structured and regulated forms of poetry, the sonnet first came to prominence in the Italian Renaissance and has long been associated with a given topic – unrequited love – as well as with a social class – the aristocratic élite – and cultural milieu – male courtiers seeking patronage. Over the centuries of European sonnet writing, many of these features have been fundamentally changed. And yet, the cultural connotations it involves are still sufficiently precise to be re-activated and ironically used in post-colonial writing, for instance by the Irish poet Seamus Heaney (see 3.1), by the Zimbabwean writer Dambudzo Marechera (1992), who has produced a different version of Shakespeare's sonnets to the so-called Dark Lady, or by the Black British poet Patience Agbabi (2000), who has written caustic female verses of wooing.

Similarly, other poetic subgenres have been cross-culturally translated and rewritten, thereby exploring their ideological profile and exposing the specific cultural attitudes enshrined or expressed in them. For instance, "Guyana Pastoral" by David Dabydeen (1988) is a poem consciously couched in the language of English pastoralism, but juxtaposed here with disturbing references to the harsh conditions of black life on West Indian sugar plantations. The poem thus explores what language and generic forms might be available for creole culture. In some way, it actually repeats the efforts of eighteenth-century English poets who, according to the cultural agenda of their time, were trying to transfer the classic forms and literary precepts of antiquity onto their own unclassical domestic scene. On the other hand, Dabydeen's "Pastoral" questions and subverts these strategies of ennobling and idealizing barbarous homegrounds, as it insists that the age of neoclassicism was also the age of slavery. On a large and truly impressive scale, the classic genre of epic has also been subjected to such cultural translations into postcolonial writing, as in Derek Walcott's *Omeros* (1990) and Les Murray's *Fredy Neptune* (1998). Based on the great Homeric models, epic has long been seen to be especially closely tied to a certain ideological agenda of heroism, conquest, settlement, foundation and empire (see Quint 1993). It is therefore extremely interesting and challenging to observe how a contemporary Caribbean and an Australian writer have turned to this eminent genre and how they have transformed it.

Postcolonial uses of established genres: pastoral and epic

Redrawing the conventions

Postcolonial genre writing, these examples all suggest, can thus be understood as a continued and extended strategy of rewriting (see 2.4.4), i.e. a literary project that draws on given forms and structures in order to redraw them. Whereas for most rewriting projects the intertextual connections are to identifiable texts and titles, postcolonial genre writing pursues and explores the connections to basic patterns and conventions of familiar literary forms whose ideological premises and cultural effects are often defamiliarized in the process (see Döring 2002).

Crime fiction and genre (re-)writing: transcultural examples

This also concerns genre writing in the second sense outlined, above all, postcolonial crime fiction. A relatively new development in postcolonial literatures (with some notable historical forerunners), narratives of mystery, crime and detection have recently come to wider critical attention because they do not just include extremely popular books such as the series about *The No. 1 Ladies' Detective Agency* in Botswana by the Scottish writer Alexander McCall Smith (1998ff) which has steadily acquired cult status, but also because they offer a very rich and rewarding field of cross-cultural investigation. As a recent study of crime fiction from a transcultural perspective argues (Matzke/Mühleisen 2006), there are cases where the detective is a migrant or comes from a transcultural background; to solve the crime, the investigator is called upon to decipher hidden clues and meanings that require alternative forms of cultural understanding. For the reader, such fictions may therefore disclose new interpretative methods and indeed challenge facile interpretations of the postcolonial world.

Sherlock Holmes in his colonial world

Such disclosures and challenges are so significant because traditional crime fiction, in the conventional form developed in the nineteenth century, has strong political affinities to a conservative and often explicitly colonial agenda. In many cases the classic plot structures proceed to re-establish a given social order, temporarily disturbed or shaken by the crime but eventually reinforced as the result of a successful investigation which manages to have all foreign, threatening or unfamiliar elements eliminated. In Arthur Conan Doyle's Sherlock Holmes stories, for instance, with their popular investigations in the Home Counties of late-Victorian England, villains typically are of Indian, "Eastern", "Southern" or, at any rate, outlandish stock (some of them are also German). As in much Victorian fiction, the imperial outside world here functions as a backstage area whence dangerous illnesses, crime and corruption come to Britain but where, conversely, Britain must still go for business, consumer goods and power. The dark places of the colonies are thus assumed to be suffused with light and legal trade, an assumption which forms a topos in colonial discourse. As Patrick Brantlinger has argued, "Sherlock Holmes cannot tolerate a mystery without solving it, nor can Doyle; the darkness of this world will soon disperse, and light, radiating especially from England and Sussex, will be universal." (1988: 252) In this way, classic crime fiction contributes to the production and circulation of colonial world views.

It is therefore crucial to acknowledge how writers in the postcolonial field have used the crime genre and shifted its fundamental structures into a transcultural frame. In *When We Were Orphans* (2000), for example, the Japanese-British writer Kazuo Ishiguro undertakes a radical dissection and disenchantment of the English detective figure, sending him to failure in war-torn Shanghai, with many allusions to classics of the Sherlock Holmes genre and subtle intertextual links to golden age mystery writing. Other examples include the Bengali Holmes-figure called "Feluda", who features in a large number of stories by Satyatjit Ray published since the 1960s (and available in English as *The Adventures of Feluda*, 1988), or novels by the Black British writer Mike Phillips, who has produced a series of urban thrillers set in London, modelled on Dashiel Hammett's hard-boiled private eye of 1930s America, but this time with a black investigator. In *Anil's Ghost* (2000) Canadian writer Michael Ondaatje uses the narrative pattern of detective fiction for a haunting novel investigating the traumatic past in contemporary Sri Lanka (the country where Ondaatje was born and grew up), trying to recover from the violence of civil war. All these suggest how productive it is to focus on genre writing, or indeed genre rewriting, in postcolonial literatures.

Postcolonial detective fiction: investigating the tradition

In each case, readers' expectations are first raised and then disturbed or redirected as the literary conventions by which a genre is defined, are first evoked but ultimately often displaced, reconsidered, rejected or transcended. Another genre in which such moves are especially telling and important is, finally, the case of travel writing. Since the early modern accounts by explorers and discoverers who ventured into the New World or other unknown areas, travel writing has a long and close connection to imperial politics and colonial projects (see Pratt 1992, Spurr 1993). The very act, by an

The genre of travel writing and its post-colonial uses

outsider, of making a record of some foreign place and setting down momentary impressions in textual or visual representations that often suggest permanence, must be seen as an act of power by which authority attempts to be established (see 2.2.1). Postcolonial critical engagements with this genre, going back for quite some time, are therefore highly significant. Rehearsing the traditional rhetoric of discovery and adventure, they turn its trajectory around and shift the contact zones of cultural encounter to familiar territory such as England or the metropolis, whose outlines become defamiliarized as a result. Examples of such travelogues about England include *Sir Apolo Kagwa Discovers Britain* (1904/75) by Ham Mukasa from Uganda, *Land of Hope and Glory* (1949) by Frank Clune from Australia, or *Passage to England* (1959) by Nirad Chaudhuri from India. Equally interesting are postcolonial travelogues by migrants, such as V.S. Naipaul's *The Middle Passage* (1962) or Amryl Johnson's *Sequins for a Ragged Hem* (1988), who return from England to revisit the former home – in the two cases cited: Trinidad – they left behind.

Critical explorations

That the rhetoric of travel continues to offer a useful language for various modes of research, cultural discovery and intellectual probing is also suggested by the title of our present chapter, "explorations". Looking at some aspects of the history, culture, criticism and of the texts involved in postcolonial literatures, the chapter has not just tried to give a survey of this field, but also to explore – in the sense of careful thinking and discussion – the central strategies and issues which are at stake when engaging with postcolonial writing.

SUMMARY

This chapter has

▶ looked at ways in which postcolonial writing has employed and changed established literary formulas and forms
▶ discussed some such examples as special cases of rewriting
▶ in particular turned to the genres of crime writing and travel writing, since their Victorian rise to popularity closely allied to colonial practices and world views
▶ argued that recent postcolonial literature has critically and creatively investigated these traditions from transcultural perspectives

This chapter gives a survey of the geographical and cultural areas where postcolonial writing in English, or some variety of English, has emerged and continues to play a role in contemporary literature. These areas are – principally, but not exclusively – the former colonies, dominions, protectorates or mandates of the British Empire; since decolonization, many of them – but not all – are now members of the Commonwealth of Nations (or British Commonwealth, as it used to be called until 1949), a loosely organized association of sovereign states, several of them republics, which still pay some allegiance to the British crown. Hence the traditional name "Commonwealth Studies", prevalent until the 1980s, for what is now more often known as Postcolonial Studies (see 1.2.1). The union of the Commonwealth has purely symbolic, no actual political power, yet it involves a common frame of reference in historical and cultural matters, such as sports. For instance, all major cricket playing nations of the world are Commonwealth members, a remarkable and much-studied development because historically this very game used to represent colonial attitudes. While it was never really played nor understood outside the British Empire, cricket has long become a training ground for postcolonial moves of self-assertion in the anglophone world (see James 1963) and continues to symbolize shared aspects in the cultural construct of the Commonwealth.

Commonwealth and cricket: how to survey postcolonial territories

The survey undertaken in this chapter is focussed on a number of relevant areas and should serve three purposes. First, it offers exemplification of the critical and textual strategies discussed in the previous chapter, with reference to some of the concrete historical developments and cultural contexts in which they operate. Second, it offers basic information on these developments and contexts, i.e. the political, social and linguistic situation we should take into account when engaging with the literature that has emerged from it and that may, in turn, reshape this situation. Third, the survey would like to suggest points for further reading, i.e. introduce some well-known postcolonial writers and texts which students of this field might want to engage with in more detailed readings. (For more comprehensive and theory-informed critical interpretations of twelve relevant novels, see *A History of Postcolonial Literature in 12½ Books*, Döring 2007).

The agenda for the present survey chapter

But this straightforward agenda is, in fact, quite problematic. The problems begin with the critical value of the categories used.

Critical problems and omissions in this chapter

What, for instance, should terms like "African writing" or "Indian writing" refer to when the territories in question are large continents, containing a great number of ethnic, linguistic, social and literary traditions, with different degrees of involvement in the field of postcolonialism (which, for practical reasons, here only covers anglophone writing anyhow). Furthermore, we rarely find a clear relationship between territorial and cultural placing, because a lot of "African" or "Indian" writing is actually produced in diasporic situations, especially in North America and Britain. In fact, for historical reasons, much of the writing we are looking at cannot really be classified in regional or national terms at all, because the writers have migrated and have significant connections to more than just one place. This is what a category like "Black British", not based on geographical but political terms, is used to signify. But above all, the survey given in this chapter is problematic because of the limited number of areas included in it, as a mere glance at the list of subchapters – with their focus on Irish, African, Indian, Australian, Caribbean and Black British literature – will show. To note just the most glaring omissions: New Zealand and Canada, or various South Asian countries like Pakistan, Sri Lanka or Hong Kong, even some European places such as Malta, all used to be part of the British Empire and have become postcolonial territories in which the English language is a major medium of literary production. So, clearly, they would all need more detailed study in our context. However, as argued at the outset (see 1.1), the present introduction does not aim at a comprehensive account that might cover all aspects, but tries to highlight strategies and give relevant examples which show what is at stake.

Imperial world maps: a Conradian example

The six parts of this chapter should be taken as a kind of map, which may give orientation precisely because it is selective and schematic and can never be confused with the actual territory covered. As a matter of fact, the notion of mapping is rather apt in our context because the Empire, whatever else it may have been, was fundamentally a cartographic construction: a particular view of the entire world on paper, with divisions and claims of possession marked in a cartographic code. This notion is well captured in a scene from Conrad's *Heart of Darkness* (see 2.4.4) where the narrator looks at a map of Africa "marked with all the colours of a rainbow". What these colours indicate is brought out with his following observations: "There was a vast amount of red – good to see at any time because one knows that some real work is done in there – a deuce of a lot of blue, a little green, smears of orange, and, on the East Coast, a purple patch, to show where the jolly pioneers of progress drink the jolly larger-beer." (Conrad 1988: 13) The imperial partition of the African continent, and the colonial claims over each part by the various European powers, are starkly illustrated here: "red" signifies the British territories, "blue" the French, "purple" the German and so on, resulting in a grotesque patchwork of interests manifest in such a clownish cartographic image.

As a rule, imperial borders were all drawn on a map, in accordance with the different spheres of European interest, but with no regard to any of the ground realities, ethnic groups or local cultural connections involved in each case. And yet, these arbitrary borders later came to define many of the postcolonial nations that emerged in the twentieth century. In *Imagined Communities*, an important study on the origin and spread of nationalism, Benedict Anderson has emphasised this point and argued that it was precisely the colour code derived from the imperial map which made the cartographic image of the colonies serve as a logo for postcolonial liberation movements: "Dyed this way, each colony appeared like a detachable piece of a jigsaw puzzle. As this 'jigsaw' effect became normal, each 'piece' could be wholly detached from its geographic context." That is to say, the physical outline constructed on and by the map took on a rather different function: from a marker of imperial convenience it became a mark of recognition and identification by a new alliance of local peoples who began to organize themselves under its auspices: "Instantly recognizable, everywhere visible, the logo-map penetrated deep into the popular imagination, forming a powerful emblem for the anticolonial nationalisms being born." (Anderson 1991: 175) For instance, a country like Nigeria, which came about as a result of the 1914 "amalgamation" of two British protectorates, i.e. simply through an act of colonial administration, in later decades still developed a sense of nationhood on the basis of this act: the different ethnic, cultural and religious groups externally identified as "Nigerian" began to identify themselves with this colonial marker from the map – at least temporarily, until the wake of independence in the 1960s. It follows that the map as medium of imperial domination has historically been effective in constructing and strategically using postcolonial identities.

Nationalism and post-colonial uses of the map

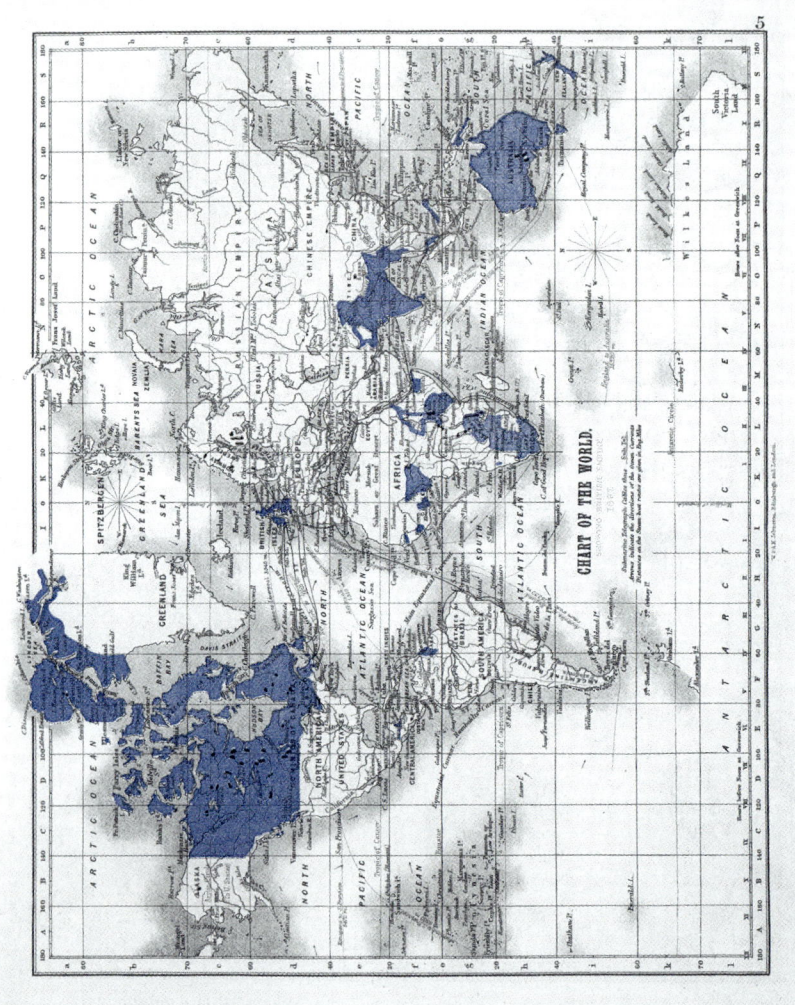

Quelle: A Historical Companion to Postcolonial Literatures/The British Library London

In the same way as maps are made of abstractions and reductions, history writing always leaves out more than it includes. And yet, just as with maps, the historical surveys offered in this chapter, sketchy and selective as they are, may nevertheless help to suggest what issues and developments Postcolonial Studies should take into account. The lists of historical dates are presented here from an English point of view and, in many cases, begin with colonial discoveries, conquests, take-overs or interventions. This is not to deny the long and significant indigenous history of many areas – for instance the Aboriginal presence in Australia, predating European landfalls by several thousand years. However, the historical survey deliberately adopts a colonial perspective and pattern, so as to highlight those aspects of history which postcolonial views and writing have subsequently questioned. The term "literary paradigms" is used in the sense of literary 'model' or 'example' to show how something works; so the following sub-chapters on cultural developments and trends do not give comprehensive nor continuous narratives of literary history, but introduce some central issues, writers and their work.

How to read the following surveys and charts

1 Focus on Irish Literature

In the general framework set up by Postcolonial Studies, the case of Ireland has long been debated. The question is whether Irish literature, for centuries produced under English domination, should be included in this frame so that it is aligned with postcolonial writing from Africa or India and, if so, how we should then address the issue that many Irish were functionaries of the British Empire, involved in maintaining colonial rule in Africa or India and many other places. No-one can doubt that Ireland was England's oldest colony and, in the twentieth century, the first to fight successfully for independence. Yet many have followed *The Empire Writes Back* (see Ashcroft et al 1989: 33) in doubting how useful it might be to see the literature and culture of a white European country, long complicit with colonial enterprises overseas, in line with anti-colonial resistance movements and their cultural agenda or with writing from newly decolonized countries. What is more, as soon as Irish literature is considered part of postcolonialism, there is no reason to exclude Welsh and Scottish writing any longer, because these nations with their common Celtic background, too, have been early victims of English expansion.

Is Ireland a postcolonial country?

Critical uses of comparison and contrast

Nor should they be excluded. In the understanding of the term suggested in this introduction (see 1.1 and 1.2.1), postcolonialism is not a matter of colour and political correctness, but of emplacement and perspective, a term which clearly should allow for such historical complexities and cultural entanglements as emerge in the case of Ireland, Scotland or Wales. The focus on Irish literature offered in this chapter, then, should not make us forget the salient contrasts that separate, say, a contemporary Australian Aboriginal writer like Mudrooroo from a European Irish modernist like Yeats. And yet, the complex moves and counter-moves of cultural affiliation and personal identification which both these writers have performed, constructing not just a tradition for themselves but also an embattled sense of audience and literary commitment, can usefully be studied against the frame set up by English literary traditions on which both writers draw in order to seek difference from them – a paradigmatic postcolonial strategy they share. Strictly speaking, each place and culture, every single writer and every one of his or her works demand to be studied on their own terms, since all comparisons or generalized claims involve distortions. But, taken to its final consequence, this view would not allow for any concepts to be used beyond a single instance. Therefore, comparisons, transfers, contrasts and generalizations must be risked. So the concepts available in postcolonial approaches may well be helpful to engage with Ireland, too.

"White chimpanzees": the Irish in Victorian English views

In the eyes of the English, the Irish have traditionally occupied an uneasy position between brothers and others, i.e. between views of sameness and difference. This is powerfully illustrated by the Victorian writer Charles Kingsley, who in the 1860s travelled through the Irish West and noted, in a letter to his wife, that he felt "haunted by the human chimpanzee" in the country. Referring to the Irish peasants he saw, he confessed "to see white chimpanzees is dreadful: if they were black, one would not feel it so much, but their skins [...] are as white as ours." (Kingsley 1901: 111) The statement is remarkable for its admission of uneasiness. The English traveller is troubled by the irritating mix-up of the categories usually keeping things apart: white versus black, human versus ape, colonizer versus colonized. But in the case of Ireland, he must note, the natives do not look sufficiently different from their masters since their skins are "white as ours". This conceptual confusion is captured in the telling phrase "white chimpanzee" or "human chimpanzee", using Darwinian vocabulary so as to combine two contradictory terms into one – the rhetorical figure of oxymoron – in order to indicate the peculiar in-between position of the Irish. It is important to realize, however, that this position is here formulated and assigned by an English observer; thus, it says more about *his* frame of reference or thought system than anything about the Irish he refers to. Generalizing from this example, we can say that postcolonial perspectives on Ireland rest not so much on any inherent features of the writing studied, but on the interests of the observer and the critical concerns at stake.

For a long time, Irish writing, especially its great modernist period with authors like Joyce or Beckett, who dissociated themselves from nationalist politics and spent their working lives in Europe, has fully been subsumed under the teaching canon of English. Yet for this very reason, it can be all the more productive to reposition such authors from the etablished mainstream and consider what critical insights might be gained when placing them in Irish and postcolonial contexts. The same has been done with recent readings of classic eighteenth-century writers like Jonathan Swift (1667–1745) or with a celebrated nineteenth-century figure like Oscar Wilde (1854–1900), whose life and work is best known for its intimate concern with upper-class manners, masks and myths in late-Victorian England. However, precisely by taking on the idiom and guises of the English aristocracy, like in a cultural masquerade, and by making them his chosen medium of mimicry and self-invention, Wilde can be seen to undermine their status of superiority and rob them of exclusive claims. Besides, the wit and verbal bravura of Wilde's famous quips and aphorisms in the English language have been set in line with linguistic strategies elaborating verbal worlds in resistance to, or compensation for, the political reality denied. In the phrase of Declan Kiberd, "words have always been the last weapons of the disarmed" (1989: 233), hence key instruments for cultural decolonization. That is to say, there can be basic literary strategies at work which need not be "about" the struggle for national emancipation so as to be relevant for postcolonial perspectives.

Swift, Wilde and their writing: words as "weapons of the disarmed"

1   Historical Survey

The history of English involvements in Ireland does not only go back long into the past, it also comes down right to our present, with the special case of Northern Ireland. Since the medieval

Early modern Ireland: divided between pale and Gael

Norman conquest of Ireland in 1171, led by King Henry II and supported by Pope Adrian IV, the country was repeatedly subject to large military campaigns trying to establish feudal or colonial English power structures so as to transform Gaelic society and subdue its leaders. Significantly, none of these campaigns managed to take the entire island, usually leaving out some parts of the Western country where cultural, linguistic and political realities remained unassimilated to English influence. Areas within the immediate sphere of English power were known as **the pale**, beyond which **the Gael** continued to exist, from an English point of view representing native barbarism. When in the sixteenth century the Tudor monarchs, especially Henry VIII and Elizabeth I, enforced the establishment of a Protestant Church of Ireland, most parts of the Irish population beyond the pale remained Roman Catholics. Thus began the long-term division and close association of religious with political alignments that has dominated Irish politics ever since. Following successive attempts at rebellion, the Gaelic earls and their resistance movement under Hugh O'Neill, Earl of Tyrone, were routed in the Battle of Kinsale in 1601.

The eighteenth century: plantations, the ascendancy, and a failed uprising

In the seventeenth century, after punitive campaigns by Cromwell's army in 1649–50, England intensified efforts to have Protestant settlers establish themselves on Irish lands, mostly in the Northern province of Ulster, but also in some other parts. For the purpose of these so-called **plantations** (the same term as used in colonial America and the West Indies), land was confiscated from Catholic owners and given to English settlers for further development and exploitation. This created a pattern of Protestant landlords and large estate owners, many of whom spent much of their time in England, dominating Irish tenants who had to scrape a living on the ground. In July 1690 William of Orange, recently made King William III in the Glorious Revolution, defeated the Stuart King James II in the Battle of the Boyne, destroying last hopes for a restoration of Catholic power. (To the present day, this victory is triumphantly re-enacted in Northern Ireland by the Orange Orders, i.e. determined unionists, with their so-called marching season in July.) Penal Laws were introduced to curb civil rights for Catholics and prevent them from participating in public life. But the ensuing rise of the **Protestant Ascendancy**, i.e. the class of established power-holders based on property and religion, also led to a growing sense of division between their cultural connections to England and their local loyalties in Ireland. Increasingly, this Anglo-

Irish class began to see themselves as different from the English and to assert this new awareness also in political terms, setting up a local parliament and government. When the United Irishmen, with the help of revolutionary France, tried to stage a serious rebellion against English domination in 1798, they were led by the Protestant Wolfe Tone. Its failure resulted in the **Act of Union**, making Ireland part of Britain under Westminster rule.

The nineteenth century saw continued conflicts and alliances between the different segments of Irish society. Daniel O'Connell successfully encouraged Catholics to turn away from Gaelic backgrounds and, through embracing the English language, seek new opportunities in middle-class and urban life styles. In the 1840s, the economic principles of the liberal government in London, refusing to interfere with market forces, resulted in a catastrophic situation that caused the starvation of a million Irish tenants, dependant on subsistence work, when the potato crops which were their staple failed. Many lives were also lost on emigration ships, due to appalling conditions. In the later decades of the century, various groups and movements formed to campaign for Home Rule, i.e. Irish self-government, for land reform, i.e. redistribution of property, and for a revival – or indeed reinvention – of the linguistic, literary and cultural heritage of Gaelic Ireland, including Gaelic sports like hurling, that was near the point of total loss. Collectively referred to as the Irish Renaissance, this nationalist project was pushed forward and decisively championed by Protestant leaders like Parnell and Anglo-Irish intellectuals like Yeats. Several of these leading figures spoke no or little Gaelic but still sought passionately to forge an alliance with the Irish peasantry, as guardians of myths and spiritual traditions, against the filthy modern tide they identified with English materialism. Their movement found a major platform on the stage of the Irish National Theatre, since 1904 known as the Abbey Theatre (see 3.1.2), where cultural nationalism was articulated and fiercely debated.

The nineteenth century: Catholic emancipation, the famine, and the Irish revival

Political developments came to a head with World War I. After the failed Easter Rising in 1916 under Connolly and Pearse, Sinn Féin led a war of independence against the British which ended with the Anglo-Irish Treaty in 1922, partitioning the island between three Southern provinces and the Northern province Ulster, whose Protestant majority demanded it remain in the United Kingdom. The question whether or not this treaty was acceptable was fought

The twentieth century: independence, civil war and the colonial legacy in the North

SOME DATES IN IRISH HISTORY

1801	Act of Union: Irish parliament abolished, Ireland becomes fully part of Britain and is ruled from Westminster
1839	Catholic Emancipation Act: permits Catholics into parliament; Daniel O'Connell leader of Catholic emancipation
1846–49	The Great Famine: more than a million people die, many others emigrate, mainly to North America, so that the population is halved
1858/59	Irish Republican Brotherhood and Fenian Brotherhood: resistance movements founded in Dublin and the USA
1873	Home Rule League founded: campaigning for self-government and, together with National Land League (founded 1879), for land reform, 1877–90 with Charles Stewart Parnell as leader
1893	Gaelic League: with Douglas Hyde as leader, campaigning for the deanglicization of Ireland
1905	Sinn Féin founded by Arthur Griffith: campaigning for full political independence of Ireland
1916	Easter Rising: nationalist rebels proclaim Irish Republic in Dublin, followed by martial law, rebel surrender and 16 executions
1919–21	Anglo-Irish War: Sinn Féin sets up Dáil Éireann (Irish Assembly) and proclaims independence, Britain partitions Ireland in 1920 and grants Southern Ireland dominion status as the Irish Free State
1922–23	Irish Civil War between supporters and opponents of the Anglo-Irish Treaty; the supporters under Eamon de Valera win, Northern Ireland (province of Ulster) remains part of the United Kingdom
1937	Irish Free State becomes republic, renamed Eire
1949	Republic of Ireland: constitution ratified
1967	Northern Ireland Civil Rights Association founded: campaigning for civil rights for Catholic minority in Northern Ireland; rising tensions with Protestant and Unionist establishment
1969	Irish Republican Army (IRA), founded in the Civil War, reorganized as military unit in the North
1972	"Bloody Sunday": civil rights march in Derry fired upon by British troops, 13 demonstrators immediately killed, another dies later; direct rule from Westminster imposed on Ulster
1970s–1980s	"The Troubles": IRA bombings in Northern Ireland and on the British mainland as well as Protestant paramilitary action demands higher death toll than Anglo-Irish War and dominates all subsequent political initiatives
1981	IRA members in Maze prison go on hunger strike to demand recognition as political prisoners; ten hunger strikers die
1994	IRA declares cease fire
1998	Good Friday Agreement ends sectarian violence in the North
2007	joint government led by Paisley and McGuinness in the North

out in the Irish Civil War, won by the supporters of the treaty. Subsequent developments in the South led to a consolidation of the Irish Free State, which later became fully independent and in 1949 was renamed the Republic of Ireland. The situation in the North, however, where Protestants resorted to drastic measures in order to defend their status of privilege and power against Catholics, continued to resemble colonial conditions. Tensions mounted with the civil rights movement of the 1960s and erupted in 1972 when a Catholic protest march in Derry (after Belfast the second biggest city in the North, known to Protestants as Londonderry) was fired upon by British troops, killing 14 demonstrators. As officially established in the Saville Inquiry in 2002, this was an act of military violence against peaceful civilians. Subsequent decades saw very serious sectarian violence, with killings, bombings and military action on both sides and a higher death toll than in the Anglo-Irish War. Strong international involvement, especially from the US, and joint peace initiatives from Dublin and London, eventually succeeded in the 1990s to set up a peace process.

2   Literary Paradigms

It is clear that Ireland has an ancient Gaelic literary tradition, consisting of bardic poetry and songs, epic warrior cycles and heroic narratives just as of fairy tales and myths and other oral forms. Many strands of this tradition have survived in the modern age and in the written medium; they have combined with other cultural strands and been transformed into specific genres such as the *aisling* or dream poems of the eighteenth century, fusing erotic with political desire by speaking of Ireland as a beloved woman. All these, however, are for students and scholars of Celtic to consider. What matters for a postcolonial view of Irish literature, and for Irish writing in English, is rather to consider how aspects of this literary heritage were rediscovered, recreated and, in parts, reinvented in the English language under specific historical conditions where they came to serve as elements for cultural identities set up against colonial domination. This took place around 1900, as part of what is known as the Irish Renaissance, a broad movement which offers a paradigm for the political relevance of literary activity as well as for postcolonial approaches in exploring it.

Oral Gaelic poetry and the revival around 1900

Until 1890, constitutional efforts to establish Irish Home Rule were led by the charismatic Protestant Charles Stewart Parnell (1846–

W.B. Yeats and the Abbey theatre: a stage for Irish national debates

1891), but he fell into disgrace when his involvement in a divorce case became known. After this failure, the nationalist movement split into more radical political formations like Sinn Féin and cultural nationalists who sought to renew their country by tapping into the heroic, spiritual or occult energies they thought dormant in the Irish people, especially peasants in the West, far removed from urban and anglicized life-styles. Ironically, many active and articulate explorers of these energies, like the writer W.B. Yeats, were themselves part of the life-styles they condemned. With an Anglo-Irish Protestant background, Yeats spoke no Gaelic; his early poetry was deeply immersed in late-Romantic English and French symbolist aesthetics, while he consciously set out to construct, through English poets like William Blake, the kind of alternative tradition to which he wanted to belong. He found allies in the Protestant estate owners Edward Martyn and especially Lady Augusta Gregory, whose command of Gaelic brought about an important series of fairy tale collections and translations. Together they founded the Irish Literary Theatre in 1897, which in 1904 turned into the Abbey Theatre and, under Lady Gregory's management, soon became the main stage for nationalist consciousness, conflicts and debates.

J.M. Synge's plays at the Abbey: de-anglicizing English

The Abbey presented folkplays centred on the Irish peasantry, many of them written by Lady Gregory to counter English clichés of stage Irishmen, as well as literary parables and allegories written by Yeats. But most of all, the theatre first had to create its own audience, often through public scandals, rallies and enormous rows. In 1907, performances of John M. Synge's comedy *The Playboy of the Western World* could only be defended against angry crowds by calling in the Dublin Metropolitan Police, in effect a colonial force, because the play was felt to offend the idealized image of pure Irishness and Irish maidenhood entertained by many middle-class spectators. As such, Synge's play offers an example for postcolonial predicaments, between a version of the country imagined or desired and its actualities. Set in a rural pub on the West coast, it centres on a young vagrant who arrives one day and turns into a hero for the local villagers, especially the girls, when he claims to have killed his father. What enraged Dublin audiences was the blatant reversal of moral standards. Yet what makes the play politically significant is not just its reversed emphasis on fantastic talk, pretence and play-acting instead of real action, but also the use of the dramatic language Synge constructs. When, for example, the hero admits "I killed my poor father, Tuesday was a week, for doing the like of that" and another figure responds "Is it killed your father?" (Synge 1958: 117), the words are familiar but the syntax is not: drawing on his study of Gaelic, Synge fabricates an English that appears to be de-anglicized, an idiom based on the local modes of oral communication among the people where the play is set. His written text therefore conveys, just as other post-colonial "palimpsests" in Africa and elsewhere (see 2.2.2), an alternative cultural presence through the medium of English.

The Abbey theatre produced several other memorable plays and rows, like later Sean O'Casey's trilogy of Dublin plays all dealing with recent Irish history, *The Shadow of a Gunman* (1923), *Juno and the Paycock* (1924) and *The Plough and the Stars* (1926). But the short career of J.M. Synge (1871–1909) best exemplifies the promise as well as the problem of the kind of literature that cultural nationalists championed. Claiming to write not just about Irish peasants but on their behalf, Synge constructed himself as a spokesman for "the people" and so assumed a patronizing position toward them. His own background was strictly Protestant and urban. He learned Gaelic at the Sorbonne in Paris and, following Yeats's suggestion, went from there to spend some time on the remote Aran islands off the Irish West coast, like a participant observer, studying local life and customs. The precarious position of his work therefore suggests the uncertainties in struggling to create, not just a language adequate for Irish writing beyond colonial stereotypes and nationalist clichés, but also an audience conversant in that language and, as such, metonymic of the imagined community of the emergent nation. This is why the theatre became a major medium for the nationalist project: performance is a speech act that can bring about such new realities through utterance.

Synge's cross-cultural career and his views of "the people"

Before considering another, more recent theatrical example, a brief look at modernist Irish fiction. James Joyce (1882–1941) was born and educated in Dublin, but left the country at the age of 22, never to concern himself with Irish nationalist aspirations, except through mockery and parody. Yet central aspects of his novels, often celebrated for their stylistic and narrative innovations, are also relevant for postcolonial perspectives. For example, the protagonist of his early autobiographical novel *A Portrait of the Artist as a Young Man* (1916), a student in a Jesuit college, observes when talking to his English dean: "The language in which we are speaking is his before it is mine." On one level, this reflects the general situation by

Joyce's writing from a post-colonial perspective: style and language

Augusta Gregory (1852–1932), dramatist, folklorist; founder and manager of the Abbey theatre; collected myths and wrote more than forty plays, e.g. *Spreading the News* (1904)

Oscar Wilde (1854–1900), play: *The Importance of Being Earnest* (1895); novel: *The Picture of Dorian Gray* (1890); poetry: *The Ballad of Reading Gaol* (1897); essay: *The Portrait of Mr. W.H.* (1889)

William Butler Yeats (1865–1939), poet, dramatist, essayist; leading figure in the Irish National Theatre movement, later Senator of the Irish Free State; poetry: *The Rose* (1893), *Responsibilities* (1914), *The Tower* (1928); plays: *Cathleen Ni Houlihan* (1902), *On Baile's Strand* (1904), *Purgatory* (1939); philosophy: *A Vision* (1925/37); Nobel Prize 1923

John Millington Synge (1871–1909), plays: *Riders to the Sea* (1905), *The Playboy of the Western World* (1907); prose: *The Aran Islands* (1907)

Sean O'Casey (1880–1964), plays: *The Shadow of a Gunman* (1923), *Juno and the Paycock* (1924), *The Plough and the Stars* (1926)

James Joyce (1882–1941), fiction: *Dubliners* (1914), *A Portrait of the Artist as a Young Man* (1916), *Ulysses* (1922), *Finnegans Wake* (1939)

Elizabeth Bowen (1899–1973), novels: *The Last September* (1929), *Friends and Relations* (1931), *To The North* (1932), *The Heat of the Day* (1949)

Patrick Kavanagh (1904–1967), poetry: *Ploughman and Other Poems* (1936), *The Great Hunger* (1942), *Soul for Sale* (1947)

Samuel Beckett (1906–1989), plays: *Waiting for Godot* (1952/54), *Endgame* (1957/58), *Krapp's Last Tape* (1959); novels: *Molloy* (1951/55), *Malone Dies* (1951/56), *The Unnameable* (1953/58); Nobel Prize 1969

Flann O'Brian (Brian O'Nolan) (1911–1966), novels: *At Swim-Two-Birds* (1939), *The Third Policeman* (1940/68)

Brendan Behan (1923–1964), plays: *The Quare Fellow* (1955), *The Hostage* (1957)

Brian Friel (*1929), plays: *Philadelphia Here I Come!* (1964), *The Freedom of the City* (1973), *Translations* (1980), *Making History* (1988); fiction: *The Diviner* (1983)

Seamus Heaney (*1939), poetry: *Death of a Naturalist* (1966), *North* (1975), *Station Island* (1984), *Electric Light* (2002); Nobel Prize 1996

Medbh McGuckian (*1950), poetry: *The Flower Master* (1982), *Selected Poems: 1978–1994* (1997)

Anne Devlin (*1951), plays: *Ourselves Alone* (1985), *After Easter* (1994)

Frank McGuinness (*1953), plays: *Observe the Sons of Ulster Marching to the Somme* (1985), *Carthaginians* (1988), *Mutabilitie* (1994)

Marina Carr (*1964), plays: *The Mai* (1994), *Portia Coughlan* (1996), *By the Bog of Cats* (1998), *Woman and Scarecrow* (2006)

which language always exists socially and so precedes all individual usage: "His language, so familiar and so foreign, will always be for me an acquired speech." (Joyce 1988: 194) But this sense of having to appropriate the master's words in order to debate with him is particularly acute for postcolonial writers (as, in another context, the figure of Caliban exemplifies, see 2.4.4). Against this background, chapter 14 of *Ulysses* (1922), Joyce's great modernist novel and stylistic odyssey, is relevant. Set in a maternity ward in Dublin, this chapter deals with birth and issues of biological growth; it is presented in a series of elaborate pastiches, i.e. stylistic parodies, suggesting the historical 'growth' of the English language and its literature. In this way, it highlights the construction of the English canon that is often taught and seen as if it were the outcome of a natural development rather than a contigent historical product. In this way, *Ulysses* shows how the English language, at once so familiar and so foreign to many Irish writers, is retaken and revealed as an acquired matrix, used in Ireland to give birth to very different cultural offspring.

Issues of language, finally, have also been central for the work of a Northern theatre company called Field Day, which formed around the playwright Brian Friel (*1929) in 1980. Based in Derry, where the 'troubles' had erupted in 1972 (see 3.1.1), this group was comprised of the actor Stephen Rea, the poets Seamus Heaney and Tom Paulin and the critics Seamus Deane and David Hammond. Without anything resembling a fixed agenda, their plan was to produce a play each year that would address Irish predicaments without aligning themselves with either side of the sectarian divide but instead explore what has been called "a fifth province of the mind" (Richtarik 1994), i.e. an imaginative space beyond the frontlines of the conflict. Their first production was Friel's *Translations* (1980), a historical drama set in 1830s Ireland when British soldiers were engaged in mapping the country and producing English versions of all local place names. This cartographic project is effectively combined in the play with topical allusions to recent British military action and used as a dramatic model for colonial dispossession. At the same time, the play argues for the necessary changes in a process of cultural translation by which traditions need to be continuously transformed.

The Field Day Company from Derry: performing in postcolony

As part of their attempt to initiate new debates, Field Day also launched a series of publications, like short pamphlets and a monu-

Field Day's intellectual challenges: postcolonizing Ireland

mental anthology of Irish Writing. It was mainly due to these publications, and to the critics associated with them, especially Seamus Deane (1986) and Declan Kiberd (1995), that Irish literature and culture began to be debated in postcolonial terms. In 1988 Said published a Field Day pamphlet on "Yeats and Decolonization", for the first time suggesting to see the cultural achievements of the Irish Renaissance in the same perspective as the political agenda of anti-colonial movements in the Third World, headed by writers such as Senghor, Césaire or Neruda. The idea was taken up by Kiberd when he pointed out in his book-length study *Inventing Ireland* that "some shapers of modern Africa, India and the emerging world looked at times to the Irish for guidance" (1995: 4). Precisely because of the ambivalent attitudes among many Irish writers towards English cultural models, therefore, it has turned out to be particularly productive to approach their work from postcolonial points of view.

2   Focus on African Literature

What does it mean to speak of "Africa"?

To speak of a "focus" on "African" literature must sound rather absurd, like a contradiction in terms: Africa is so vast, varied, heterogeneous and challenging a continent, with so many different languages, cultures, countries and literatures, that no single "focus" can ever behold it. The least we should do when turning to African writing – as most introductory textbooks do in this case – would be to draw a distinction between the Northern countries of the Maghreb (i.e. Arabic and largely francophone; nothing will be said about these here) and sub-Saharan Africa, which should then be further divided into West Africa, East Africa and Southern Africa. Such a subdivision into broad regions might at least acknowledge the importance of variety and the internal differences in the continent we are looking at.

The need for differentiated and specific views of African cultures

On the other hand, we may wonder what could actually be gained from it. Surely, "East", "West" and "South" are also concepts of convenience and far too general to talk about local realities with any specificity. For serious literary studies one should rather focus on individual languages and look at, say, Yoruba poetry or focus on individual countries and study, say, Ethiopian literature. This is the approach adopted in specialist writing and handbooks (see

Irele/Gikandi 2004). This is also the approach that redresses the eurocentric misconception, perpetuated over centuries of colonial thinking, that the entire continent was basically the same – like the more famous case of "the Orient" and its assumed homogeneity (see 2.3.2). It long used to be a standard attitude in European politics, philosophy and literature to conceive of Africa as one large, entirely black, dark, timeless, static and benighted whole, eventually to be salvaged from this state through outsiders and their engagement. So the idea that "Africa" could ever form a single reference point as such has been historically tied to racist notions and colonial discourse.

And yet, to use a term like "African literature" for the purposes of our introduction is not only dictated by the desperate need to look at postcolonial literatures from around the world in just one chapter. There is a sense in which this term can be employed – indeed has been employed – with a strategic purpose, so as to emphasize commonalities in the many forms of African writing across the great diversity of languages: a sense of shared concern which may either derive from connecting cultural elements or from shared experience in recent history. Cultural heritage, for instance, is the basis of the claim by which a well-known specialist opens the *Cambridge History of African and Caribbean Literature* calling Africa "the oral continent par excellence" (Gunner 2004: 1). This sweeping phrase suggests a fundamental trait in all the cultural patterns across the entire continent: the prevalence and prominence of orality in constituting social life. In fact, it seems hard to overestimate this point. With regard to African societies it could be argued that oral modes of communication, whether improvised or formalized, are basic and pervasive means of interaction, clearly also of importance for contemporary literature (see 2.2.2). Many African writers, for example, have said they see themselves in the role of "griots", i.e. professional story tellers and their popular art. For we are not looking at some ancient or outdated feature but at a living practice. In multilingual societies where literacy is limited not just to educated segments of the population but, more importantly, to certain languages and communicative domains, orality cannot die out. On the contrary, in recent decades modern media like radio or television have given it new boost.

Orality as a common feature shared by African societies

If orality, then, offers one possibility to suggest a common basis to speak of Africa provisionally as a whole, another possibility lies in

Colonial legacies as a shared feature of contemporary Africa

emphasizing the historical realities that have shaped the continent over the past five hundred years and have imposed common structures on its existing diversity. The result is clearly visible, for instance, in the map of Africa where almost all current borders derive from imperial rivalry or arbitration and yet have come to define modern African nations (see 3 for some remarks on mapping and nationalism). With the exception of Ethiopia (where only Mussolini's Italy tried to establish a short-lived colonial presence), the entire African continent used to be subjected to colonial dominance by European powers. Although in many areas this was just a temporary episode in an age-old history of internal conflicts, conquests and cross-cultural engagements, colonialism has left indelible marks and deep effects on the social and cultural fabric. Chief among these is not just the imposition of European languages such as English, French, Portuguese, Dutch or German onto many areas, where these languages have since undergone significant developments and sometimes turned into vernaculars of local expression. Another far-reaching effect of European involvement in African societies has also been the wider use of writing. Prior to missionary and colonial encounters, many indigenous languages in sub-Saharan Africa existed without an alphabet (Arabic, used also in Eastern Africa, is a special case). Thus, African *literature*, as a *written* genre in whatever language, in central ways perpetuates this common legacy.

Pan-African perspectives: publications and decolonization

In fact, when African intellectuals and writers first began to organize and think about their situation, their views were entirely pan-African: all emphasis lay on the continent as a whole, without reference to local specificities, including even the black diasporas in America and Europe. Senghor's concept of négritude (see 1.2.5) just as his pioneering *Anthologie de la nouvelle poésie nègre et malgache de langue française* (1948) first set the theme also for anglophone debates. Jean-Paul Sartre's foreword to this anthology, entitled "Orphée Noir", gave its name to the important journal *Black Orpheus*, dedicated to "African and Afro-American Literature", which began publication in 1957 Nigeria and was first edited by two German scholars, Ulli Beier and Janheinz Jahn. The first writers' conferences, too, championed all-embracing perspectives. In 1962 in Accra, Ghana, the following definition of African literature was proposed: "any work in which an African setting is authentically handled, or to which experiences which originate in Africa are integral" (in Riemenschneider 1983: 39). Though rather unsophisticated and remarkably inclusive, this definition continued to serve as a point of reference. In the same year, the African Writers' Conference in Kampala, Uganda, celebrated the current mood of decolonization with enthusiastic Pan-Africanism. It was at this conference that Heinemann publishers first discussed their African Writers Series with Chinua Achebe as founding editor, embracing writing from across the continent – a book series whose influence cannot be stressed enough. All these are arguments, in short, for ways of seeing African literature also as a whole.

1 Historical Survey

African societies, in the diversity of their traditions and historical dynamics, over the centuries developed many different forms of organization and cultural expression, including the mighty kingdoms of Dahomey in the West or of Zimbabwe in the South-East (see Ki-Zerbo 1990). But it has only been in rather recent times that Europeans took any notice of this. Until well into the twentieth century, it used to be received wisdom to consider Africans "the people without history" (Wolf 1982), thus establishing a timeless image of the continent as a storehouse of the primitive where simple forms of human life – or, in racist discourse, subhuman life – had somehow been preserved. This notion is also reflected in the list of dates given in this chapter, where the main focus and agency concerning African history since 1800 seem to lie with the imperial powers such as Britain – a blatantly one-sided and distorted view. But ironically, it was this view which has become central for African writers, especially of the first generation in the period of decolonization, who set out to show, in the words of Chinua Achebe, "that Africans did not hear of culture for the first time from Europeans" (in Riemenschneider 1983: 154).

Ancient history against modern prejudice: African affirmations

Since early modern times, Africa was used by European sea powers primarily as a stop-over on their Eastern voyages to India and Asia where more lucrative trade was available. With the conquest of the New World, however, and the increasing demand of labour for mines and plantations there, most Western parts of Africa were soon turned into major sites of slave trade. More than ten million people were shipped to America. For a long time, from a European point of view, this business remained a strictly coastal affair. Although many African élites co-operated with the slavers, trying to safeguard their own people by handing over others, Europeans

The slave trade and its impact

seem to have spent little thought on the complex social structures and cross-cultural dynamics in the hinterland which must have sustained this trade. The African interior, to them, remained the ultimate dark mystery. Only very few spots on the continent, like the Cape of Good Hope where the Dutch East India Company established a revictualling station in 1652, were used for white settlement. With growing philanthropism in the later eighteenth century, Africa was turned into a space for utopian experiments: in 1787 an English gentleman took four hundred emancipated slaves and a few dozen prostitutes (for child-bearing) from London to Sierra Leone, where they were to form a "Province of Freedom"; the project failed, yet it shows how the continent was used as a *tabula rasa* onto which white horrors just as hopes for improving the world could be inscribed.

Slavery abolished – confrontations and migrations in Southern Africa

In 1807 Britain abolished the slave trade, in 1833-4 slavery as an institution. The motives were not entirely humanitarian. As Eric Williams argued in a famous analysis (1944), Britain was then fully entering the industrial age and, through abolition, trying to oust the United States with their plantation-based economy. In the South of Africa, where Britain for strategic reasons had taken the Cape in 1806, the abolition put pressure on the Boers, farmers and descendants of Dutch settlers, who in 1836 began to trek North so as to get away from the sphere of British control and establish their own states, Transvaal and the Orange Free State. Their "Great Trek" coincided with the rise of the Zulu empire under Shaka (see 2.4.3) and large migratory movements among other peoples of the region, the so-called *mfecane*. In an area first inhabited by the Khoisan, these various moves created the complex situation of ethnic confrontations and layers of domination that resulted in many wars, with the rivalling colonial powers fighting against Xhosas and Zulus but also, at the turn to the twentieth-century, fighting against each other, Boers versus British.

Imperial engagements in the interior: the Scramble for Africa

In other parts of Africa, abolition paved the way for sustained colonial engagements (see Brantlinger 1988). With the alleged aim to root out the evil of slavery from tribal life – slavery was now construed as an "African" practice – and to establish forms of "legitimate" trade, the exploitation of resources began. Victorian traders, explorers and missionaries jointly ventured into the interior to bring enlightenment through Commerce, Civilization and Christianity – the three Cs – and so set up the important network of outposts and stations, even without governmental directives, which established spheres of interest and which has been called the "informal" Empire. When in the later nineteenth century imperial rivalries among the European nations intensified with the "Scramble for Africa", i.e. the race for power footholds and economic bases overseas, the formalization of colonial rule largely followed these informal outlines. This happened at the Berlin conference in 1884 with the administrative division of the continent. But in actual fact, the degree to which African societies were affected by European domination varied greatly. The main difference was between settler colonies like Kenya where large parts of the fertile land were given to white farmers, and colonies like Uganda or Nigeria where Britain in the early twentieth century implemented so-called "Indirect Rule": for this purpose, local élites were recruited or, if not available, created so as to serve as stand-in for the colonial authorities which, in effect, remained largely absent.

By far the greatest impact on local cultural realities and transcultural developments came from the Christian missions. Their ambition to spread the gospel was not just crucial for all attempts to codify and write down the indigenous languages (so that the Bible could be translated into them – often demanding risky compromises in adapting lexical features of the text to local horizons), but also for introducing formal education, printing presses and other elements which later enabled the development of African writing. In the Victorian era, when the rhetoric of elevating child-like natives onto the higher levels of humanity was going strong, missionary activity could still serve as a benevolent guise for economic interests. But this changed fundamentally in the twentieth century, when the products of colonial education turned out to be ever harder to control. The rhetoric of Africans as children to be educated rests on an unstable figure: children grow up and become adults who want to manage their own affairs. This is why, roughly since World War I, colonial administrators began to resent the missionary zeal for education and conversion and instead emphasized rigid cultural identities, idealizing the "unspoilt", "genuine" and "proud" tribal African because this figure allowed them to continue their status of superiority. In subsequent decades, in fact, the most decisive action towards postcolonial moves came from Africans who had gone through missionary schooling and colonial education, often in a European metropolis, and who became successful political leaders precisely because they represented more than just one world.

Missionary work and the unstable rhetoric of education

1806	Britain captures Cape of Good Hope from the Dutch
1807	Britain officially ends slave trade
1833	slavery abolished in the British Empire
1851	Britain captures city of Lagos
1859	London Missionary Society establishes Matabele Mission
1870	diamonds discovered in Southern Africa
1884–85	Berlin Conference: partition of Africa among European powers
1885	German rule begins in Tanganyika (East Africa)
1886	gold discovered in Transvaal (Southern Africa)
1899–1902	Anglo-Boer War in South Africa: Britain fights for domination
1904–05	Herero war in German South-West Africa: indigenous population systematically starved and slaughtered
1910	Union of South Africa formed, Louis Botha first prime minister
1912	South African Native National Congress founded (later: ANC)
1908–12	Maji Maji uprising in German East Africa
1919	Pan-African Congress in Paris (W.E.B. DuBois)
1936	Italy invades Abyssinia
1945	Pan-African Congress in Manchester
1948	National Party in South Africa installs apartheid
1952–56	violent Mau Mau campaign in Kenya against colonial presence
1954–62	Algerian war of independence
1956	Morocco and Tunisia become independent
1957	Ghana independent, Kwame Nkrumah first president
1958	All-Africa Conference in Ghana to co-ordinate anti-colonial forces
1960	Nigeria and many other countries become independent
1960	Sharpeville massacre in South Africa; ANC banned, leaders jailed
1963	Kenya independent, Jomo Kenyatta first president
1966	first military coup in Nigeria (followed by several others)
1967–70	Nigerian civil war over secession of Biafra
1976	rioting and police crack-down in South Africa after Soweto student uprising against compulsory tuition in Afrikaans
1979	Tanzanian invasion ends dicatorship of Idi Amin in Uganda
1980	Zimbabwe independent, Mugabe Prime Minister
1990	Nelson Mandela released from prison (after 27 years); post-apartheid era in South Africa begins
1991–93	Somali civil war
1994	first democratic South African elections won by Mandela and ANC
1994	Rwandan genocide: a million Tutsi killed by Hutu militias
1995	writer Ken Saro-Wiwa executed by military government in Nigeria

After various anti-colonial revolts and campaigns, such as the 1929 Igbo women's uprising in Nigeria or the forceful Mau Mau movement in 1950s Kenya, and with the break-up of the Empire after World War II, most African countries (with the important exception of South Africa and Zimbabwe) gained independence around 1960. The enthusiasm of these years, however, soon waned into bitter moods when in many countries national liberators turned into dictators, frequent military coups and civil wars took place, neo-colonial élites repressed other ethnic groups and violated human rights, while most of the new nations were quickly aligned to the power blocks of the Cold War. Also in the so-called new global order established in the 1990s, when institutionalized white domination ended even in South Africa, many of the old problems, conflicts and attitudes persist and often escalate. For instance, the Rwandan genocide in 1994, where a million Tutsis were murdered by Hutus, in many ways reflected legacies of the colonial era, with German, Belgian and French involvement in the country, when the difference between these two ethnic types or social classes was first established (see Stockhammer 2005).

Twentieth-century developments: decolonization and neo-colonial violence

2   Literary Paradigms

The various forms of poetry and theatrical activity which writers and performers have produced in postcolonial Africa can generally draw on aspects of indigenous tradition and recreate or reinvent communal practices of oral culture for contemporary purposes. The case is very different for the novel, a modern European form (whose rise is often seen to begin with Defoe's *Robinson Crusoe*, 1719, in which Africa features as a place of slavery and danger), a written genre closely tied to middle-class values and habits of individual readership. African novels are therefore often marked by crucial and creative tensions: they negotiate different, sometimes opposing tendencies – including linguistic, cultural and social elements of varied backgrounds – and thus manifest, more clearly than either poetry or drama, the transcultural realities that inhabit postcolonial writing.

The novel in Africa as a colonial heritage transformed

Among the earliest examples of this genre is Sol T. Plaatje's *Mhudi*, a historical novel about the *mfecane* of the 1830s, published in 1930 in South Africa. Centred on a remarkably independent heroine, the narrative pays tribute to the spectrum of traditions that inform it: structured around starkly emblematic scenes reminiscent

Some early examples: *Mhudi* and other African "palimpsests"

perhaps of oral epics of the past, it is rendered in elaborate English dialogues containing literary references as well as Biblical and Shakespearean allusions. Yet the author (1876–1932), a linguist and black activist, founder of the South African Native National Congress, has interwoven these different strands with ease. Like Mofolo's *Chaka*, published in Sesotho under missionary tutelage five years earlier, after being long withheld for fear of spreading superstition (see 2.4.3), Plaatje's novel does not just document a period of transition and transculturation but actively helps to shape it. The same holds true for the earliest East African and West African novels which came out with London publishers, Akiki Nyabongo's *Africa Answers Back* (1936) from Uganda and Amos Tutuola's *The Palm-Wine Drinkard* (1952) from Nigeria. Especially Tutuola's exuberant and linguistically wonderfully innovative text (as even the title shows) has often been noted for its recreation of Yoruba myths and idioms in the medium of English, using familiar words in rather unfamiliar structures – a prime example of "the African palimpsest" (Zabus 1991, see 2.2.2) that combines written and oral modes and could well have been inspired by the strategies of Irish writers such as J.M. Synge (see 3.1.2).

The significance of Achebe's *Things Fall Apart*

The watershed event for African literature, however, was the publication of Chinua Achebe's *Things Fall Apart* in 1958 (see Innes 2007). Set in a fictive Igbo village around the turn of the century, this Nigerian novel depicts the mounting pressures in a rural community which escalate with the arrival of Christian missionaries and colonial administrators. Yet it would be a serious misreading to see the final confrontation between black and white protagonists as central; the crucial lines of conflict rather lie within Igbo society and concern the question of how to deal with cultural change. The main protagonist, a warrior hero proud of ancient custom, is destroyed precisely because of his rigidity and failure to accommodate to new developments. Main features of the text are its subtle use of Igbo tales and proverbs, its "thick description" (see 2.2.1) of a specific cultural setting and yet its highly modulated narrative voice, including also pointed references to European literary traditions, as in the ironic quote from Yeats's poem "The Second Coming" in the title. Achebe's second novel, *No Longer At Ease* (1960), borrowing its title from T.S. Eliot, continues this ambiguous engagement with canonical writing while also continuing the story, now set two generations later, at the eve of Nigerian decolonization when new conflicts emerge. Far from idealizing African village life as idylls outside the modern world, as some Western readers chose to see it at the time, Achebe's fiction rather offers cautious explorations of the cultural transformations that have always taken place and of which his books, sold in millions throughout Africa, have themselves become strong agents.

Criticism of Achebe, long regarded as a father figure of African literature, has concentrated on two points: his use of the English language and his portrayal of women. The linguistic issue, which concerns anglophone African writing in general, has been most forcefully put forward by Ngũgĩ wa Thiong'o, himself a prominent novelist, dramatist and political activist from Kenya, who argues in *Decolonizing the Mind* (1986) that the use of the former colonizer's language basically compromises all attempts to construct post-colonial perspectives in writing. As a consequence, Ngũgĩ then announced that he would continue his own work exclusively in Gikuyu and, for purposes of wider circulation in Africa and beyond, rely on the age-old medium of translation. This radical stance, reflecting the more rigid language policies in colonial Kenya, has since been questioned and nuanced in several ways. Many writers, also of younger generations, have rather followed Achebe's practice in making English "bear the burden" (as he put it) of African experience. The gender issue, by contrast, continues to cause debate. Women writers from Nigeria and elsewhere, like Flora Nwapa or Buchi Emecheta, while appreciating the fuller version that his fiction offers about social life in Africa, have pointed out the marginal female presence in this version and have tried with their own novels to redress this.

> **Criticism of Achebe: issues of language and gender**

A powerful example, from a different context, is the novel *Nervous Conditions* (1988) by the Zimbabwean writer and film-maker Tsitsi Dangarembga (see Matzke 2007). Beginning with the shocking opening sentence "I was not sorry when my brother died" (1988: 1), this narrative explores a process of female education in late-colonial Rhodesia as a series of cultural substitutions: the girl is send to missionary school *instead of* her dead brother; she is trained in certain social roles *instead of* self-realization; her English educated cousin begins to rebel *instead of* her, while devouring books *instead of* food, etc. The dynamics of education as powerful trans-culturation, which historically troubled colonial administrators in the high imperial age (see 3.2.1), is here turned into a figure of the gender trouble from which new social constellations may emerge.

> **A female *Bildungsroman* in late-colonial Rhodesia**

SOME AFRICAN WRITERS

Amos Tutuola (1920–1997), Nigeria; novels: *The Palm-Wine Drinkard* (1952), *My Life in the Bush of Ghosts* (1954)

Gabriel Okara (*1921), Nigeria; novel: *The Voice* (1964)

Nadine Gordimer (*1923), South Africa; novels: *The Conservationist* (1974), *Burgher's Daughter* (1979), *July's People* (1981), *None to Accompany Me* (1994); Nobel Prize 1991

Chinua Achebe (*1930), Nigeria; novels: *Things Fall Apart* (1958), *No Longer at Ease* (1960), *Arrow of God* (1964), *A Man of the People* (1966), *Anthills of the Savannah* (1987)

Flora Nwapa (1931–1993), Nigeria; novel: *Efuru* (1966)

Athol Fugard (*1932), South Africa; plays: *The Island* (1974), *Siswe Banzi Is Dead* (1974), *'Master Harold'… and the Boys* (1982)

Wole Soyinka (*1934), Nigeria; plays: *A Dance of the Forests* (1960), *The Road* (1965), *Death and the King's Horseman* (1974); novel: *The Interpreters* (1965); memoir: *Aké* (1981); Nobel prize 1986

Bessie Head (1937–1986), Botswana; novel: *A Question of Power* (1974)

Ngũgĩ wa Thiong'o (*1938), Kenya; novels: *A Grain of Wheat* (1967), *Petals of Blood* (1977), *Devil on the Cross* (1982), *Matigari* (1987)

Ayi Kweyi Armah (*1939), Ghana; novel: *The Beautiful Ones Are Not Yet Born* (1968)

J.M. Coetzee (*1940), South Africa; novels: *Waiting for the Barbarians* (1980), *Life and Times of Michael K* (1983), *Foe* (1986), *Disgrace* (1999), *Slow Man* (2004); Nobel Prize 2003

Ken Saro-Wiwa (1941–1995), Nigeria; novel: *Soza Boy* (1986)

Ama Ata Aidoo (*1942), Ghana; novel: *Our Sister Killjoy* (1977)

Buchi Emecheta (*1944), Nigeria; novels: *The Joys of Motherhood* (1979), *Destination Biafra* (1982), *Gwendolen* (1989), *Kehinde* (1994)

Nuruddin Farah (*1945), Somalia; novels: *Sardines* (1981), *Close Sesame* (1983), *Maps* (1986), *Gifts* (1992), *Secrets* (1998)

Jack Mapanje (*1945), Malawi; poetry: *Of Chameleons and Gods* (1981)

Mafika Gwala (*1946), South Africa; poetry: *No More Lullabies* (1982)

Abdulrazak Gurnah (*1948), Tanzania; novel: *Paradise* (1994)

Dambudzo Marechera (1952–1987), Zimbabwe; prose: *House of Hunger* (1978), *Black Sunlight* (1980); poetry and prose: *Mindblast* (1984)

Tsitsi Dangarembga (*1960), Zimbabwe; novels: *Nervous Conditions* (1988), *The Book of Not* (2006)

Ben Okri (*1959), Nigeria; novels: *The Famished Road* (1991), *Songs of Enchantment* (1993), *Astonishing the Gods* (1995)

Yvonne Vera (1964–2005), Zimbabwe; novels: *Nehanda* (1993), *Without a Name* (1994), *Under the Tongue* (1996), *Butterfly Burning* (1998)

Chimamanda Ngozi Adichie (*1977), Nigeria; novels: *Purple Hibiskus* (2004), *Half of a Yellow Sun* (2006)

In the double voice of a first-person narrator (see 2.4.1) and modelled on the English *Bildungsroman* tradition represented in such books as *Jane Eyre*, the novel thus modulates the classic forms of life writing to suggest that African women, trying to combat their double domination by colonial and patriarchal structures, can best construct their own lives, not through openly confronting, but cautiously manipulating the powers that be. In the context of a recently independent country, this point bears far-reaching political implications.

These concern, above all, the perennial issue of so-called committed literature: in a manifestly unjust world, can or should or must writing be part of the political struggle? If so, how? If not, what is the legitimacy of poetic and aesthetic products? These questions are relevant for African and postcolonial writing in general, but they were especially urgent in the apartheid context of South Africa. Here the social wrongs were long felt to be so enormous that literature could never adequately respond; the critic Lewis Nkosi once provocatively quipped that literature therefore should best be renounced to solve "the problem" first, before there might be time for poetry again. A different response is formulated in Mafika Gwala's poem "In Defence of Poetry" (1982: 10). The title takes up an early modern English classic, Sidney's *Defense of Poesy*, and gives it a topical note: "What's poetic/about Defence Bonds and Armscor?/What's poetic/about long-term sentences and/deaths in detention? [...] Can there be poetry/in fostering Plural Relations?" In this way, the poem raises a series of bitter questions that expose the vocabulary of apartheid and explore its brutal exclusion of all poetic language. Yet the poem closes with a curious turn: "As long as/this land, my country/is unpoetic in its doings/it'll be poetic to disagree." The solution is not escapism; rather, this ending insists that, under such political conditions, poetry turns into committed writing precisely by not committing itself.

Literature and politics: how to defend poetry in adverse times

3   Focus on Indian Literature

The term "Indian literature" should be understood in the same way as "African literature" (see 3.2) or indeed "European literature", covering an entire continent with a great variety of languages, ethnicities, religions, cultures and traditions. The sheer linguistic spectrum is enormous. When India gained independence in August

The plurality of Indian languages and literatures

1947, the new constitution singled out fourteen languages which gained official status; these were Sanskrit, Assamese, Bengali, Gujarati, Hindi, Kannada, Kashmiri, Malayalam, Marathi, Oriya, Punjabi, Tamil, Telugo and Urdu. In subsequent years, several others have been added to this list, which now also includes English, Sindhi, Maithili, Dogri, Rajasthani, Mainpur, Konkani and Nepali. Yet even this extended list is not exhaustive of the several hundred languages, dialects or vernaculars (depending on the socio-linguistic criteria applied in defining such distinctions) spoken in the country. Some of the major languages listed are mainly regional in usage. Others are used, in some variety or other, across the entire subcontinent, such as Hindi and Urdu; these two are very closely related but written in different scripts. However, few Indian languages would in fact be used exclusively by their speakers. In a multilingual country, individual monolingualism is quite rare.

Sanskrit epics and their orientalist translations

As with the other areas surveyed here, the discussion will be limited to literature in English. But it is necessary to take note of a few more points about the wider linguistic context, such as the special case of Sanskrit. Though listed among the national languages of India, it is not (or no longer) a spoken tongue. With a literary tradition of some 3,000 years, Sanskrit is the language of the ancient epics, like the *Ramayana*, the *Bhagavadgita* or the *Mahabharata*, whose heritage lives on in many ways – also in contemporary anglophone Indian writing – but which has long become a matter of study, expert knowledge and scholarship. In fact, it was the heritage of Sanskrit that first attracted English and European philologists around 1800 and was central in their establishment of Orientalism as a discipline (see 2.1.1). Significantly, Indian intellectuals and reformers of the time, such as Rammohan Roy from Calcutta, who published his version of the Upanishads in 1816, made equally great efforts in translating and editing the ancient Sanskrit texts in English so as to make their legacy available to a larger audience of modern and non-expert Indian readers.

English in post-colonial India: resented and championed

The role of English in India, however, has always been highly politicized and embattled. Interestingly, it was officially recognized as an "Indian" language in 1954 by the National Academy of Letters, following a move by Prime Minister Nehru, at the academy's first annual convention. Established in the eighteenth century as the language of colonial administration, English in the nineteenth century became a language of formal education and, more and more openly, imperial domination, which has therefore been resented and rejected in many anti-colonial and nationalist contexts. But its function to operate as a shared medium across the many regions and cultures is not easily taken on by any of the other choices available in India. While Hindi is officially recognized as the language of the Union (in Pakistan, the national language is Urdu), it remains closely associated with religious allegiances not necessarily shared by many of its speakers. Before independence and the breakaway of Pakistan, Gandhi hoped to establish a hybrid colloquial variety of Hindi and Urdu as the common language for both the Hindu and the Muslim segments of the population. Today, this is the vernacular best known through Bollywood movies, yet its political agenda has not been fulfilled.

Today, English is actively used by no more than five percent of India's population, situated mainly in higher education, international business and other formal domains. However, in recent years English has gained a new prestige through India's vigorous participation in the computer, media and communication boom. It is no longer rare, for instance, to see US-based companies set up call centres in Bangalore, with local personel trained to adopt American mid-Western accents, so that customers calling from suburban Fargo about maintenance for their deep freeze units are in fact served by Indian staff. More upmarket choices for Indian speakers of English lie in computing and information technology. In this way, the former status of the English language in India is undergoing rapid transformation, but the basic sociolinguistic structure remains diglossic (see 2.2.2). As an externally imposed language of social power and upward mobility, English was installed in the cultural hierarchy of India historically in the same position as Persian had been for centuries. Until the late eighteenth century a shared language of culture as of domination, Persian had come to India with the Mughal emperors who, through several waves of North-western invasions, subjected large parts of the country to their rule. With the colonial rise of English, this diglossia remained largely intact, just the high-prestige language was now different. In the foreword to his novel *Kanthapura* (1938), Rao calls English "the language of our intellectual make-up – like Sanskrit or Persian was before – but not of our emotional make-up" (1989: iii) and looks forward to a time when Indian English will have become as distinctive a variety as Irish or American English.

Indian diglossia: Persian or English as languages of domination

Macanly's "Minute": the argument for English education

The extent to which Indian people should receive instruction in English, as opposed to keeping their various indigenous and ancient tongues for schooling, was long a central issue of colonial debate. It was effectively decided in 1835 with a famous "Minute on Indian Education", which the English historian and young colonial adminstrator Thomas B. Macaulay delivered to the board of education in London. In this much-cited speech, he argued forcefully for the adoption of a fully anglicized curriculum, dismissing the entire heritage of Eastern languages and Oriental literature as insignificant while candidly admitting his own ignorance of them: "I have no knowledge of either Sanscrit or Arabic. But I have done what I could to form a correct estimate of their value. [...] I am quite ready to take the Oriental learning at the valuation of the Orientalists themselves. I have never found one among them who could deny that a single shelf of a good European library was worth the whole native literature of India and Arabia." (Macaulay 1972: 241) Building his argument on a supposed link between the 'value' of literature and the 'virtue' of the language in which it is composed, Macaulay managed to promote English literature and learning as the best and only way to improve Indian society. This move was part of the larger debate in England between Orientalists, supporters of the old approach to colonial government on the basis of local authorities and their cultural standing, as opposed to Anglicists, who favoured the assimilation of local élites into the dominant culture. Both approaches required different kinds of knowledge, and they licensed different administrative measures. The Anglicist position, which was not without support from Indian intellectuals and reformers like Roy (s.a.), eventually won and led towards far-reaching changes.

Teaching literature in India: defining the English canon

In central ways, such issues actually reflect the cultural situation in Britain because what was at stake in them had strong domestic repercussions. In a comprehensive study of literary education and British rule in India, Gauri Viswanathan (1989) has shown that, following Macaulay's minute, the introduction of English literature as key part of the curriculum in India preceded similiar developments in England. That is to say, English Literature as a school subject was *first* established in the colony *before* it was eventually introduced at home in 1871. The reason for this remarkable reversal lay in the concern of colonial authorities that Indian education was dominated by the Christian missions, who put rather too much emphasis on Biblical instruction. In order to hold ground against the missionaries and to provide a viable alternative to religious teaching, civil administrators therefore installed English literary study so as to teach superior civilizational values to the natives – without, however, exposing them to church influence. Yet in order to do so, the new subject first needed definition. Simply put, to teach the natives who we are we must first know ourselves. According to Viswanathan, therefore, the canon of English was initially defined for purposes of colonial export, to be implemented in schools overseas before it was, a generation later, re-imported for domestic use. India thus became a testing ground for secular literary education.

1   Historical Survey

English colonial involvement in India is known as the Raj. It was arguably the most splendid and powerful of all imperial ventures, the "jewel in the crown", as the Victorians used to call it, and has often come to serve as a paradigm of colonial politics at large. For a long time, it used to be said that Britain acquired India and her imperial status generally in "a fit of absent-mindedness". Such a notion is misleading and dangerously ameliorating, but it contains an element of truth. This lies in the fact that, especially in India and the East, the Empire began with trade ventures and private business transactions rather than with official policies or military campaigns (which only came much later). In 1600 the East India Company was granted a trade monopoly by Queen Elizabeth I. At first a loose association of merchants and ship owners, the Company established trade bases at Madras (in 1639), Bombay (newly acquired from the Portugese in 1664) and Calcutta (in 1696), but soon seized or demanded greater administrative power. By the mid-eighteenth century, though still a private company, it had effectively become the governmental body running all British affairs in India. The turning point came with the British victory in 1757 over the Nawab of Bengal, making Bengal the main base for the expanding colonial influence.

The East India Company and early English involvements

With the subsequent permission to collect tax revenue and take control over much of the land, the Company now filled the social space vacated by the disintegrating Mughal empires, i.e. the Persian élite who had conquered and ruled large parts of India for centuries. In 1773, the Company's governor-general of Bengal, Warren Hastings, was made head of all British operations, before the 1784

Centralization and reform: British rule established

SOME DATES IN INDIAN HISTORY

1600	East India Company founded in London
1690	English settlement at Calcutta: Bengal becomes colonial stronghold
1757	Battle of Plassey: Robert Clive defeats the Nawab of Bengal; the Company gains right to collect tax and administer justice in Bengal
1784	India Act centralizes the expanding British presence in India
1813	Company's monopoly broken: trade and missionary activities open
1835	Macaulay's "Minute on Education" anglicizes colonial curriculum
1845–49	British-Sikh wars end with defeat of the Sikhs
1857–58	Great Indian Rebellion ("Mutiny") brutally suppressed; India turned into Crown colony, with Viceroy as queen's representative
1858	India Act ends Company rule; new India Office established
1859–60	Indigo rebellion: peasant revolts
1871	British PM Disraeli declares Queen Victoria "Empress of India"
1885	formation of Indian National Congress
1905	Viceroy decides to partition Bengal, sparking resistance campaigns
1906	All India Muslim League established
1913	Bengali writer Rabindranath Tagore wins Nobel Prize for Literature
1916	Lucknow Pact of Muslim League and Indian National Congress
1919	Gandhi leads first all-India *satyagraha* (peaceful resistance)
1919	Amritsar massacre: British troops kill 400 peaceful demonstrators
1929	Congress calls for "complete independece"
1940	Muslim League demands separate state for Muslims
1942	"Quit India" resolution issued by Congress; leaders jailed
1943–44	severe famine in Bengal
1947	at midnight, 15 August, India gains independence, with Nehru as Prime Minster; bloody partition of the subcontinent along lines of religion; mass migration and expulsion; Pakistan becomes Muslim country; severe fighting over Kashmir
1948	Gandhi assassinated by orthodox Hindu fanatic
1965	Nehru dies, his daughter Indira Gandhi becomes Prime Minister
1965–66	second Indo-Pakistani war over Kashmir
1971	civil war in Pakistan: East breaks away and declares independence as Bangladesh; mass migrations; Indo-Pakistani war won by India
1975–77	state of emergency gives PM Indira Gandhi dictatorial powers
1984	PM moves against Sikh separatists in Punjab; assassinated by two of her own Sikh guards; her son Rajiv Gandhi becomes PM
1990	mass march of determined Hindus to Ayodhya to reclaim the site of an existing mosque as originally Rama's birthplace and location of old Hindu temple: major confrontation with rioting in many cities
1991	Rajiv Gandhi assassinated by Tamil woman suicide bomber
1993/2006	terrorist bomb blasts in Mumbai (Bombay) kill hundreds

India Act further centralized British rule. The Company's policy towards India was then based on a principle of cultural non-intervention, trying to keep local élites largely intact so as use them as a basis for political power and economic exploitation. For this reason, the Company also encouraged and sponsored Orientalist scholars to produce translations and digests of ancient Sanskrit texts, like Sir William Jones's versions of Kalidasa, a fourth-century dramatist whom he liked to call "the Shakespeare of India". With the admission of Christian missions into the country in 1813 and the rise of laissez-faire liberalism in the nineteenth century, however, attitudes began to change. Ushering in an age of reform in the 1820s and '30s, the Company's administrators now sought to transform Indian society, often in close competition with the missionaries, by introducing free trade, English education and legal reforms, such as the suppression of *sati*, so-called widow-burning, in the name of civilization, enlightenment and progress (see the comments on Spivak's discussion of this issue in 2.3.4).

The 1857 Indian uprising against British rule, generally known as "the Mutiny", but more appropriately referred to as the First War of Independence, was triggered by religious objections to introduce cartridges greased with pig fat. Yet the agenda of the rebellion included popular outrage against territorial annexations and economic oppression and soon took on a seriously nationalist attitude, culminating in the attempt to restore the last of the Mughal rulers to the throne of Delhi. Shocked by the power of this anti-colonial challenge, Britain responded with sheer military force, suppressed the rebellion and ended the Company's rule. Henceforth India was a crown colony with a viceroy – a splendid and much-coveted post for English high aristocrats – as the monarch's representative. In 1871, Prime Minister Disraeli declared Queen Victoria to be Empress of India (a move which was mainly prompted by the fact that the Prussian king had just been declared German Emperor). Since this formalization of colonial rule in India, in the period of late-nineteenth-century rivalries growing among European powers, the Raj provided much of the pomp and pageantry for the self-fashioning of the British Empire while, at the same time, Indian intellectuals grew increasingly restless and estranged from their distant rulers.

Indian uprising and Victoria's triumph: the Raj in its most splendid period

With the 1885 foundation of the Indian National Congress, this political unrest created its first major platform. Though initially

Congress and the twentieth-century moves towards decolonization

conceived as a comprehensive organization to include all segments of India's population, Congress became increasingly identified with Hindu politics and culture. For a long time, British administrators had successfully played off Indian communities – Hindu, Muslim, Sikh, to name just the most significant – against one another. The same strategy was at work, when Viceroy Lord Curzon declared the administrative partition of Bengal in 1905, which potentially made Hindus a minority in either of the two new parts. Seen as an act of colonial arrogance, the partition quickly gave a major rallying point to anti-British sentiment and anti-colonial campaigns and was eventually withdrawn. Still, it served to deepen the rift between Hindu and Muslim communities. Politically, this rift began to be institutionalized with the 1906 foundation of the All India Muslim League, since 1913 with Muhammad Ali Jinnah as its leader. In 1916, however, the two main nationalist movements joined forces when the Pact of Lucknow established a temporary agreement between the Muslim League and Congress. At that point, their common aim was not to overthrow British rule altogether, but to demand greater Indian participation on all levels of government and administration.

After and before world war: Gandhi's great campaigns of *satyagraha*

After World War I, in which many Indian regiments had fought for the Empire, the situation quickly escalated, as demobilized British officials returned from the army to their former colonial posts and ousted the Indian subordinates who had done the job in the meantime. Unrest went especially high in Punjab and in 1919 reached a bloody climax in Amritsar when some four hundred civilians were killed in a massacre, an ill-guided British attempt to restore public order. This opened the way for a series of new anti-colonial campaigns staged by Gandhi, a London-trained lawyer from Gujarat who had first become politically active fighting racist politics in South Africa. His concept of *satyagraha*, i.e. the peaceful violation of laws recognized as unjust, was demonstrated in a number of highly visible mass boycotts and movements, which even managed to unite India's social and religious groups. In 1921-22, at a high point of Hindu-Muslim unity, Gandhi launched a Non-Cooperation Movement, calling for the use of hand-woven cloth as a symbol of India's economic self-sufficiency. In 1931, Gandhi launched a Civil Disobedience campaign with a 287-mile march to the Gujarati coast where he made salt in defiance of British tax claims on this basic commodity. Gandhi's vision for India was based on the peasantry and the revival of a rural, non-industrial economy; hence his emphasis on spinning and other traditional crafts as the backbone of Indian self-reliance. With his ascetic life-style, constant acts of faith and keen awareness of his own iconic power, Gandhi held formidable charisma and managed to present his ideas as expressing the true Indian spirit. But in fact, his thinking owes a great deal to the anti-industrial discourse of the Victorian English critic John Ruskin (see Gandhi 1997: xxxix-xli). Gandhi's historical importance, however, lies in discovering and defining weapons of the weak which could effectively challenge the giant machinery of Empire.

Britain first responded to the mounting pressure of the masses with a number of London roundtables, negotiating constitutional reforms, which neither satisfied Congress nor the Muslim League nor helped to stem popular unrest. Matters came to a head when in 1939 the Viceroy, in line with British politics, declared war on Germany without consulting Indian leaders and so lost all nationalist support for Britain's war efforts. In 1942 Congress issued a "Quit India" resolution, while Muslim leaders openly campaigned for a separate Muslim state in the Northwest. Rising tensions between religious factions led to a bloody civil war in 1946. When therefore Lord Mountbatten, Britain's last viceroy, was briefed in 1947 to transfer power into 'responsible hands', the break-up of the Raj into India and Pakistan was both a failed solution to rampant violence and a political necessity. Especially in the Punjab, but also in many other provinces, the new border created by partition could not neatly separate Muslim, Hindu and Sikh populations and so gave rise to mass migrations of some ten million refugees. In horrendous massacres another million lost their lives. On the subcontinent, then, the postcolonial period began with trauma.

Hindu-Muslim confrontations: violence, migration and partition in 1947

In the decades since, military conflicts between India and Pakistan have repeatedly escalated, especially about Kashmir. But also within India, violent political confrontations have frequently taken place in the name of religious affiliations and separatist demands. Indian governments, long led by Congress and the dynasty of Nehru's family, have tried a hard hand to contain the conflict, yet recent developments suggest that religious radicalization, on various sides, will continue to be used for politics of terror and violence.

Current conflicts

2 Literary Paradigms

Indian writing in English cannot easily be defined

As mentioned above (3.3), India has not only a venerable literary tradition of the ancient past, but also a multitude of present-day literatures, comprising all genres in all Indian languages. To confine our attention to anglophone writing, then, means to focus on a small fraction of a broad cross-linguistic spectrum of literary activity. But even 'Indian writing in English' is a difficult category with very fuzzy edges, due mainly to two factors: the Indian diaspora and the problem of distinguishing 'outsiders' from 'insiders' in Indian writing. **Diaspora**, as we have seen (1.2.5), is a common postcolonial experience, but it has special relevance for postcolonial Indian literature, much of which is produced elsewhere – in Britain, North America, the Caribbean, Australia or East Africa – and often explores the condition of so-called NRIs (non-resident Indians), as they are known today. The second factor is about the status of English writers in India. It is common to distinguish **Anglo-Indian** from **Indo-Anglian** literature: the latter refers to the work of Indian writers who chose English as their creative medium; the former refers to writing by Englishmen and -women who spent a formative time of their lives on the subcontinent, perhaps were even born there, and used local experience for literary purposes.

Anglo-Indian writers and their ambiguous position

It could certainly be argued that Anglo-Indian writers are not part of Indian literature at all; as 'outsiders' to the country and its culture, their work should properly belong to British literature with its various colonial inflections. To cite a roughly parallel case: the simple fact that writers like Joseph Conrad, Graham Greene or William Boyd have travelled through West and Central Africa and written about it does not make their work part of African literature (even though Boyd was actually born and raised in Ghana). But this parallel is misleading. If anything, we should compare Anglo-Indian with Anglo-Irish writing (see 3.1) and acknowledge that, historically and biographically, the Raj brought about some areas of cultural entanglements where all too neat distinctions between white, colonial 'outsiders' and non-white, colonized 'insiders' are difficult to maintain. To say the least, some of the English expatriates or *sahibs*, as they used to be known in colonial India, cultivated or imagined such remarkably strong bonds to local realities that Anglo-Indian writing has become a clear segment in the broad spectrum of Indian literatures. As always in the cultural legacies of Empire, issues of home and belonging are hard to disentangle. One of the best-known novels for this issue is E.M. Forster's *A Passage to India* (1924), a powerful modernist tale of cultural uncertainties and cross-cultural misunderstandings, steeped in the rhetoric of classic travel writing.

The classic example, however, is Rudyard Kipling (1865–1936). Born in Bombay to parents in the highest Anglo-Indian society, he spent his childhood in India, went through unhappy school years in England and America, to eventually return to India in the 1880s and make his name as a short-story writer. His popular fiction, like *Plain Tales from the Hills* (1888) or *The Jungle Books* (1894/95), offers a clear case of place writing, in the sense discussed earlier (2.4.2), because it tries to lay creative claims to a locality not previously part of English literature. In the late-Victorian heyday of the Raj, Kipling soon became the unacknowledged bard of Empire, so his work, with its many racist overtones, has long been studied in colonial discourse analysis (see 1.2.2). Yet there is a sense in which some of his best-known texts, despite their adolescent boy-scout quality, remain so interesting today precisely because they cannot be accounted for in simple terms. His novel *Kim* (1901), for instance, tells the story of a young orphan, son of an Irish soldier, who spends his time in colonial Lahore and eventually joins up with an old lama to travel and spy in North India. Through its title hero, this novel constructs a figure of surveillance, penetrating all and encompassing everything with his powerful capacity of seeing – which we must surely see as a figure of imperial wish fulfilment. At the same time, however, postcolonial readings of the novel (e.g. Suleri 1992) have suggested that the orphaned half-breed Kim can also be seen as a hybrid, in the sense defined by Bhabha (see 2.3.3), i.e. a figure of colonial anxiety. The example serves to show that the hyphenated identity of Anglo-Indian writing – that is to say, an identity that can only be named with two terms, combined or perhaps divided by a hyphen – has produced lastingly challenging fictions.

> **The case of Kipling: the bard of Empire in postcolonial reviews**

Indo-Anglian writing began in 1794 with *The Travels of Dean Mahomet, a Native of Patna in Bengal, Through Several Parts of India [...], Written by Himself*, the first book in English written by an Indian. In several ways comparable to Equiano's *Narrative* (see 2.1.2 and 2.4.1), this native travelogue was produced for a readership in England. The author, S. D. Mahomet (1759–1851), who had entered service of the East India Company as a teenager and

> **Indo-Anglian writing around 1800**

later accompanied his master to England, thus offers an early example of the transcultural career and double consciousness characteristic of most Indo-Anglian writers right into our days. A classic study of their literary achievements therefore speaks of "twice-born fiction" (Mukherjee 1971) to indicate that in India, just as in other postcolonial contexts, no writer relates to a single literary tradition nor to just one strand of cultural knowledge. Arguably, this also holds true for the nineteenth-century Indian intellectuals who used English as just one among their several literary languages. The poet Henry Derozio (1809-31), for instance, composed verses closely modelled on the Romantic idiom of contemporary English poetry; still, in poems like "The Harp of India", he managed to employ the received cultural forms to articulate nationalist concerns.

Social realism in twentieth-century novels: Anand and Rao

The same case can be made for the three major novelists, Mulk Raj Anand, R.K. Narayan and Raja Rao, whose debut work emerged in the last decade before India's independence. Born in the early years of the twentieth century, all three were shaped by the tumultuous times of Gandhi's great campaigns and all three sought for literary ways to come to a fuller understanding of what India, as a new nation beyond imperial confines, could mean or could become. For this purpose, they all wrote novels in the tradition of social realism, which explore specific regional and social spaces at the margins of official India but at the heart of what they see the true country to be. Anand, who studied in London, fought in the Spanish civil war and lived for a time in Gandhi's ashram, deliberately turned to the low lives of an outcast in *Untouchable* (1935) or of landless peasants in *Coolie* (1936), so as to evoke humanitarian compassion for the exploited. His political vision was socialist and he clearly conceived of his literary art as a means towards social change. Rao, by contrast, who lived for a time in France, then took part in India's liberation struggle and was also associated with Gandhi, entertained more spiritual and religious concerns, especially in his later work. His debut novel *Kanthapura* (1938) constructs a village to portray the social dynamics and changes in rural India under Gandhian influence. Written in colloquial, oral style, with many digressions and asides, the narrative consciously tries to tap on the resources of local history and the legendary annals of village life; as the author notes in his preface, "the tempo of Indian life must be infused into our English expression" (1989: iii).

Narayan, who spent all his life in India, consistently denied a social or political agenda for his work. Yet for more than half a century, his novels gave a realist portrait of a fictitious South Indian little town called "Malgudi", where all his plots are set and explore, in quiet and often humorous ways, the unheroic lives of ordinary people. The young title figure of his first novel, *Swami and His Friends* (1935), grows up and re-occurs together with some of the other characters in subsequent novels, suggesting a literary series and establishing Malgudi as a microcosm of Indian society. In *The Guide* (1958) Narayan shifts the scene to a village temple just outside the city where a former prisoner takes refuge; the villagers mistake him for a holy man and he eventually begins to like this new identity, beginning also to believe his own stories he tells them. Not unlike Synge's *Playboy of the Western World* (see 3.1.2), the novel thus explores the power of story telling and narrative inventions in producing, rather than merely reproducing, lived realities.

In postcolonial fiction, this tradition of large-scale realistic narrative has continued into the present period, for instance in Vikram Seth's *A Suitable Boy* (1993), an extended middle-class family saga set in post-independence North India and presented with such characterizations and plot developments that might derive from Trollope and Victorian fiction (whereas in other works, the same author has used very different literary styles). It is against this realist background that the postmodern and experimental narrative modes in Salman Rushdie's fiction, exploring the making and unmaking of Indian history and historiography (see 2.4.3) in novels like *The Moor's Last Sigh* (1995), can best be appreciated (see Schülting 2007). When the unreliable narrator of *Midnight's Children* (1981), for example, refuses to correct the false date he gave for Gandhi's assassination ("in my India, Gandhi will continue to die at the wrong time", 1982: 166), this is also an ironic comment on the confident representation of historic figures and national events in Anand's, Rao's or indeed Seth's novels. Similar ironies are at work, and are directed also against Rushdie, in Shashi Tharoor's monumental *The Great Indian Novel* (1989), a retelling of India's liberation struggle in cultural guises borrowed from the *Mahabharata*. With a curious blend of myth, folklore, literary allusions and historical implications, the novel creates the rambling voice of a cantankerous old man, bastard son of mixed parents, who presents his narrative as a "twice-born tale".

Narayan's fictional microcosm of ordinary India

Experimental and postmodern Indian fiction: Rushdie and Tharoor

SOME INDIAN WRITERS

Rabindranath Tagore (1861–1941), poetry: *Gitanjali* (1912), *The Fugitive* (1921), *The Child* (1931); Nobel prize 1913

Mulk Raj Anand (1905–2004), novels: *Untouchable* (1935), *Coolie* (1936), *The Sword and the Sickle* (1942)

R.K. Narayan (1907–2001), novels: *Swami and His Friends* (1935), *The English Teacher* (1945), *Waiting for the Mahatma* (1955), *The Guide* (1958)

Raja Rao (1908–2006), novels: *Kanthapura* (1938), *The Serpent and the Rope* (1960), *The Cat and Shakespeare* (1965)

Nissim Ezekiel (1924–2004), poetry: *A Time to Change* (1952), *The Unfinished Man* (1960), *Collected Poems* (1989)

Kamala Markandaya (*1924), novels: *Nectar in a Sieve* (1954), *Possession* (1963), *The Nowhere Man* (1972)

Nayantara Sahgal (*1927), novels: *A Time to Be Happy* (1958), *This Time of Mourning* (1965), *A Situation in Delhi* (1977), *Rich Like Us* (1985)

Anita Desai (*1937), novels: *Cry, the Peacock* (1963), *Clear Light of Day* (1980), *Baumgartner's Bombay* (1989), *Fasting, Feasting* (1999)

Bapsi Sidhwa (*1938), Pakistan; novels: *The Crow-Eaters* (1978), *The Bride* (1983), *Ice-Candy Man* (1988)

Shashi Deshpande (*1938), novels: *The Dark Holds No Terrors* (1980), *That Long Silence* (1988), *The Stone Woman* (2001)

Bharati Mukherjee (*1940), novels: *The Tiger's Daughter* (1972), *Jasmine* (1989), *Desirable Daughters* (2002)

Salman Rushdie (*1947), novels: *Midnight's Children* (1981), *Shame* (1983), *The Satanic Verses* (1988), *The Moor's Last Sigh* (1995), *The Ground Beneath Her Feet* (1999), *Shalimar the Clown* (2005)

Rohinton Mistry (*1952), novels: *Such a Long Journey* (1991), *A Fine Balance* (1995); *Family Matters* (2002)

Vikram Seth (*1952), verse novel: *The Golden Gate* (1986); novels: *A Suitable Boy* (1993), *An Equal Music* (1999), *Two Lives* (2005)

Romesh Gunesekera (*1953), Sri Lanka; fiction: *Reef* (1994), *Monkfish Moon* (1992), *Sandglass* (1998), *Heaven's Edge* (2002)

Amitav Ghosh (*1956), novels: *The Circle of Reason* (1986), *The Glass Palace* (2001); travel fiction: *In an Antique Land* (1992)

Shashi Tharoor (*1956), novels: *The Great Indian Novel* (1989), *Show Business* (1992), *Riot* (2001)

Amit Chaudhuri (*1962), novels: *A Strange and Sublime Address* (1991), *Afternoon Rag* (1993), *Freedom Song* (1998), *A New World* (2000)

Vikram Chandra (*1961), fiction: *Red Earth and Pouring Rain* (1995), *Love and Longing in Bombay* (1997), *Sacred Games* (2006)

Arundhati Roy (*1962), novel: *The God of Small Things* (1997)

Jhumpa Lahiri (*1967), fiction: *The Interpreter of Maladies* (1999), *The Namesake* (2003)

Kiran Desai (*1971), novel: *The Inheritance of Loss* (2006)

A different and no less significant challenge to the central tradition of Indian fiction as established in the 1930s has come from the remarkable number of powerful women writers, whose work has made a strong impact on national debates and international readers since the 1950s. In Kamala Markandaya's *Nectar in a Sieve* (1954), as in much of her later work, we find explorations of Southern village life which are strongly reminiscent of *Kanthapura* and yet portray the rural world from a distinctly female point of view. Women's experience of patriarchal India and feminist commitments to redefine women's places are just as central in Nayantara Sahgal's as in Anita Desai's novels, but both writers have also given several examples of their political concerns beyond the domestic sphere. Sahgal, who is Nehru's niece and grew up at the hub of India's independence struggle, has used her later work to explore how Indira Gandhi's state of emergency in the '70s affected public life. In *Baumgartner's Bombay* (1988), Desai (who has a German mother) has explored the double exile of a Berlin Jew who finds himself a perennial stranger also in his Indian refuge. Shashi Deshpande, another Indian woman writer to emerge in the 1980s, has recently written a novel, *Small Remedies* (2000), about the personal effects of the Ayodhya crisis and the Bombay riots in 1992. Diasporic conditions of Indian women, their search for identity and struggle in North American society have long been a main focus of Bharati Mukherjee's fiction, such as *Jasmine* (1989).

Indian women writers and their creative achievements

Yet the most notable success in Indian literature, since the international triumph of Rushdie's *Midnight's Children* in 1981, was the publication of Arundhati Roy's *The God of Small Things* (1997), the first non-diasporic Indian novel to win the prestigious Booker Prize in Britain. Set in rural Kerala in the 1960s, the novel tells a family story of love and death that is indebted to the mainstream of Indian village fiction just as its linguistic inventiveness clearly follows Rushdie's prompting, but it manages to use the various inherited traditions creatively for its own purposes. Perhaps its most remarkable feature is the narrative use of a child's consciousness as a central focalizer, which suffuses all observations of everyday life in Southern India with a sustained sense of wondering and slight alienation. Published fifty years after Indian independence, this novel marks a new stage in critical engagements with colonial and Anglo-Indian legacies, moving towards newly defined communal and national concerns. It is therefore a bitter irony that the international marketing of Roy, especially in the US, has tried to exoticize

Indian fiction on the global market: problems of the "postcolonial exotic"

and commodify her person and her book to such a point that it can serve as an example of what has been called "the postcolonial exotic" (Huggan 2001).

4   Focus on Australian Literature

Australia and its "peripheral" location

It has not been a coincidence that *The Empire Writes Back* (Ashcroft et al, 1989), the pioneering textbook for Postcolonial Studies which first defined or popularized the term "post-colonial", was written by Australian critics (see 1.2.1). The basic pattern they employ to discuss what they call "dominated" literatures, i.e. literatures under the continued spell of the powerful mother country Britain and the metropolis London, is a pattern well suited to describe Australian developments. In fact, the major criticism raised against their book has focussed on the question of whether such a model, suggesting a constitutive tension between the imperial "centre" and the colonial "periphery", could be transferred to other former colonies around the world where very different cultural and historical realities may come into play. With regard to Australia, however, the centre-periphery model and, consequently, the conceptual framework of postcolonialism has long been seen as quite compelling.

Antipodean attitudes in Australian culture: looking towards England

Historically a British settler colony of a special kind (see 3.4.1), Australia has been a federal state with its own government since 1901 but, as a constitutional monarchy, continues to recognize the British monarch as the head of state. Geographically, Australia is of course a continent almost as far away from Europe as anyone can travel – hence its early modern designation as "the antipodes", which used to be synonymous with the end of the world. In Shakespeare's comedy *Much Ado About Nothing*, for instance, a character who would like to escape from undesirable present company says "I will go on the slightest errand now to the Antipodes that you can devise to send me on" (act 2, scene 1). But despite this geographical remoteness from Britain – or perhaps because of it – Australia has long been closely tied to British norms and standards in the symbolic and cultural spheres. When for instance in the early twentieth century the new national capital was designated, the minister for home affairs and member of the first federal Australian government seriously proposed calling it "Shakespeare". In the event, it was called Canberra, yet this curious anecdote suggests the cultural predicament of a peripheral society deriving its main notions of what is valuable and viable from elsewhere, i.e. from a far-away metropolitan centre whose canon has been transferred and adopted.

As a matter of fact, a distinct sense of 'Australianness', i.e. of local differences in literature and culture, has been defined and defended since the late nineteenth century – which is precisely the postcolonial move which Ashcroft et al describe as the change from cultural assimilation to abrogation and eventually appropriation (see 1.2.1). But the spurious idea that Australia, at least as long as it regarded itself programmatically as a white and Anglo-Saxon nation, should look towards Britain for high culture has been surprisingly long lived. It used to be captured in the term "cultural cringe": the notion that antipodean creativity in literature and art were all somehow second-hand and second-rate and in need of English imports. Complex as the background to such cultural attitudes may be, the early settler history of the country offers at least one way to explain them. For, strictly speaking, Australia has been named and constituted entirely through imports. The name of its best known city, for example, is derived from Lord Sydney, the British secretary of home affairs and in 1788 the authority responsible for setting up the first white settlement in a place which, eight years earlier, an English captain had named New South Wales. What such place names, imposed from outside, generally signify is a colonial condition of cultural displacement in which all important reference points lie elsewhere. It is just this condition which Paul Carter, in his classic postcolonial study of Australian spatial history (1988), has analysed at length (see 2.4.2).

"Cultural cringe" and the colonial legacy of naming

Since the 1970s, challenges to this condition, and departures from its conceptual basis, have occurred through two related developments: the official abandonment of the White Australia policy which restricted immigration for non-Europeans, and the increasing awareness of the Aboriginal civilizations on the continent, or rather their present-day remains, which predate the European presence by many thousand years. Clearly, the entire notion of a largely homogeneous white Australia – an ideological notion which had dominated colonial mind-sets for almost two centuries and looked on Irish immigrants as the most exotic parts of the local settler population – could only work as long as the existence of indigenous people, as original owners of the land, was entirely suppressed,

The aboriginal presence and postcolonial challenges to White Australia

135

denied or actively combatted. To the extent, therefore, that Aboriginals succeeded in making their case known and demand public recognition of their rights – a case often made in and through Aboriginal literary production – the foundation of the whiteness myth crumbled away and revealed its exclusivist assumptions as blatant, racist prejudice. In a concurrent development, spurred also by the protests against American atrocities in Vietnam (in which Australian forces were actively involved), Australia began to see itself increasingly in terms of its Asian location and its Pacific connections, rather than continue to position itself either in relation to the old British mother country or a new American imperial power. Thus, throughout the 1980s, '90s and beyond, vigorous debates have explored issues of Australian identity and tried to redefine the postcolonial nation in multicultural and multicentred networks, rather than perpetuate the centre-periphery model.

1 Historical Survey

European landfalls and discoveries: the penal colony established

European involvements in Australia or, as we should perhaps more accurately put it, the European invasion of Australia first began with Dutch explorers in the early seventeenth century. Through early travellers' reports about an unknown Southern continent in the far East, a *terra australis incognita*, the place attracted much attention and eventually received its name. But British interests in the region, mainly based on economic and strategic thoughts about a stronger naval presence in the East, began to be established considerably later. The decisive explorations were the three Pacific voyages by Captain Cook, on behalf of the Admiralty, whose landfall at Botany Bay in 1770 claimed the land as British and prepared the way for subsequent colonial settlement. Yet when in 1788 the First Fleet arrived and brought some 1,500 settlers, about half of them convicts from overcrowded English prisons, Britain's imperial status had recently suffered a serious set-back, due to the American declaration of independence. The breaking away of the former New World colonies in 1776, however, urged Britain to seek other places in partial compensation of this loss, and so Australia was seen as suitable for this purpose. The early convict settlement established in New South Wales, the founding event of white Australia, therefore suggests how the colonial periphery used to function as a marginal social space to which unwanted, 'criminal' elements could be transferred and eliminated from society at home. In the social economy of empire, the colony thus serves like a safety valve so as to reduce domestic pressures.

The foundational event of this penal colony continued as a major factor shaping Australian realities for a long time. It accounts, for example, for the strong military presence in New South Wales, for the strictly authoritarian forms of administration under the imperial governor and, generally speaking, for the male dominance in a settler population that long attracted more immigrants and fortune seekers from the lower social classes. But, even in these early decades, tensions arose in the colony, which erupted in the 1808 rebellion against Governor Bligh when officers of the New South Wales Corps led an "emancipist" faction against central and imperial control. The other major shaping factor for social realities was the vastness of the land apparently available for settlement. Before long, various explorations around the continent and into its interior undertook to map and claim this space for white development. This led to the eventual foundation of several colonies: apart from New South Wales (in the Southeast), Queensland (in the Northeast), Victoria (in the South), South Australia, Western Australia and the Southern island of Tasmania, each consolidating their distinct characteristics. But this also led to many bloody campaigns against Aboriginals, which drastically decimated the indigenous population and, with European farming methods, robbed them of the basis for their age-old nomadic life-styles. Apart from this so-called "pacification by force", as the massacres used to be known, diseases introduced from Europe (hence fatal for indigenous immune systems) further contributed to the Aboriginal decline. Until well into the second half of the twentieth century, indigenous life and culture were widely seen – and widely hoped – to be rapidly on their way to extinction.

The vast natural spaces of the so-called Outback and the availability of endless and unsettled bushland have long been recognized as central for the development of a specifically Australian imagination (see 3.4.2). But it is equally important to remember that nineteenth-century Australia also saw the rise of vibrant urban lifestyles, particularly in Sydney and Melbourne, which in the 1880s ranked among the largest cities in the world. The remarkable expansion in population numbers through increasing immigration, fuelled by a liberalist economic climate and hopes for individual progress, came about with the discovery of copper, silver and, especially, gold in various parts of the country. So besides farming, the settlers and fortune seekers now saw even greater opportunities for starting brilliant new lives in the colony. During this entire period,

Nineteenth-century developments

The Outback as opposed to urban culture

the various colonies did not have strong political relations with one another. This changed in 1901 when the first Commonwealth parliament opened and Australia became a federal state, with its own national government, officially ending the colonial period.

Military engagements and political repercussions

Yet political and social ties, let alone cultural and personal relations, to the Empire and England remained intact. This became brutally evident in World War I when in April 1915, as part of the campaign of allied forces in Turkey, the Australian and New Zealand Army Corps fought in the ranks of the British at Gallipoli and incurred very heavy losses. Nationally commemorated to this day as Anzac Day, this event symbolizes both the selfless heroism of a young nation and its continued bonds with a mother country whose distant wars Australian soldiers came to pay for with their lives. World War II, by contrast, marks the period when Australia openly began to move away from political allegiance to Britain and seek closer alliance with the US. As soon as the Far East and the Pacific became a major theatre of war, with the Japanese attack on Pearl Harbour, the Australian government made it clear that the country would now look fully to America, as Prime Minister Curtin put it, "free from any pangs about our traditional links of friendship to Britain". Three decades later, this new friendship led to the Australian involvement in the Vietnam war, which, in turn, gave rise to the demonstrations and student protests of the late '60s. At that point, the postwar immigration policy accepting people from Southern and Central Europe had already substantially transformed society. Yet the rising social movements also created a new awareness for the dismal Aboriginal situation and led to a change in the constitution, allowing Aboriginals to vote.

Fundamental changes since the 1970s: aboriginal land rights established

Further changes in the same direction came with a short-lived but significant Labour government in the early 1970s, establishing an Aboriginal Consultative Committee in 1973 (later renamed National Aboriginal Conference). At the same time, White Australia policy was officially abandoned, so that the country opened for broad and continuing Asian immigration from China, Korea, Vietnam and other neighbouring countries. The 1988 Bicentennial Celebrations, and the protests against its exclusivist vision of Australian history, have prompted ongoing searches into the image and self-understanding of the nation and more debates about its cultural make-up. In 1992, the Australian High Court ruled in a historic decision that the idea of "terra nullius", which had served the

SOME DATES IN AUSTRALIAN HISTORY

1616	Dirk Hartog (Dutch) makes first recorded European landing
1770	James Cook lands in Botany Bay, on behalf of British Admiralty, names and takes possession of New South Wales
1788	First Fleet arrives: eleven British ships bearing some 1,500 people, half of them convicts; penal settlement established at Sydney
1802	first Australian book printed (NSW General Standing Orders)
1803	settlement established in Van Diemen's Land (Tasmania); Sydney Gazette first issued
1808	rebellion led by New South Wales Corps deposes Governor Bligh
1829	entire Australian continent declared British
1836	South Australia established as colony of free settlers
1840	no more British convicts transported to New South Wales
1850	University of Sydney established
1851	discovery of gold in Victoria, New South Wales and later Queensland spurs economic growth and development
1850–60	population quadrupled through immigration
1880	bushranger Ned Kelly captured and hanged in Melbourne
1894	women's suffrage in South Australia
1901	Australia becomes a federation, with British monarch as head of state; federal government adopts White Australia policy, Canberra declared federal capital (1908)
1915	allied landing at Gallipoli (Turkey) in World War I: among the British forces, many Australian and New Zealand soldiers lose their lives; to the present day commemorated as Anzac Day (April 25)
1947	European immigration programme to boost white population
1962	Chair of Australian Literature established at University of Sydney
1965–71	support for US forces in Vietnam strengthens ties to the US
1967	referendum allows Aboriginals to be recognized as citizens
1972	Labour party wins government and withdraws troops from Vietnam
1973	White Australia policy officially abandoned: increased Asian immigration; Sydney opera house opens; writer Patrick White wins Nobel Prize
1975	Racial Discrimination Act makes it unlawful to discriminate on grounds of national or ethnic origin
1988	Bicentennary Celebrations; strong Aboriginal protests
1992	Mabo land rights decision: High Court of Australia acknowledges Aboriginal land claims
1998	"stolen generations" report puts pressure on government to apologise for mistreatment of Aboriginal peoples
1999	republic referendum held (unsuccessful)
2000	Olympic Games held in Sydney

British Crown in the eighteenth century to occupy the continent, was invalid, thus accepting for the first time the priority of Aboriginal land rights.

2   Literary Paradigms

Oral traditions and their traces

Like in most other parts of the world, literary traditions on the continent began with oral performance, but as a result of racist politics in colonial Australia, it has taken an extraordinarily long time before any of these old traditions have ever been acknowledged, translated and appreciated. Much of them in fact is no longer available and has been forgotten. Whereas the Western canon was firmly built on the Homeric epics, remembered and reworked throughout the centuries, Aboriginal writer Mudrooroo has pointedly asked "how many know of the long epic poems", like the *Djanggawul* epic, "that belong to Australia?" (1997: 17)

Early English writing in the colony

The first contributions to white Australia's literary culture were made by some early pioneers, settlers and explorers, often in the form of journals, letters or expedition records, framed largely by pragmatic purposes and a quest for knowledge. With the 1824 foundation of *The Australian*, a Sydney-based newspaper which soon became a platform for emancipist and early nationalist sentiment, writers had a potential medium of publication. Yet most novels serialised there were, in fact, contemporary English fiction popular at the time such as Charles Dickens's works. The first Australian novel, *Quintus Serviton* (1830-31), was written by the convict Henry Savery; the first novel of greater note is *The Recollections of Geoffry Hamlyn* (1859) by Henry Kingsley, a family romance and emigrant success story, partly set in England. It was preceded by Catherine Helen Spence's *Clara Morrison* (1854), a domestic tale of South Australia during the gold fever and the first book published by an Australian woman.

Outback and mateship: the promises of simple bush life

Generally speaking, life in the Victorian colony was not much given to literary or intellectual activities; often it was clearly averse to them and instead championed the ideal of the unsophisticated, independent, strong-willed and nature-loving bushranger, whose need for books was very limited. This notion derives from the vast spaces of unsettled land and their impact on the Australian imagination. In the context of white settler thinking, the so-called Outback sets up a perennial frontier between culture and nature, civilization and wilderness, social bonds and personal freedom, control from without and self-control, a frontier which every Australian may feel free to cross at his own peril and so, as a self-reliant pioneer, become the maker of his fortune. In the nineteenth century, this Australian dream was roughly similar to North America and its experience of the "Wild West". But in the US, the frontier was officially declared closed in the 1890s when civilization had covered the entire continent, whereas in Australia the promise of the bush has remained fresh almost to the present day. It has created social attitudes of toughness, perseverance and endurance and has cultivated a strongly masculine ethics of mateship, defying all superior authority just as all cultural refinement. Since the 1880s, such attitudes were prominently voiced in a nationalist journal called *The Bulletin*, published in Sydney and generally known as "the bushman's bible" because it propagated republican sentiments: anti-British, isolationist and thoroughly in favour of simple bush life as the real Australian thing. Among its best known writers was Henry Lawson, who also tried to make his name in England. It might be felt that the very medium of a printed periodical, as a literary and commercial enterprise, belies the entire notion of an individual, unsophisticated, natural existence which *The Bulletin* championed. Still, the mateship myth of the Outback has remained a central feature of Australian self-fashioning.

For all their chauvinistic tendencies, such publications served a crucial purpose in abrogating English cultural dominance, negotiating a sense of Australian identity and thus moving towards post-colonial perspectives (in the way discussed above, 3.4). Many of Australia's best-loved folk-heroes are bushrangers and outlaws, such as Jack Donohoe in the 1820s and especially Ned Kelly in the 1870s, often turned into the subject of ballads, popular myth-making and writing. In recent years, the Kelly story has been subjected to a postmodern rewriting by Peter Carey (2001; see Brosch 2007). But also *Voss* (1957), an early novel by Patrick White, later Australia's first Nobel laureate for literature, draws powerfully on the outback myth. In a plot of epic simplicity, it tells the story of the first cross-continent expedition in the 1840s, which ends in failure, death and mystery (it is based on the German explorer Leichhardt, whose expedition vanished without trace). The novel ends in puzzlement about the lasting record of this failing hero, asking how to disentangle a desire for legends from the need for facts: "Come, come. If we are not certain of the facts, how is it possible to give the

Literary legacies of bushrangers: Ned Kelly and White's *Voss*

answers?" a character remarks (1960: 448). But the narrative implies that it is just the lack of any answers which compels story telling and myth making to continue.

Clichéd perceptions of the Aboriginal presence

In white bush writing, the Aboriginal presence is very stereotypically portrayed, always framed by two conflicting attitudes which set up indigenous people as objects of either fear or of temptation. White representations thus reflect a split cultural desire for dominating the indigenous ('fear') or, alternatively, for submitting to its power ('temptation') in the wish to break out from civilizational rules. In a study of this issue, Terry Goldie argues that "our image of the indigene has functioned then as a constant source for semiotic reproduction in which each textual image refers back to those offered before" (1989: 6), that is to say, the textual images do not relate to experience or observation but just to previous images constantly reproduced. With explicit reference to Said's *Orientalism* (see 2.3.2.), Goldie analyses this semiotic pattern in the literature of Canada, Australia and New Zealand. What emerges is a series of clichés with which indigenous people are invariably associated: nature, sex, violence, orality, mysticism and the prehistoric. Against this background, we can understand the urge and power of Aboriginal writing since the 1960s, combatting such clichés from white writing while critically redefining the political premises on which they rest. In Mudrooroo's words, "indigenous writers who arose in the sixties were the products of assimilation revolting against assimilation" (1997: 14).

Postcolonial strategies on different levels: targeting multiple domination

All this shows that cultural and literary developments in Australia, as in other former settler colonies (like Canada, New Zealand or even South Africa), follow complex patterns and suggest a double process of postcolonial emancipation. In the first place, white Australian writers work against the dominance of English cultural norms and try to define local forms and standards of their own so as to articulate their sense of cultural difference. But secondly, indigenous writers must also work against the forms they are confronted with in the dominant white tradition and question the clichés by which Australian literature long used to represent their world. In the terms of *The Empire Writes Back* (see 1.2.1), postcolonial strategies like abrogation and appropriation are not directed at one and the same "centre" all the time, but at various points of cultural dominance and literary authority. Nor does the process end there. Aboriginal women writers, for instance, may also see the need to address patriarchal structures within indigenous societies – another power centre, as it were – and thus add a third level of critique and concern for their writing to work on.

Chief among the Aboriginal writers and activists emerging in the 1960s were poets like Oodgeroo Noonuccal or Kevin Gilbert, whose place writing (as noted earlier, 2.4.2) set out to redescribe local landscapes. Their efforts were, however, soon joined by white nature poets like Judith Wright or Les Murray whose environmental concerns combine with a search for Australian icons and identities. One of Wright's poems is entitled "The Eucalypt and the National Character" (1976) and playfully explores the possibilities of seeing the tree's "sprawling and informal", "dishevelled, disorderly" nature, though tough and "graceful asymmetry", as embodying the Australian character (1994: 362). In a larger sense, this image might also suggest the manifold asymmetries and creative coalitions, across gender, race and class, that take place in Australian literature.

Nature poetry and Aboriginal writing

This may also help to account for the fact that narratives of adolescence are so prominent in Australian literature, especially in its recent multicultural period, because the personal process of growing up and coming to consciousness can usefully be allied to the social process of coming to terms with new realities (see 2.4.1). Three examples bear this out. *Johnno* (1975), David Malouf's debut novel, set in mid-century Brisbane, tells the story of second- and third-generation immigrants from Asia Minor wondering about the place in which they find themselves: "What an extraordinary thing it is that I should be here rather than somewhere else", the narrator reflects. "If my father's father hadn't packed up one day to escape military service under the Turks […], I wouldn't be an Australian at all. It is practically an accident, an entirely unnecessary fate." (1984: 52) And yet, the experience of entering adulthood, the novel shows, rather lies in finding out about extraordinary necessities. In a historical framework, and from an Aboriginal perspective, the same experience is explored in Mudrooroo's novel *Doctor Wooreddy's Prescription for Enduring the Ending of the World* (1983), depicting the lives of the last Tasmanians as they face their white destroyers in the 1830s: "Wooreddy waddled his way towards adulthood in an awful world that became less and less familiar" (1983: 5); in such wry yet compassionate prose the narrative combines personal with historical transformations.

Growing up in Australia: three formative narratives

Adam Lindsay Gordon (1833–1870), poetry: *Bush Ballads and Galloping Rhymes* (1870)

Henry Lawson (1867–1922), stories: *The Country I Come From* (1901), *Joe Wilson and His Mates* (1901), *Children of the Bush* (1902)

Miles Franklin (1879–1954), novels: *My Brilliant Career* (1901), *Old Blastus of Bandicoot* (1931), *All That Swagger* (1936)

Christina Stead (1902–1983), novels: *Seven Poor Men from Sydney* (1934), *For Love Alone* (1944), *The Man Who Loved Children* (1940)

A.D. Hope (1907–2000), poetry: *The Wandering Islands* (1955), *Collected Poems* (1966), *Orpheus* (1991)

Patrick White (1912–1990), novels: *The Aunt's Story* (1948), *The Tree of Man* (1956), *Voss* (1957), *Riders in the Chariot* (1961), *The Vivisector* (1970), *The Eye of the Storm* (1973), *A Fringe of Leaves* (1976), *The Twyborn Affair* (1979); Nobel prize 1973

Judith Wright (1915–2000), poetry: *The Moving Image* (1946), *Woman to Man* (1949), *Collected Poems 1946–1985* (1994)

Jack Davis (1917–2000), plays: *The Dreamers* (1983), *No Sugar* (1986), *Barungin: Smell the Wind* (1988)

Oodgeroo Noonuccall/Kath Walker (1920–1993), poetry: *We Are Going* (1964), *The Dawn is at Hand* (1966), *My People* (1970)

Dorothy Hewett (1923–2002), poetry: *Selected Poems* (1991)

David Malouf (*1934), novels: *Johnno* (1975), *An Imaginary Life* (1978), *Harland's Half Acre* (1984), *Remembering Babylon* (1993)

Randolph Stow (*1935), novels: *To the Islands* (1958/82), *Tourmaline* (1963), *Visitants* (1979), *The Girl Green as Elderflowers* (1980)

Thomas Keneally (*1935), novels: *The Chant of Jimmy Blacksmith* (1972), *Schindler's Ark* (1982), *The Playmaker* (1987)

Les Murray (*1938), poetry: *Selected Poems* (1976), *Translations from the Natural World* (1992), *Fredy Neptune* (1998)

Mudrooroo/Colin Johnson (*1939), novels: *Wild Cat Falling* (1965), *Doctor Wooreddy's Prescription for Enduring the Ending of the World* (1983), *Master of the Ghost Dreaming* (1991)

Jeanette Turner Hospital (*1942), novels: *The Ivory Swing* (1982), *Borderline* (1985), *The Last Magician* (1992)

David Williamson (*1942), plays: *Don's Party* (1973), *Travelling North* (1983)

Peter Carey (*1943), novels: *Oscar and Lucinda* (1988), *Jack Maggs* (1997), *True History of the Kelly Gang* (2001)

Louis Nowra (*1950), plays: *Inside the Island* (1981), *The Golden Age* (1985)

Sally Morgan (*1951), memoir: *My Place* (1987); play: *Sistergirl* (1992)

Richard Flannagan (*1961), novel: *Gould's Book of Fish* (2001)

Christon Tiolkas (*1965), novels: *Loaded* (1995), *Dead Europe* (2005)

This combination is just as central for Sally Morgan's memoir *My Place* (1987), probably the most successful and controversial Australian publication over the last decades and a set text in all schools (see also 2.4.1). Debates have centred on issues of authenticity and the author's claim of ethnic belonging, but the point of her own Aboriginal family history she discovers actually lies in seeing identification as a cultural process beyond genetic determinations. With chapter headings such as "Owning up" and "A Beginning", the narrative dramatizes a personal quest for more inclusive versions of the past, bringing out the skeletons from the family closet. The most notable literary device is Morgan's presentation of various other stories in the story – so-called intradiegetic narratives – which widen the scope of personal memories to include the older generation and which emulate oral story telling situations with the communal sharing of knowledge and experience.

Morgan's place and the debate about authenticity

5   Focus on Caribbean Literature

One of the most productive and paradigmatic areas of postcolonial culture, the Caribbean comprises the islands and coastal countries of the central American region where centuries of conquest, colonization and migration have brought about intense social encounters and entanglements. Different terms have been used to designate this area and especially the archipelago, i.e. the long chain of tropical islands, many of them rather small, that stretches between Florida and the South American mainland. In francophone contexts, the term **Antilles** is often used for them; in anglophone contexts, the term **West Indies** is still common (in a narrow sense, "West Indies" refers exclusively to Caribbean Commonwealth countries, i.e. former British colonies). This latter term is sometimes avoided or resented because of its Eurocentric bias: it transparently derives from an early modern cartographic error, namely Columbus' famous misconception that he had come to India. However, the term **Caribbean** also holds Columbian legacies: it derives from the designation **Caribes** for one of the indigenous peoples he thought to have identified, a designation first recorded in the Admiral's diary in 1492 and etymologically related to the "cannibals" which he also claimed to have discovered there (see Hulme 1986). The terminological issue thus highlights the extent to which outside notions and involvements have historically shaped the area.

The territories and the names of Caribbean culture

A "hybrid" region after centuries of outside influence and domination

Geologically, the chain of islands all belong to a volcanic mountain range, largely submerged in the ocean, which connects North and South America and marks a broad sphere of shared geographic features. Yet the Caribbean area includes important mainland countries, too, such as Guyana (formerly British Guiana), Belize, Cayenne and Surinam on the Southern continent, with their vast hinterland of rainforest, mountains and rivers. Since 1492, the history of the entire region around the Caribbean Sea (including also Venezuela, Colombia and other Latin American countries) has been dominated by Spanish, English, French and Dutch colonial projects, especially the plantation economies established there and staffed with slave labourers from Africa and later Asia. Resulting from these centuries of enforced dislocation and violent resettlement, however, the social culture of the Caribbean now is unique for its variety, diversity and amalgamation of different cultural and ethnic elements from around the world. Whether with regard to local languages and their many creole forms or with regard to local religions and their syncretic mixtures or to any other aspect of life, the Caribbean is the "hybrid" place *par excellence* (for a definition of this term, see 1.2.6). As Caribbean cultural theorists and critics like Edouard Glissant (1989) have therefore often argued, any notion of cultural purity, homogeneity or even stable boundary has no true ground in this archipelagic area.

Diaspora, displacements, disparities and the search for home

And yet, the Caribbean is the place whence black pioneers like Aime Césaire or Marcus Garvey came to develop concepts such as négritude (see 1.2.5) and religious practices like Rastafarianism (see 3.5.1), which emphasize African origins and black identity. This may be due to the fact that the area has long been subject to a history of fragmentation and violence, of constant passages and ongoing diaspora. Despite claims to the contrary (see Torres-Saillant 1997 and 2006), there is little sense of unity or cultural coherence that would encompass the whole region. The postcolonial Caribbean continues to be primarily seen – and continues to see itself – in relation to the four main colonizing powers (Spain, Britain, France, the Netherlands) and their cultural legacies, with the United States as a major new presence and cultural model for most countries to contend with. By contrast, since the days of the short-lived West Indian Federation (1958-62), inter-island relations tend to be rather weak and only follow the former colonial affiliations (the University of the West Indies, for example, has campuses in Trinidad, Jamaica and Barbados). This has far-reaching consequences, for instance in communication services. St Lucia and Martinique are neighbouring islands, their coasts within sight and easily reached by boat. But until the 1970s, a letter posted in St Lucia would first be transported to London, then to Paris and then on to Martinique (to this day, a French département where the local currency is Euro), i.e. the letter would have to cross the Atlantic twice, before it reached an addressee just a few miles across the St Lucian Channel. This postal problem typifies the larger political predicaments of a fragmented region.

The rich linguistic situation follows from the multilingual history of this cultural contact zone. Throughout, the social structure is diglossic (see 1.2.4), i.e. most formal communication domains, such as administration, international business, higher education and print culture, are defined in a local variety of the former colonial language (e.g. English or French), which in most places still holds a high prestige position (even if this is undergoing rapid change, see Mühleisen 2002); all informal domains, such as personal and oral communication, popular culture, but increasingly also radio and television programmes, some newspapers and even elementary schooling, make use of one of the local contact languages, variously known as **creole** languages or **patois**. The complex features of these creoles relate closely to their origins in the history of slavery and are studied in one of the most fascinating fields of linguistics (see Sebba 1997). Principally, they are the result of language contact between (a) the West African languages brought to the New World plantations by African slaves with (b) the European languages of their colonial masters, mainly English, French or Dutch. Roughly speaking, the grammatical structures of creoles derive from the African side (so-called **substrate** elements), while their lexical items derive from the European side (so-called **superstrate** elements). Because we therefore recognize most words, this has the effect that, for instance, English-based creoles look quite familiar to English speakers, just the grammar looks odd; thus, in a colonial mind-set, creoles used to be looked down upon and thought of as "bad English".

The language situation: creole and diglossia

But this notion is wrong. Creoles are fully developed, highly elaborate and functioning languages, spoken as the mother tongue in their linguistic communities (though rarely the only tongue used there) and increasingly used also in writing, especially in literature. Since the early modern genocide left the Caribbean without indige-

Creoles as opposed to pidgin languages

nous tongues, creoles have come to stand in for the native languages. This is captured in the term "nation language" that Kamau Brathwaite (1984) has suggested for them. For this reason, creoles must be sharply distinguished from pidgin languages, which are widely used in some African countries and Pacific territories and also sometimes employed for literary purposes. **Pidgins** are contact languages without native speakers, i.e. they exist always in addition to a mother tongue and are employed for specific purposes of cross-cultural communication, such as business transactions. Pidgins are thus limited in their communicative range, specified in their uses and simplified in their resources. However, when a pidgin, with the birth and growth of a new generation, becomes the first language that children acquire, it undergoes restructuring, expansion and eventually becomes a creole. According to one hypothesis of creole genesis, this is what must have happened on eighteenth-century West Indian plantations, where slaves used to be kept in multilingual groups and the use of mother tongues was prohibited in order to prevent rebellion. Since the nineteenth century, the linguistic situation has been further enriched with the introduction of Hindi, Chinese and other Asian languages through indentured labourers and migrants.

Further meanings of the term *creole*

Confusingly, the term *creole* is used also in various other, even contradictory senses, namely (1) for a person of mixed European and black descent, (2) for a descendant of Spanish, French or other white settler families in the Caribbean (especially in the historical context of plantation culture), or even (3) for a member of an Afro-Caribbean, i.e. black community (especially in Trinidad). But this remarkable spectrum of meanings only serves to highlight the prevalence and prominence of creole culture in the Caribbean. Like the languages, African and Asian religious practices, too, have come to the New World and undergone extensive transformation in Caribbean societies. This syncretic heritage is manifest, for instance, in Haitian voodoo cults, Jamaican Shango rituals or so-called obeah just as in the religious celebrations and enactments of Indian communities in Trinidad. In their displaced context, often actually in resistance against colonial oppression, all these traditional practices commemorate the cultural background of the different ethnic groups in Africa, India or wherever they once came from; but none of these traditions have remained quite the same. They are changed, as a result of their exposure and response to other elements in the Caribbean contact zone, and so undergo a process of creolization. What follows, therefore, is a cultural reality impossible to categorize in simple terms: hybrid, polyphonic and deterritorialized, the fragments of Caribbean culture always suggest different, but never complete wholes.

1   Historical Survey

On 12 October 1492, after crossing the Atlantic, Christopher Columbus arrived on an island he named San Salvador and claimed for the Castilian Crown. His project had of course been to establish a Western sailing route to India; though he never realized where he landed, his accidental discovery of an unmapped continent was in fact even more useful for his patrons, opening a New World for imperial domination. The early sixteenth century saw the Spanish conquest of America, destroying ancient civilizations, plundering their riches and brutally obliterating Amerindian populations in the entire region through a combination of military and medical effects (many died from diseases introduced by Europeans). Except in some remote places in the South American hinterland, no descendants of the six million indigenous inhabitants of the pre-Columbian Caribbean survived the early modern onslaught. Among intellectuals at the time, especially members of the church, this did not go unnoticed and sparked off theological debates. A Spanish friar called Bartolomé de Las Casas wrote an American history and strong indictment of imperial policies (*Breve Rélacion de le Destruycíon de Las Indias*, 1532). The pope eventually issued a bull, declaring that native Americans were humans, not beasts, hence available as objects of missionary teaching. But the mythic quest for gold and the unspeakable riches allegedly to be found in "El Dorado", continued to keep a powerful hold on the European imagination.

Columbus and the Spanish conquest of America

When the first English sailors and explorers travelled to the region in the 1560s to '80s, they were late-comers, desperate to secure a part of these legendary shores for the glory of the budding British Empire. But English colonization in the New World, with the haphazard and rather luckless colony in Virginia, took a slow start. It was only in 1623 that Thomas Warner occupied the island of St Christopher (St Kitts), gained a royal charter for its settlement and thus began the period of intense engagement and exploitation. Sugar cane, which had been introduced into the region, turned out a most successful crop; together with cocoa, coffee and tobacco it

Early English settlements and sugar plantations

soon became the main product of the new plantation economy. Labour-intensive in cultivation and very demanding in its further processing, sugar was a key factor in imperial commerce and power, comparable only to oil in the twentieth century. So the profits to be made from it set the agenda for colonial Caribbean societies which, in the words of a historian, "as traditionless and artificial new creations on depopulated land, were the most radical sociotechnical experiment of the age" (Osterhammel 1997: 31).

Colonial social hierarchies and imperial rivalries

Highly stratified, with a tiny white élite trying to control huge numbers of black slaves, Caribbean societies were extremely volatile and had to reinforce their hierarchies through military force and naked violence. Evident from the long history of slave rebellions throughout the region, planters were forever struggling to maintain their standing, while also struggling to keep up relations with their European homeland (not always keen to support the tropical expatriates). Especially in the larger islands like Jamaica, where the mountainous interior provided ample space for hiding, runaway slaves or so-called **maroons** soon formed their own communities, which operated as radical elements of unrest and resistance against colonial structures. Yet the main manifestations of colonial power resulted from the constant rivalries between the imperial nations, especially Britain, Spain and France, which set up the Caribbean and the New World as a theatre of war to make or break their own status. This is why nearly all places in the area have been under changing rule, often captured as trophies or given as pawns in European power games. St Lucia, for example, changed hands fourteen times and so became known, in colonial and patriarchal parlance, as 'the Helen of the West Indies'.

The Atlantic slave trade: triangular passages

The slave trade which Britain joined on a large scale in the 1620s, was organized as a sequence of three voyages, in a triangle between Europe, Africa and the New World. Ships would set off from British ports like Liverpool, London or Bristol and sail to West Africa with certain goods (like the notorious glass beads) which they traded in for slaves; the human cargo would then be shipped across the Atlantic, often incurring heavy losses through mistreatment, misery and illness, to be sold at Caribbean slave markets in exchange for sugar and other plantation products, which were finally shipped back to Britain. The middle section of this triangle, the so-called **Middle Passage** across the Atlantic, was the central voyage, traumatic for the ten million Africans who were thus deracinated and brutally displaced from their home. In the imagination of the diaspora, cultural memories of the Middle Passage have therefore been turned into key tropes for the recovery of African identities.

In the 1790s, a slave rebellion in Saint-Domingue, stimulated by the French Revolution and under the charismatic leadership of Touissant L'Ouverture, managed to defy the Napoleonic army and in 1804 established the first independent Caribbean state, the republic of Haiti (its former Arawak name). Not unlike revolutionary France, Haiti went through a long period of terror and bloody dictatorships, but still set an example for postcolonial developments. Major changes in the region came with the official emancipation of slaves in the 1830s. In order to save their labour force for the plantations, the British began to recruit workers from India on so-called **indenture** contracts: East Indians (in colonial language referred to as "coolies") were promised free passage to the West Indies and economic opportunities in exchange for ten years labour. In effect, the indenture system, which lasted until 1917 and dislocated roughly half a million people, was just a new version of slavery and few coolies ever made their voyage home. As a result, countries like Guyana and Trinidad now have a large Indo-Caribbean population, with distinct linguistic, religious and cultural characteristics; to the present day, political confrontations and affiliations in these countries tend to correspond to ethnic background.

Revolution and emancipation: indentured labourers from India

By contrast, countries like Jamaica where few indentured labourers arrived, have developed more pronounced forms of black nationalism, reasserting African identities. The Jamaican Marcus Garvey (1887–1940), a pan-African activist, writer and founder of the Universal Negro Improvement Association in the 1920s, who also lived in the US and Britain, was central in formulating the ideas of black separatism and African repatriation at the heart of **Rastafarian** religion. Radically reinterpreting the Bible so as to identify the black diaspora with the plight of Israel in Babylonian captivity (see 1.2.5), Rastafarians cultivate a life-style, language and philosophy of their own (manifest through visible markers such as dread locks or their use of the African colours), strongly aimed at a return to the Promised Land. When Hailee Selassie was crowned Emperor of Ethiopia in 1930, then the only African country not under colonial rule, he was seen as the black messiah, known as Jah Rastafari, fulfilling the prophecy of Isaiah (9: 6). Especially in Jamaica, Rasta-

Jamaican culture and Rastafarian religion

SOME DATES IN CARIBBEAN HISTORY

1492	October 12, Columbus arrives in Guanahani/San Salvador
1494	Treaty of Tordesillas: Pope Alexander VI divides Spanish and Portuguese spheres of interest in the New World
1504/07	Amerigo Vespucci (an Italian traveller and trader) and Martin Waldseemüller (cartographer) name the New World "America"
1520s–30s	Spanish conquest of Aztec and Inca empires
1564	John Hawkins begins English slaving voyages
1584	Walter Ralegh's expedition to Guiana
1623	Royal charter to Thomas Warner for plantation of St Christopher
1620s	British join large-scale trafficking of slaves from Africa
1739	British peace agreement with rebellious maroons in Jamaica
1760s	slave rebellions in Jamaica and several other islands
1756–63	Seven Years War (Britain vs France over New World hegemony)
1790–1804	revolution in Saint-Domingue: black Republic of Haiti founded
1802	peace treaty between Spain and Britain over Caribbean colonies
1834	official emancipation of slaves in British colonies
1838–1917	indentured labourers brought from India to work on Caribbean plantations, mainly in Trinidad and Guiana
1865	Morant Bay rebellion in Jamaica ("Gordon riots") suppressed
1887	conservative writer J.A. Froude tours the West Indies and urges liberal government in London for stronger commitments in the region
1902	volcanic eruption of Mount Pelée kills 30,000 in Martinique
1919	riots in Jamaica, British Honduras and Trinidad
1946	Martinique and Guadeloupe become French départements
1948	*SS Empire Windrush* takes Caribbean immigrants to England
1953	in British Guiana, Cheddi Jagan's socialist party wins election; Britain sends troops and suspends constitution; Jagan jailed
1958–62	West Indian Federation
1959	Cuban revolution: socialist leader Fidel Castro takes power
1961	'Cuba crisis': United States and Soviet Union reach the brink of nuclear confrontation in Cold War climax
1962	Jamaica, Trinidad and Tobago gain independence
1966	Barbados and Guyana gain independence
1966	Haile Selassie, Emperor of Ethiopia, visits Jamaica
1972	PNP with Michael Manley wins Jamaican parliamentary elections
1973–81	oil boom brings rapid prosperity to Trinidad
1978	reggae artist Bob Marley holds "One Love"-concert in Jamaica
1979	St Lucia, St Vincent and the Grenadines independent
1986	Haitian dictator Duvalier ("Papa Doc") overthrown after 30 years
2007	St Kitts, as the last Caribbean country, ends sugar production

farian communities have introduced a radical and utopian element in society; yet their influence is strong throughout the Caribbean and the diaspora, especially prominent also in popular culture and music, i.e. Reggae. Hailee Selassie's visit to Jamaica in 1966 marked a high point of the anti-colonial struggle. For all its emphasis on blackness, Rastafarianism is in fact a highly syncretic movement and offers a powerful example of postcolonial appropriations, wresting the central Christian text, the Bible, from white and missionary control by infusing it with different meanings.

Independence was won in the larger Caribbean countries in the 1960s, in the 1970s for most others. Prominent among the political pioneers who became figureheads in the years of decolonization was the Oxford-educated Trinidadian Dr Eric Williams (1911–1981), long Prime Minister of Trinidad and Tobago, historian and author of an important Marxist study, *Capitalism and Slavery* (1944).

Decolonization since the 1960s

2   Literary Paradigms

Anglophone writing from the Caribbean used to be strongly affected by the "daffodil gap", as we might call it, i.e. the cultural predicament discussed in the introduction (see 1.1) of seeing one's own world in terms derived from elsewhere. The lush tropical flora and fauna on the islands, for instance, has mostly been known by names imported by colonial settlers, transferred from very differnt natural environments, hence often felt to be at odds with the Caribbean realities they are meant to describe. This was not just a problem for white settler poets like James Grainger, whose epic *The Sugar-Cane* (1764) set out to render plantation life in neo-classic literary form. The problem has equally been felt by postcolonial and black writers in their efforts to engage with their own locality in English or English-based creole. For, with the historical erasure of indigenous peoples and their tongues, what names and terms should any Caribbean writer employ, other than adopt imported ones? This issue of making landscape and language cohere is also highlighted by V.S. Naipaul in his 1964 essay "Jasmine" where he describes how this flower's name had long been just an empty signifier for him: "The English language was mine; the tradition was not" (1976: 27).

How to name Caribbean plants: the daffodil gap

Local literary traditions began to be defined in the 1930s. The novel *Minty Alley* (1936) by the Trinidadian writer and political

153

Fiction: social realism and carnival narratives

historian C.L.R. James offers a closely observed portrait of the unheroic goings-on in an urban backyard, rendered in naturalistic prose including a great deal of dialogue. This set the style for things to come. Naipaul's first book, *Miguel Street* (1959) is just such a backyard novel, and even his great international success, *A House for Mr Biswas* (1961) owes much to this model. The narrative of an insignificant and failed life in late-colonial Trinidad, full of missed opportunities and vain ambitions, *Mr Biswas* unfolds an epic panorama of an extended Indian family (based in fact on Naipaul's father's fate), told with very pointed humour and Dickensian love of detail. Here, as in all Naipaul's fiction, the only solution for the stagnation and stupor of peripheral island life, is the escape to England. By contrast, other novelists have emphasized the strength of local visions and the need to reconnect personal lives with hidden ancestries. Earl Lovelace, one of the few major writers who has stayed in Trinidad, explores the local Carnival tradition in *The Dragon Can't Dance* (1979), powerfully evoking creative forces of the imagination and, at the same time, the tensions they must overcome (see also 4.2). The common claim for social unity at carnival time, "All o' we is one", at any rate, is here subjected to critical scrutiny. Jamaican novelist Erna Brodber, a professional sociologist, has used her fiction like *Jane and Louisa Will Soon Come Home* (1980) to map the space of local women's experience, their psychic struggles in a quest for belonging and for overcoming alienating structures.

Anti-realist writing and transculturation

Brodber's narratives, drawing on oral story-telling traditions, often go beyond the frame of realism. In this way, they are connected to the work of Wilson Harris from Guyana, the most prominent and productive Caribbean writer in a programmatically non-naturalist tradition. Beginning with *Palace of the Peacock* (1960), the story of a river journey in search of El Dorado, his visionary prose delves deeply into the South American hinterland of myth and ritual, drawing on Amerindian symbolism just as on the European canon, forever offering new allegories for contemporary cross-cultural society. For this reason, Harris's complex fiction can be seen to renew and manifest the central insight first articulated by the Cuban writer Fernando Ortiz in 1940, when he argued to conceive of Caribbean culture, even plantation products like sugar and tobacco, as products of transculturation, always transforming given realities. An eminent father figure for the younger generation, Harris has many followers among contemporary writers; his effects may also be traced in the postmodern experiments of Robert Antoni's dazzling text *Divina Trace* (1991).

In Caribbean poetry, it has long been a major strategy to draw on modes of expression and oral performance derived from African tradition, i.e. to make creative uses of non-European cultural heritage. Poetry, as a genre, is less reliant on print publication than the novel and so allies itself more easily with local and performative approaches, just as with music and dancing. After some notable forerunners in the 1930s, like the Jamaican Una Marson, a pioneer for these approaches was Louise Bennett, equally gifted as writer and comedian, who in the 1950s created the character "Miss Lou", a witty, gossipy and down-to-earth Jamaican woman, as her speaking persona. In this voice she managed to depict and satirize contemporary developments, as in the poem "Colonization in Reverse" about Jamaican immigrants in Britain, a parodistic turning around of convention: "An week by week dem shippin off/Dem countryman like fire/Fi immigrate and populate/De seat a de Empire" (1982: 106). A pioneer also in putting creole, an oral language without established orthography, onto the page, Bennett opened many new creative pathways for Caribbean writing to explore.

Poetry: women pioneers and writing in patois

These did not just lead into Jamaican DJ culture, reggae lyrics and dub poetry as central modes of black expression (see Habekost 1993), but also since the late 1960s to the poetry of Kamau Brathwaite from Barbados, historian, writer and one of the strongest researchers for contemporary ways to reconnect Caribbean culture with African origins. His epic cycle *The Arrivants* (1973) is a new world trilogy about the double process of displacement and recovery, written in creolized verse forms and incantatory rhythms. It gives impressive evidence of the poetic search to create models for Caribbean poetry beyond European conventions, an agenda which Brathwaite put into the memorable phrase: "The hurricane does not roar in pentametre." (1984: 10) In the 1970s, his work was therefore regarded as spearheading "the oral tradition" in Caribbean poetry and polemically opposed to "the literary tradition", which engages more decisively with the canonical heritage from Europe and its given forms. As the main representative of the literary approach, the cultural debate cast Derek Walcott from St Lucia, whose work indeed lends itself to such a role. In his verse autobiography *Another Life* (1973), for instance, Walcott is scathingly critical of négritude, black consciousness and all back-

Debates about African presences in 1970s poetry: Brathwaite and Walcott

to-Africa movements, accusing their proponents of taking a "free ride on the middle passage" (1992: 269). Instead, his poetic work has always sought expression for the specific Caribbean condition of constant transfer and translation, a condition of metaphor and multiplicity, which Walcott, in a variation of the postcolonial hybridity concept (see 1.2.6), likes to call mongrelization.

Walcott's drama and the Trinidad Theatre Workshop

To be sure, the blunt oppositions of the "Walcott versus Brathwaite"-debate have always been far too simplistic. In the 1960s and 1970s Walcott spent decisive decades in Trinidad, where he founded the Trinidad Theatre Workshop in 1959 and made it a laboratory for developing new, integrative Caribbean artistic styles, fusing language, design, dance and music like in alchemical experiments. His *Dream on Monkey Mountain* (1967), an allegorical dream play about masks of identity, or *The Joker of Seville* (1974), his creolized rewriting of an early modern Spanish Don Juan comedy, are among the best-known products of this quest. The comic double-act *Pantomime* (1978) draws on the Trinidadian Carnival tradition to rehearse postcolonial repeats and reversals of the master-slave dialectics in Defoe's colonial classic *Robinson Crusoe*. Similar role changes, masquerades and carnival subversions also take place in Mustapha Matura's drama, like the bitter comedy *Play Mas* (1974) or his ingenious Trinidadian adaptations of early twentieth-century European classics, *Playboy of the West Indies* (1984) and *Trinidad Sisters* (1988).

Genre, language and gender in more recent writing

Most recent Caribbean writing, in whatever genre, has been more or less closely associated with diasporic conditions and has mainly come from writers based in metropolitan centres like New York, Toronto or London. A general trend in recent fiction, however, has been to further stress the use of creole languages as a literary medium in its own right, employing it no longer just for character speech (as, for example, in Naipaul's early novels) but also for authorial narration. Another common trend is the increasing prominence of gender issues, established in the 1980s with novelists like Joan Riley and, since then, ever more urgently explored, often transcending ethnic identities. US-based novelists Jamaica Kincaid and Michelle Cliff, for instance, though from very different backgrounds, have both successfully recreated scenarios of Caribbean adolescence memories. *Aelred's Sin* (1998), a novel by the London-based white Trinidadian writer Lawrence Scott, is notable for its foregrounding of gay identity.

SOME CARIBBEAN WRITERS

Jean Rhys (1894–1979), Dominica; novels: *Voyage in the Dark* (1934), *Good Morning, Midnight* (1939), *Wide Sargasso Sea* (1966)

C.L.R. James (1901–1989), Trinidad; novel: *Minty Alley* (1936); historical studies: *The Black Jacobins* (1938), *Beyond a Boundary* (1963)

Louise Bennett (1919–2006), Jamaica; poetry: *Verses in Jamaican Dialect* (1942), *Jamaica Labrish* (1966), *Selected Poems* (1982)

Wilson Harris (*1921), Guyana; novels: *Palace of the Peacock* (1960), *The Infinite Rehearsal* (1987), essays: *The Womb of Space* (1983)

Samuel Selvon (1923–1994), Trinidad; *The Lonely Londoners* (1956), *Moses Ascending* (1975), *Moses Migrating* (1987)

George Lamming (*1927), Barbados; novels: *In the Castle of My Skin* (1953), *Water With Berries* (1971); essays: *Pleasures of Exile* (1960)

Derek Walcott (*1930), St Lucia; drama: *Dream on Monkey Mountain* (1967), *Pantomime* (1974), *A Branch of the Blue Nile* (1986); poetry: *Collected Poems* (1989), *Omeros* (1990); Nobel prize 1992

Edward Kamau Brathwaite (*1930), Barbados; poetry: *The Arrivants: A New World Trilogy* (1973), *X/Self* (1987)

V.S. Naipaul (*1932), Trinidad; novels: *A House for Mr Biswas* (1961), *The Mimic Men* (1967), *The Enigma of Arrival* (1987); travelogues: *The Middle Passage* (1962), *A Way in the World* (1994); Nobel Prize 2001

Earl Lovelace (*1935), Trinidad; fiction: *The Dragon Can't Dance* (1979), *A Brief Conversion and Other Stories* (1988), *Salt* (1996)

Mustapha Matura (*1939), Trinidad; plays: *Play Mas* (1974), *Meetings* (1980), *Playboy of the West Indies* (1984), *Trinidad Sisters* (1988)

Erna Brodber (*1940), novels: *Jane and Louisa Will Soon Come Home* (1980), *Myal* (1988), *Louisiana* (1994)

Lawrence Scott (*1943), Trinidad; novels: *Witchbroom* (1992), *Aelred's Sin* (1998)

Michelle Cliff (*1946), Jamaica; novels: *Abeng* (1984), *No Telephone to Heaven* (1987), *Free Enterprise* (1996)

Jamaica Kincaid (*1949), Antigua; fiction: *Annie John* (1985), *Lucy* (1991), *The Autobiography of My Mother* (1996), *My Brother* (1997)

David Dabydeen (*1955), Guyana; novels: *The Intended* (1991), *A Harlot's Progress* (1999); poetry: *Slave Song* (1984), *Turner* (1994)

Caryl Phillips (*1958), St Kitts; novels: *The Final Passage* (1985), *Higher Ground* (1989), *Cambridge* (1991), *The Nature of Blood* (1997)

Joan Riley (*1958), Jamaica; *The Unbelonging* (1985), *Waiting in the Twilight* (1987), *Romance* (1988), *A Kindness to the Children* (1992)

Robert Antoni (*1958), Trinidad; novels: *Divina Trace* (1991), *Carnival* (2005)

Patricia Powell (*1966), Jamaica; novels: *Me Dying Trial* (1993), *A Small Gathering of Bones* (1994)

**Walcott's
Omeros: a
postcolonial
New World epic**

With Walcott's later work, Caribbean literature has also produced memorable feats of epic, a generic form classically associated with the politics of empire and the need to glorify imperial warrior heroes (see Quint 1993). Yet in *Omeros* (1990), a book-length poem in terza rima, Walcott has subjected the ordinary lives of fishermen, taxi drivers and waitresses in St Lucia to such epic treatment, trying out possibilities to see their dignified but unheroic fate in terms and names derived from Homer's *Iliad* and *Odyssey*. Freely ranging between the New World and the Old, widening its cultural scope also to include North America, West Africa and Southern Europe, this text launches readers on an open-ended passage towards a fuller understanding of West Indian and American existence constituted always by historic transfers (see Döring 2002). What Naipaul famously derided as Caribbean mimicry, for instance in his novel *The Mimic Men* (1969), i.e. the need to imitate and take on outside standards, is thus redefined by Walcott as a powerful creative principle following the primal human impulses in art as mimesis (see Terada 1992). But finally, *Omeros* suggests, the best way to study Caribbean history and culture is to seek it in the pages of the sea, "an epic where every line was erased/yet freshly written in sheets of exploding surf" (Walcott 1990: 296).

6   Focus on Black British Literature

**What kind of
category is
"Black British"?**

After the period of decolonization and the demise of Britain's global power, it used to be said that England was the last remaining colony of the British Empire. The point about this bitter irony was to shift attention from historical developments outside Europe towards the political situation at home where practices of dominance continued and where, after decades of black immigration, some of the social realities especially in urban areas may indeed have recalled colonial boundaries. At the same time, migration experience has been worked through in a significant body of writing which offers a fast growing and now highly popular literary area for Postcolonial Studies to focus on. The final section of this chapter, then, takes a focus rather differently constructed than the previous five sections. "Black British literature" is a category not just defined by geographical basis, but also with the designation "black". This introduces yet another key term into our field, which needs consideration and which also serves to put the other terms we use into perspective. For again, terminology is not simply a side-issue but leads us into the heart of cultural debates. As noted at the outset (see 1.2), how to name a certain field and how to focus on its literature, always involves acts of power.

The term "Black British" has emerged from the political struggles and controversies about the social make-up of contemporary Britain. It came up in the later 1960s, in conjunction with black power movements, and gained wider currency in the '70s as an umbrella term for the entire spectrum of non-white British citizens and their communities, all living under difficult conditions in white-dominated society, as "second class citizens" – to quote the title of a novel by Buchi Emecheta (1976). It is crucial to realize the broad nature of this category. Unlike "Black American", which is usually reserved to speak about African-American people, "Black British" was introduced to speak about people with African, Caribbean and Asian backgrounds, especially South Asian (i.e. Indian, Pakistani and Sri Lankan), but sometimes also including East Asian, e.g. Chinese. As such, the term is clearly *not* a marker of ethnic identity *nor* of cultural belonging. It refers to people of many different ethnicities and diverse cultures, and subsumes them all under the same label "black" only with regard to their shared political position: socially marginalized and often institutionally oppressed. These are certainly no inherent, unchanging traits in any of the people so designated, but consequences of their place, at a particular time, outside the social mainstream. "Black British", then, serves as a marker for this contingent placing.

The term derives from politics of positioning people

This definition of the term derives from Stuart Hall (see 2.3.5), the most prominent and productive thinker on this issue in British Cultural Studies. In his much anthologized 1988 article "New Ethnicities" about black film and British cinema, Hall explains that the term "black" was coined "as a way of referencing the common experience of racism and marginalization in Britain and came to provide the organizing category of a new politics of resistance, among groups and communities with, in fact, very different histories, traditions, and ethnic identities" (1988: 27). That is to say, the term suggests a political alliance and should not make us forget that the various partners who have formed it also hold other and very distinct identities, not shared by all. In Hall's words, "'The Black Experience' as a singular and unifying framework based on the building up of identity across ethnic and cultural difference between the different communities" became a preferred way of

Hall's argument for a black alliance

speaking, even though ethnic or racial identities "did not, of course, disappear" (*ibid.*). To speak of "Black British Literature", therefore, means to focus on the work of writers who can usefully be placed in such a unifying framework, even though other frames of reference – such as Caribbean or African or Indian writing – continue to apply to them as well.

Critical responses to the term and its current uses

In this sense, "Black British" became very current in the 1980s and '90s, often employed in the publishing industry, in art, music, film and popular culture as a fashionable label. Not surprisingly, however, it has also been questioned for its popularity and criticized for its broad, inclusive usage. The Jamaican-born journalist and novelist Ferdinand Dennis, for instance, has attacked what he calls the "promiscuous use" of the term and argued in 1998 to speak of "black" only in relation to the experience of diasporic Africans whose ancestors once underwent the Middle Passage, with the trauma of cultural loss (quoted in Reichl 2002: 39). Other critics have stressed the need to acknowledge cultural specificities and avoid too general terms because they easily homogenize the field. Indeed, there are signs that, with changing politics and new social developments in Britain, the usefulness of "Black British" as a *political* term is waning. In 2000, the Parekh Report on the future of multi-ethnic Britain demanded greater emphasis on cultural diversity. Some of the more recent academic studies, too, have shifted emphasis and, like Innes (2002), speak of "Black and Asian writing in Britain", so as to mark at least one fundamental difference. Yet others, like Reichl (2002: 35), have defended the use of "Black British" as a *critical* term, strategically constructed and especially useful for literary analysis because the strategies of Black British writing, no matter what their ethnic background is, show remarkable similarities.

The United Kingdom and the realities of migration

The consequence of migration and histories of dislocation, Black British literature provides a fundamental challenge to any general understanding of what we take as "British" (see also 4.3). Black British writing is produced by immigrants or their descendants who have become part of the country's social fabric; for this reason, their contribution raises crucial questions about cultural identities and the relationship between the "national" and the various ingredients that contribute to its making. These questions are especially acute because, historically, nationhood in Britain used to operate as a divisive rather than a unifying factor. As indicated by the term

"United Kingdom", we are looking at a constellation of very different parts, i.e. England, Scotland, Wales and Northern Ireland, each with their distinct claims of nationality in language, politics and culture, which have come to be united under English hegemony and which, as every football viewer knows, continue to work separately for instance in sports. The common flag is called the "Union Jack", widely used since the union of parliaments in 1707, a combination of the Scottish St Andrew's cross (or saltire) and the English St George's cross to which, after the enforced union with Ireland in 1801, the Irish St Patrick's cross has been added for good measure. The well-known slogan "there ain't no black in the Union Jack" (the title also of a 1987 study by Paul Gilroy) therefore highlights the fact that there is more to the UK than the English mainstream and the Celtic fringe.

As a matter of fact, since the 1990s the diversity within Britain has been acknowledged in the politics of devolution, restoring political autonomy to the various regions, especially Scotland. This went along with giving more acknowledgement to the multicultural realities throughout the country. Significantly, such moves of re-inventing Britain have been accompanied or, indeed, spurred by debates on how the national, ethnic or cultural claims of Black citizens, too, should be acknowledged. In *The Black Atlantic*, an important study of this issue setting out to question the exclusive understanding of Europe as a white continent, Paul Gilroy has argued that notions of nationhood long used to be defined by what he calls "cultural insiderism" and "an absolute sense of ethnic difference", i.e. by the idea of "an ethnically homogeneous object" (1993: 3). Black experience and black identities in Europe are, by contrast, generally marked by what he describes as "doubleness" and "cultural intermixture" because they draw on more than one defining category: "The themes of nationality, exile and cultural affiliation accentuate the inescapable fragmentation and differentiation of the black subject. This fragmentation has recently been compounded further by the questions of gender, sexuality, and male domination which have been made unavoidable by the struggles of black women and the voices of black gay men and lesbians." (1993: 35) That is to say, any focus on Black British literature is, in fact, a multiple focus and requires constant adjustments and shifting points of view.

The Black Atlantic as a challenge to exclusive views of nationhood

1 Historical Survey

The *Windrush* as a common point of reference for black immigration

The history of black people in Britain used to be dated with the arrival of the *SS Empire Windrush* in June 1948 as a point of beginning, the steamship with 492 Caribbean immigrants on board. They had been actively recruited to join English workers, especially on London Transport to help rebuild the war-torn economy. With the structures of the British Empire still largely intact, their arrival was regarded as a coming to the mother country. So they were welcomed with official enthusiasm – even though tacit expectations, on the part of the British public, may have been that they had come as "guest workers" who would eventually return home. When in 1998 the fiftieth anniversary of this event was celebrated, however, it had long become apparent that the *Windrush* set in motion irreversible transformations of British society: the immigrants had come to stay and make their home away from home, thus manifesting cultural diversity in Britain on a much larger scale than hitherto experienced. Yet with present-day awareness of multicultural life-styles and concerns, it has also become very clear that the black presence in Britain goes back considerably longer and includes a much wider spectrum than the *Windrush* generation.

Black presences in England throughout history

A recent history of black and Asian writing in Britain (Innes 2002) sets the date around the middle of the eighteenth century, when British involvement in the slave trade became so strong that its effects were keenly felt on the domestic scene, with growing numbers of Africans and Indians held as servants in English households. But it is possible to go back even further. Peter Fryer opens his pioneering history of black people in Britain with the simple statement that "there were Africans in Britain before the English came there" (1984: 1). These Africans came as soldiers in the Roman armies that occupied Britannia, yet few of them would have seen the remote barbarian province as a place to stay. This must have changed in sixteenth-century Tudor England, when the early modern period of exploration and expansion started. Around 1600 the number of black servants must have been sufficiently large, at least in London, for the authorities to get concerned and order "blackamoors" to be deported. At the same time, dramatic texts like Shakespeare's *Titus Andronicus* (ca. 1592) and *Othello* (ca. 1604) show the Renaissance fascination with "moors" as central protagonists – a rather loosely defined category, however, based more on ethical than ethnic grounds and often including other types of cultural otherness such as Turks or Jews.

By the mid-eighteenth century, the black presence in Britain had not just become more numerous and noticeable – estimations vary between 10,000 and 20,000 people – but so specific that it is possible to see a black community taking shape (see Fryer 1984: 67). Their number was further boosted in 1784 when, after the American War of Independence, many former slaves, who had fought for the British in the hope of earning freedom, came to England from North America. Even if this hope was fulfilled, most of them soon found themselves among the urban poor in the streets. However, most people of colour at the time were employed in domestic service. In the upper classes, it became quite fashionable to keep African or Indian page boys as a kind of adornment and display of wealth. This can well be seen in the art of the period, especially in society paintings by William Hogarth, where black servants are depicted in the margins, as signifiers of status and exotic ostentation, just like pets (see Dabydeen 1985). And yet, the black contribution to English economy and culture was absolutely central. The wealth that went into the making of country estates and fashionable city life was largely made in the New World plantations, and the capital that fuelled Britain's lead into the industrial age actually derived from slave labour. Cultural institutions, too, were built on this basis. The Tate Gallery in London, opened in 1897, and the Booker Prize for fiction, annually awarded since 1969, are foundations by private benefactors or families who made their money in the sugar business.

Eighteenth-century culture and domestic uses of plantation money

The impact of sugar, hence black labour, on English society also works in a material sense. It has been argued that the sugar imported from the West Indies and used to sweeten English cups of tea "prefigured the transformation of an entire society, a total remaking of its economic and social basis" (Mintz 1985: 214). This is because the sweet hot drink was a quick and efficient way to give workers in English factories the high amount of calories that was needed to refresh their work force, without interrupting the production process for a full meal. Against this background we can appreciate the point of Stuart Hall's statement, cited earlier (see 2.3.5), when he declared "I am the sugar at the bottom of the English cup of tea": the history of black British culture turns out to be about the presence of transatlantic interrelations and worldwide connections at the heart of Englishness.

The impact of sugar on English society

Imperial trade and post-imperial anxieties: immigration rhetoric and laws

As a matter of fact, the global scope of Empire, with trade routes and commodity exchange reaching out to many remote places, has always meant that the mother country is exposed to outside influence from all these places, often seen as dangerous, dark and uncontrollable – and eventually always manifest in actual people. The exotic is just the reverse side of the threatening. So, many of the public debates, since the 1950s, on immigration and its threats to what is seen as traditional English life have roots in such imperial anxieties. These debates became prominent in the post-war period, as local communities, for instance in the West London district Notting Hill where many migrant workers settled, began to feel uncomfortable with their new neighbours. Fuelled also by racist right-wing organizations, the situation first escalated there in 1958 around the Caribbean carnival celebration, which ended in violent rioting. Further unrest and controversy led to repeated law enforcements, imposing ever more restrictions on people to gain entry and citizenship in Britain. Numbers peaked in 1961/62, just before new legislation came into effect, when 98,000 people migrated to Britain from the West Indies. Other areas of major immigration were West Africa and the Indian subcontinent. Yet despite high public attention and political rhetoric concerned with immigration, it should be pointed out that during the entire period, and certainly since 1983, more people actually decided to leave Britain and settle abroad than to go there (see Dabydeen et al 2007: 221).

Cultural diversity and its linguistic consequences

The 1991 census gave the ethnic minority population as three million, among them less than one million with African or Afro-Caribbean background; ten years later this group had increased to 1.14 million, clearly due to more black people having been born in the country than actually migrating there. This trend marks the most important development in the ethnic transformation of British society, where second and third generations of immigrant families bring up their children as part of both local communities and of the greater cultural diversity that now forms Britain. This diversity is manifest in many social domains, but is certainly most visible in the two domains of language and of food. Varieties of British Black English have developed since Caribbean creole languages (see 3.5), especially Jamaican creole, came to Britain with the *Windrush* generation; in urban settings they underwent further changes, combined with youth language and other non-standard idioms to form a mode of expression that has been called "London Jamaican" (Sebba 1993), a new urban vernacular whose communi-

1596	Queen Elizabeth I and her Privy Council urge slave holders in England to deport "blackamoores" from the country
1781	Captain Collingwood of slave ship *Zong* throws 132 diseased slaves overboard to let them drown in storm, so as to claim insurance
1787	Society for Abolition of Slave Trade founded
1788	Olaudah Equiano sends anti-slavery petition to King George III
1807	slave trade officially abolished in the British Empire
1834	slave emancipation in the British Empire
1919	race riots in London, Liverpool, Cardiff
1931	League of Coloured People formed by Ronald Moody
1948	on June 20, the arrival of *SS Empire Windrush* in Tilbury, with 492 Jamaicans, Trinidadians, Barbadians and Guyanese on board, marks beginning of large-scale Caribbean migration to the "Mother Country"
1948	Nationality Act creates composite UK and colonial citizenship
1956	Trinidadian carnival first celebrated in the streets of Notting Hill
1956	in Egypt, Nasser nationalizes Suez Canal Company, which precipitates the Suez Crisis: Britain realizes loss of imperial status
1958	Notting Hill riots
1962	Commonwealth Immigrants Act imposes entry restrictions
1965	Malcolm X visits England: Black Power movement takes hold
1968	Tory politician Enoch Powell gives "Rivers of Blood"-speech, warning of England's social transformation through immigration
1971	Immigration Act virtually ends all primary immigration
1974	David Pitt becomes first black chairman of Greater London Council
1978	Tory leader (and soon PM) Margret Thatcher speaks of current English fear of "being swamped" by migrants
1981	British Nationality Act introduces ethnic monitoring
1981	major riots in Brixton (London), Toxteth (Liverpool) and many other urban areas; officially investigated in the Scarman Report
1988–89	protests in Muslim communities against Salman Rushdie's novel *The Satanic Verses* (1988) become part of international crisis
1993	Stephen Lawrence, a black 18-year-old student, dies after a racist attack by five white youths at London bus stop; severe doubts about legal handling of the murder case leads to major public debate and bitter controversy about institutionalized racism
1998	*"Windrush*—Sea Change" festival celebrates immigration with four-part BBC documentary and exhibition in the Museum of London
2000	Parekh Report demands greater emphasis on ethnic diversity
2005	July 7, a terrorist group of young British Muslims cause 52 deaths in bomb series on London transport
2007	National Museum of Transatlantic Slavery opens in Liverpool

cative function is mainly symbolic as a marker of black identity, used also in popular culture and music.

"Land of Hope and Curry"? not quite and not yet for all...

In the domain of food and eating habits, the changes have been just as visible and prominent. The days are gone when fish and chips was the favourite national dish. In 2001, foreign secretary Robin Cook gave a speech in which he stressed what wonderful enrichment the variety and mixture of ethnic communities had brought to Britain, and illustrated this point with a culinary example: "Chicken Tikka Massala is now a true British national dish, not only because it is a perfect illustration of the way Britain absorbs and adopts external influences. Chicken Tikka is an Indian dish. The Massala Sauce was added to satisfy the desire of British people to have their meat served in gravy." (*The Guardian*, April 19, 2001) Public response to Cook's speech varied, yet the general drift was well captured in the *Mirror* headline which topicalized the old imperial hymn "Land of Hope and Glory" as "Land of Hope and Curry". No doubt, political rhetoric and news headlines are no sufficient indicators for cultural realities and social attitudes. Other developments of the 1990s and beyond, such as the public debates about the Stephen Lawrence murder case or, more recently, about Polish migrant workers rather indicate that narrow notions of Englishness still survive (see also 4.3). But it is now widely acknowledged that Britain has absorbed, to use Cook's words, "external influences" to such a degree that they have become internal.

2 Literary Paradigms

Eighteenth and nineteenth-century writing: no black tradition

The earliest black writers in Britain published in the later eighteenth century, in the context of abolition campaigns and mainly in some form of life writing. Offering first-hand illustrations of the plight of slavery, their life stories were avidly received and widely read – not just for their political but also their sensational use, which then fed into the cultural imagination of the gothic and its lust for horror. The seminal importance of Equiano's autobiography, the pioneer of black British literature, has already been discussed (see 2.1.2 and 2.4.1). Preceding his *Interesting Narrative* (1789) was the publication of *The Letters of Ignatius Sancho* (1782), the wide-ranging correspondence of a London grocery shop-owner and literary celebrity who had come to the country as a slave and eventually found an aristocratic patron introducing him into the world of high culture. Sancho established friendships, among others, with the Shakespearean actor David Garrick and the novelist Laurence Sterne, whom he convinced to include into the final volume of his *Tristram Shandy* (1767) an argument about the humanity of black people. Other early writers include S.D. Mahomet from India (see 3.3.2) and Mary Seacole from Jamaica, one of the most remarkably emancipated woman of the nineteenth century who worked as a nurse in the Crimean War, alongside Florence Nightingale, and published her autobiography in 1857. None of these authors, however, can be seen as part of a black tradition because "little is passed on from one writer to the next"; so their pioneering literary work is better understood "as a series of recurrent preoccupations and tropes" (Innes 2002: 2).

This changed fundamentally in the mid-twentieth century with the *Windrush* generation. Earlier twentieth-century writers were the Trinidadian C.L.R. James, who came to England in 1932 to work in journalism and pan-African politics, and the Jamaican Una Marson (1905–1965), already a published poet and playwright when she arrived the same year to join the struggle for women's rights and decolonization; during the war years she worked for the influential Caribbean programme of the BBC. With the first great wave of immigration after 1948, this radio programme, then called *Caribbean Voices*, became the major platform and outlet for aspiring writers. V.S. Naipaul has recalled the moment in a BBC room in London where "on an old BBC typewriter, and on smooth 'non-rustle' BBC script paper" he wrote the first sentence of his "first publishable book" (1985: 15). Like him, Andrew Salkey, John Figueroa, Wilson Harris, Derek Walcott, Kamau Brathwaite, Sam Selvon, George Lamming and several others thus began their international literary careers.

Twentieth-century founding figures and their support from the BBC

To look at Black British literature in the framework of Postcolonial Studies means to read it against the background of canonical English writing and explore how it engages critically with the central images and narratives established there. In the 1950s, at a time when English writers such as William Golding rewrote and reactivated colonial island myths, in *Lord of the Flies* (1954), or established writers like Joyce Cary (see 1.1) recreated history from an English point of view, the work of Black British writers was especially important for two of the postcolonial strategies identified above, namely life writing and place writing. Lamming's *In the Castle of My Skin* (1953), based on his own diasporic experience,

Post-war novels in their search for identities and black urban topographies

which set a model for many books of black life writing to come, has been discussed earlier (see 2.4.1). Equally formative was Sam Selvon's *The Lonely Londoners* (1956) about the sojourns of a Trinidadian called Moses at the centre of a hopeful group of male immigrants in post-war England. Recognizably set in the Notting Hill district "West One" between Marble Arch and Shepherd's Bush, Selvon's episodic and deeply humorous narrative transforms familiar views of London as it rewrites the cityscape into a black topography. The novel, just like its two more satirical sequels, is also pioneering in the subtle use of Caribbean creoles and Black British English, not just for character speech but also for authorial narration, making the text into a polyphonic archive of black urban experience (see Mühleisen 2007).

The Black British *Bildungsroman* as "novels of transformation"

In subsequent decades, life writing and urban place writing have continued as the two main strategies, used with great effect and flexibility in Black British novels. They are central also for novelists like Beryl Gilroy and Buchi Emecheta, whose work emerged in the 1970s and '80s to lead the way for many other women writers offering female versions and visions of immigrant identities, often suggesting critical contrasts to their earlier male counterparts. The two strategies converge in the *Bildungsroman*, a literary form with a great eighteenth- and nineteenth-century tradition (traditional examples include Dickens's *David Copperfield* and Charlotte Brontë's *Jane Eyre*), which has been prominently revived in contemporary black fiction. With the search for personal identity as a constant interplay of subjective needs and societal demands, poised also at the interface of public concerns and private aspirations, the *Bildungsroman* offers clear advantages for writers who combine a search for place with hopes for its cultural transformation. This is why the form has newly become prominent and powerful in black "novels of transformation" (Stein 2004). The seminal text, and a watershed event in the recent history of Black British literature, is *The Buddha of Suburbia* (1990) by Hanif Kureishi, a threshold narrative of adolescence set in 1970s London (see Reichl 2007). With the famous opening sentence "My name is Karim Amir, and I am an Englishman born and bred, almost", the narrator introduces himself as "a new breed" and the product of "two old histories" (1990: 3). In the unfolding story, he puts this double position to good use, among others, in revealing the ethnic status of the English, describing their quaint ways and especially exposing the follies of suburban life, with the current craze for 'Eastern' wisdom. Thus wittily constructing the point of view of a second-generation Londoner, Kureishi's novel both reverses and redraws exotic stereotypes.

The Buddha was followed by *The Black Album* (1995), exploring repercussions of the Rushdie affair, and by stories like *My Son the Fanatic* (1997) on Islamic radicalization; together also with Kureishi's films, all these works were highly controversial in the communities whose members they depicted. But in this way, they helped to launch a whole new wave of Black and Asian fiction setting out to tell yet another side of the British story. Most significant here are, again, women writers like Andrea Levy (see Richter 2007) or like Ravinder Randhawa and the members of her Asian Women Writers' Workshop, who all decided to assert their "right of way" (as a 1988 anthology is entitled) against the power of both white and patriarchal barriers held against them. The current popularity of ethnic fiction and black family sagas as best-sellers and publishing events in the new millenium, which began with Zadie Smith's *White Teeth* (2000) and climaxed with Monica Ali's *Brick Lane* (2003), would not have been possible without the struggles of this earlier generation.

Kureishi's controversial success makes Black British fiction popular

In poetry, the cultural connections between England and the Caribbean, especially Jamaica, have been particularly strong, with writers travelling frequently between these cultural places. Many poets first emerged in the context of the Caribbean Artists Movement of the '60s. The '70s saw the rise of dub poetry, as a highly politicized and urban literary form, often in creole and combined with reggae music, which British-based writers and performers like Benjamin Zephaniah and Linton Kwesi Johnson created with great verbal power and delivered forcefully as comments also on some topical events, such as the 1981 Brixton riots. Jean 'Binta' Breeze is one of the few women who has made a strong name in this male-dominated scene. By contrast, poets like David Dabydeen and Fred D'Aguiar, both from Guyana (and both also novelists and critics), have taken more self-consciously literary approaches. Dabydeen's *Slave Song* (1988) offers creole poems, Standard English translations and critical commentary, combined with images from the colonial archive, thus constructing a composite verbal-visual text; his long poem *Turner* (1994) takes this strategy even further by writing itself into the imaginative space of J.M.W. Turner's celebrated painting "Slave Ship" (1840), verbalizing the submerged

Poetry: dub, performance and more literary voice experiments

SOME BLACK BRITISH WRITERS

Ignatius Sancho (1729–1789), *The Letters of Ignatius Sancho* (1782)

Olaudah Equiano (1745–1797), *The Interesting Narrative* (1789)

Mary Seacole (c. 1805–1881), *Wonderful Adventures* (1857)

Samuel Selvon (1923–1994), see above: Caribbean writers

Beryl Gilroy (1924–2001), novel: *Frangipani House* (1986)

George Lamming (*1927), see above: Caribbean writers

Farrukh Dhondy (*1944), fiction: *Bombay Duck* (1990)

John Agard (*1949), poetry: *Mangoes and Bullets* (1985), *Lovelines for a Goat-Born Lady* (1990)

Grace Nichols (*1950), poetry: *i is a long memoried woman* (1983), *The Fat Black Woman's Poems* (1984), *Sunris* (1996)

Timothy Mo (*1950), novels: *The Monkey King* (1978), *Sour Sweet* (1982)

Ravinder Randhawa (*1952), novels: *A Wicked Old Woman* (1987), *Hari-Jan* (1992), *The Coral Strand* (2001)

Linton Kwesi Johnson (*1952), poetry: *Dread Beat and Blood* (1975), *Inglan is a Bitch* (1980), *Tings and Times* (1991)

Hanif Kureishi (*1954), films: *My Beautiful Laundrette* (1985), *Sammie and Rosie Get Laid* (1987); novel: *The Buddha of Suburbia* (1990)

David Dabydeen (*1955), see above: Caribbean writers

Jean 'Binta' Breeze (*1956), poetry: *Riddym Ravings and Other Poems* (1988), *Spring Cleaning* (1992)

Andrea Levy (*1956), novels: *Every Light in the House Burnin'* (1994), *Never Far from Nowhere* (1996), *Fruit of the Lemon* (1999), *Small Island* (2004)

Benjamin Zephaniah (*1958), album: *Dub Ranting* (1982); poetry: *City Psalms* (1993); novels: *Face* (1999), *Refugee Boy* (2001)

Caryl Phillips (*1958), see above: Caribbean writers

Joan Riley (*1958), see above: Caribbean writers

Bernadine Evaristo (*1959), novels in verse: *Lara* (1997), *The Emperor's Babe* (2001)

Winsom Pinnock (*1961), plays: *Leave Taking* (1988), *A Hero's Welcome* (1989), *Talking in Tongues* (1991), *Can You Keep a Secret* (1999)

Jackie Kay (*1961), poetry: *The Adoption Papers* (1991), *Other Lovers* (1993); play: *Chiaroscuro* (1986), novel: *Trumpet* (1998)

Meera Syal (*1963), novels: *Anita and Me* (1996), *Life Isn't All Ha Ha Hee Hee* (1999)

Monica Ali (*1967), novels: *Brick Lane* (2003), *Alentejo Blue* (2006)

Diran Adebayo (*1968), novels: *Some Kind of Black* (1996), *My Once Upon a Time* (2000)

Courttia Newland (*1973), novels: *The Scholar* (1997), *Society Within* (1999)

Zadie Smith (*1975), novels: *White Teeth* (2000), *On Beauty* (2005)

black presence that underwrites the image. Among women poets, Grace Nichols and Amryl Johnson have been noted for their subtle interweaving of myths, memory and body language with down-to-earth observations of everday life. In one of the texts from Nichols's *Lazy Thoughts of a Lazy Woman* (1989) a black woman in London reflects on the plights of migration and cultural displacements, only to conclude with a bold couplet: "Yes, divided to de ocean/Divided to de bone/Wherever I hang me knickers – that's my home" (1989: 10).

The agenda for this final chapter: the examples reconsidered

This final chapter wants to draw attention to some issues which the previous chapter has left out. As the title "Exemplifications" for Chapter 3 was meant to indicate, it aimed to give historical and literary substance to the strategies discussed in more abstract terms in Chapter 2. But examples only work up to a point. Their "exemplary" value lies precisely in looking at one particular case in view of possible generalizations, i.e. focussing on features that can also be found elsewhere. In this way, examples highlight certain things while hiding others that cannot be generalized. Therefore, examples should be reconsidered so as to see more clearly what assumptions they have made, what consequences they entail and what aspects they exclude – in short: to introduce differentiations. Two issues are especially important because they go to the heart of our understanding of the postcolonial, as defined in Chapter 1: gender and performance. The following sections would like to show, with reference to some relevant material for further reading, what difference these can make.

1   Sex and Gender: Transgressions

Why and how "sex" and "gender" are to be distinguished

Previous sections have repeatedly referred to women's writing in the postcolonial field. As a matter of fact, many women writers from this field, such as the Canadian Margaret Atwood (see Lemke 2007), have been well-known pioneers of feminist fiction, internationally celebrated for their incisive and important contributions to debates on gender. Yet to engage with their work, we should think more carefully about the ways in which gender issues enrich and complicate the critical agenda we need to address, especially what terms and concepts are appropriate here. The terms "sex" and "gender", to begin with, are not synonymous. As feminist theory since the 1970s and '80s has argued (see Hof 1995), gender is a *social* category that ascribes certain cultural norms and symbolic meanings to the *sexual* difference by which humans find themselves defined – defined especially through their anatomy. In patriarchal society, these norms and meanings privilege the masculine, thus constructing the feminine as 'weak', 'dark', 'emotional', 'deficient', 'inferior' and so setting up gender difference as a means to legitimize male power (for the male is, conversely, regarded as 'strong', 'enlightened', 'rational', 'normative', 'superior'). Nothing about this construction is inevitable, natural or unchanging; in matriarchal societies we would rather expect gender norms to be reversed. Yet the main point is to understand that anatomy need not be destiny. In this view, gender is constructed whereas sex is a given, gender is contingent whereas sex is existent, gender has to do with cultural acts and political action whereas sex has to do with materiality and nature. Since the 1990s, such clear-cut oppositions between sex and gender have been questioned and critically transgressed – or "queered", as the current idiom has it. Especially with the performative theory of gender as proposed by Judith Butler (1990, 1993), it has become possible to understand sex, too, as a socially constructed category or, rather, it has become impossible to draw the nature/culture-distinction that underwrites the sex/gender-distinction without, at the same time, also understanding sex in cultural terms.

In the field of Postcolonial Studies, these issues are highly relevant and have, over the past decades, become ever more central. This is due to several factors. For one, the critical impulse that first gave rise to Women's Studies in literature departments in the 1970s corresponds very closely to the critical impulse that led to the rise of Black Studies or African-American Studies in academia at just that time. The term "postcolonial" was not available then. But the growing dissatisfaction with a literary canon consisting almost entirely of "dead white males" prompted the search for female voices as well as black voices which had been silenced and excluded. Whether with regard to gender or to race, the first project was to discover and recover what was so evidently missing and to give it cultural visibility. This search has led, for instance, to the reprinting of many long forgotten women writers or black writers and, subsequently, to their inclusion in reading lists and teaching curricula. Yet these categories themselves, i.e. "woman" or "black", were largely taken for granted. In a second step, however, these have become the object of inquiry and critical investigation, so as to rethink the strategies and interests that go into their making.

Critical developments in Women's Studies and Black Studies

Why, for instance, have the features traditionally ascribed to women (as listed above) also been ascribed to 'the native', without any great adjustment? In colonial discourse, natives are routinely seen as 'weak', 'dark', 'emotional', 'deficient', 'inferior' – a view that corresponds point by point to the gender difference as constructed in patriarchal discourse. Illustrations for this parallel abound and can be found in many literary or visual examples. And yet, it would surely be absurd to conclude that women share inherent qualities

Woman-native-other: colonial and patriarchal views

with 'natives', for instance that they are all too easily overcome by their emotions, unable to exercise control and reason, or that they are essentially dark, mysterious, benighted and in need of receiving enlightenment. No doubt, all these attributions are prejudiced and partial. So the conclusion from any alleged parallels between 'women' and 'natives' can only be to see the power system that produces and propagates them as a means of founding itself on these terms. As in all discourse analysis (see 1.2.2), such attributes tell us a great deal more about the speaking subject who uses them than anything about the objects for which they are used. Patriarchal and colonial discourse operate in unison, indeed often in identity, because they set up women just as natives in terms of an Other whose traits and deficits legitimize male rule (see Trinh 1989). No matter whom we are specifically speaking about, the Other is always already spoken for.

Intersections of postcolonial and gender analysis: conquest as rape

In the view sketched here, the concerns and strategies of Postcolonial Studies and of Gender Studies appear to be largely the same. In just the sense that Said's *Orientalism*, for example, analyses the historical production of the East as a way for the West to gain domination (see 2.1.1 and 2.3.2), we can continue this analysis to see how this notion of the East is, in fact, a gendered notion setting up the Orient as feminine – dark, mysterious, alluring and seductive – always calling for the male to conquer and control it while threatening to engulf him. Significantly, the gender difference also functions in view of other territories, even in the West. Clearly, it does not derive from specific features of the area so described but just from the symbolic system in which the desire for conquest is articulated. For instance, in the early modern period America was consistently described as "virgin" territory, untrodden, unpossessed, uncultivated, hence inviting male inscription and insemination (see Schülting 1997). The very name "America" is the feminized version of Amerigo, the male traveller's name on whose authority the New World entered our maps and language. The gendered rhetoric of exploration is also manifest in the English texts which first described the place, for instance Walter Ralegh's enthusiastic report of Guiana (1596) as "a Country that hath yet her Maidenhead, never sacked, turned, nor wrought [...]. It hath never been entered by any army of strength, and never conquered or possessed by any Christian Prince" (Ralegh 1997: 94). Colonization, then, can be seen as an act of asserting masculinity; conquest is rape.

This discourse is pervasive, also in many literary texts. One of Seamus Heaney's best-known poems, for example, is the sonnet "Act of Union" (1975), which explores and exploits just such a parallel between political and sexual domination. Modelled on the Irish *aisling* tradition (see 3.1.2), its title refers both to the enforced union between Ireland and Britain in 1801 and to an act of violent love making or rape, evoked with the imagery of the text. So the strategic alliance of Gender Studies with Postcolonial Studies, which we are looking at in all these instances, opens many views on areas of intersecting interests. Yet crucially, these areas also include cultural nationalism and the nationalist rhetoric that was instrumental in taking up the struggle against colonial rule.

Political and sexual domination: acts of union

The history of anti-colonial movements, whether in Ireland, Africa or India, and the foundation of many postcolonial nations have been driven by a gendered rhetoric representing the country to be liberated from imperial domination as a woman. To stay with the case of Ireland – or *Erin*, as her feminized name is – the imagery and idiom of the Irish Renaissance around 1900 depicted the country as a lady in distress, alternatively a maiden seeking protection or a mother giving comfort. This allegory is at the core of Yeats's play *Cathleen Ni Houlihan* (1902), for example, featuring a mysterious female, part bride-to-be, part unforgiving mother, who incites the hero to join the rebellion against Britain. The same trope structures a great deal of Irish writing: "For Yeats and Joyce, and sometimes for Synge", a relevant study concludes, "women became identified with Ireland, both as images of an ideal order which they sought to restore, and as images of an Ireland that had been betrayed, or had collaborated in its own betrayal." (Innes 1993: 178) The nation-as-woman trope also operates in other postcolonial contexts. When Nehru describes in *The Discovery of India* (1945) how the peasants used to welcome him, he says the crowds roared "*Bharat Mata Ki Jai* – Victory to Mother India! [...] *Bharat Mata, Mother India*, was essentially these millions of people and victory to her meant victory to these people." (1959: 29) "Mother India" is also the title of a famous Indian film of the 1950s celebrating this nationalist ideal and mocked in Rushdie's *The Moor's Last Sigh* as "a piece of Hindu myth-making directed by a Muslim socialist" in which "the Indian peasant woman is idealised as bride, mother, and producer of sons." (Rushdie 1995: 138) However, this nationalist myth only licenses male action. As studies by Innes (1993) or Singh (1996) have argued, the feminization of the country has

Sexist imagery in nationalist rhetoric: Ireland and India

helped to obscure or occlude the actual part that real women played in the liberation struggle. Translated into allegory, female power has been defused.

Problematic relations between gender and ethnic difference

This shows that gender analysis, in fact, urges us to think about important differences which postcolonial analysis may not take into account – and vice versa. That is to say, Gender Studies and Postcolonial Studies are not just allied, they are also juxtaposed and direct critical attention to quite different issues. Their exact relation to each other has been at the centre of a continuing discussion. In simple terms, the question is whether *gender* difference or *ethnic* difference is the more fundamental category or, indeed, whether *class* difference is most fundamental. The interrelation between these three – gender, race and class – has been much debated. For, as our examples may suggest, postcolonial liberators and nation-builders can turn out to be traditional patriarchs; even as they fight against oppression in one field they continue oppression in another.

Postcolonial feminist debates: contesting Western concepts

In more complex terms, this debate is at the heart of Spivak's work introduced earlier (see 2.3.4). But it has also been an issue within feminist studies since the 1980s, trying to address the special role of 'third world women' in the wider struggle. Asian American critic and film-maker Trinh Minh-ha, for instance, has argued in a critical dialogue with Julia Kristeva's work that "what is known as the 'Phallic principle' in one part of the world [...] does not necessarily apply to the other parts" (1989: 103). She takes issue with the duality by which non-Western women are defined, questioning "the choice many women of color feel obliged to make between ethnicity and womanhood: how can they? You never have/are one without the other. The idea of two illusory separated identities, one ethnic, the other woman (or more precisely female), again, partakes in the Euro-American system of dualistic reasoning and its age-old divide-and-conquer tactics" (1989: 104).

Postcolonial critiques of Western feminist assumptions

In a much-cited article on feminist scholarship and colonial discourses, Chandra Mohanty takes issue with the idea that all women are world-wide "sisters in struggle" so that Western feminists have often felt the need to speak on behalf of their poor third world "sisters". In a harsh critique of American feminists and their tendency to locate postcolonial women as victims, she wants to dismantle "the production of the 'third world woman' as a singular monolithic subject" (1991: 51) and to replace it with more complex views which do not "discursively colonize the material and historical heterogeneities of the lives of women in the third world" (1991: 53) nor reproduce prevailing stereotypes: "feminist analyses which perpetrate and sustain the hegemony of the idea of the superiority of the West produce a corresponding set of universal images of the 'third world woman', images such as the veiled woman, the powerful mother, the chaste virgin, the obedient wife, etc." (1991: 73). It is important to note that Mohanty is here commenting on feminist writing committed to a politics of liberation, and yet she shows that this same writing is part of the colonial discourse system which it purports to reject. Referring to Marx's statement which Said used as an epigraph to *Orientalism* (see 2.1.1), she therefore concludes: "It is time to move beyond the Marx who found it possible to say: They cannot represent themselves; they must be represented." (1991: 74)

More recently, postcolonial gender studies have indeed moved beyond these issues and now often explore the terrains of queer, cross-gender and transsexual performances which the work of Judith Butler and others have powerfully brought to critical attention. Several postcolonial writers, too, have done much work in this direction. Novels by Lawrence Scott (*Aelred's Sin*, 1998) or Witi Ihimaera (*The Uncle's Story*, 2000) have addressed gay identities in contemporary Caribbean and Maori society (see Schulze-Engler 2007), texts by Suniti Namjoshi (1985) have addressed lesbian identities, and Jackie Kay's novel *Trumpet* (1998) reconstructs the story of a black jazz musician who performed her life as a man (see Stein 2007). In fact, performance is the key word to discuss personal or cultural moves like these which transgress given boundaries (see 4.2). So we should also note that there are prominent performers, like the Australian Barry Humphries (*1934) or the South African Pieter-Dirk Uys (*1945), who have staged their political commitment and social satire in cross-gendered roles. Dame Edna Everage, the chatty Melbourne housewife Humphries has used as a stage persona since the late 1950s, or Evita Bezuidenhout, the Afrikaans gossiper Uys has created for his shows (inspired by Dame Edna), are not just celebrated show icons but also media of social activism which includes, in Evita's case for instance, anti-apartheid and HIV campaigning.

Queer writing and performance in postcolonial fields

SUMMARY

This chapter has

▶ established the need for gender theory and difference in Postcolonial Studies
▶ looked at female figurations of colonial territories as examples where postcolonial and gender analysis often go together
▶ also looked at female figurations of the nation as examples where gender analysis questions postcolonial politics
▶ introduced further issues of debate in Western feminism from a post-colonial perspective

2 Text and Performance: Carnivalizations

Why and how oral perform-ance matters in postcolonial texts

Throughout, the focus of this introduction to postcolonial litera-tures in English has been on texts produced and mainly received in the medium of writing. There have been several points when issues of orality have come up, but by and large the emphasis of our dis-cussion has been on books, i.e. material available in print. How-ever, such a focus is quite limited. As with the gender issues just considered (4.1), we need to set this discussion into a larger frame of reference in which postcolonial literatures exist and in which interactions between orality and writing play an important cultural role (see 2.2.2). The first point is to acknowledge that the opposi-tion between literacy versus orality is neither absolute nor clear-cut; we are rather looking at a spectrum of possibilities in which they operate and interrelate. A written text can still be organized or realized in a way that manifests oral practices, whose traces be-come evident in the use of certain devices, such as proverbial or poetic expressions, forms of address or apostrophe, narrative con-ventions or structures of story telling, as illustrated in many of the postcolonial books introduced above.

Genres of per-formance and wider cultural performances

Yet we should look further. There are entire genres and modes of expression, prominent in postcolonial cultures, for which a script can only give a very limited account because the verbal level is just one among several at play there. These are the genres of perform-ance, such as theatre and drama, song and dance, performance poetry and dub, ritual enactments or ceremonial festivities, popular processions and masquerades. Many of these form highly visible events in the public life of their community, some of them also involve scripted elements, as for instance song lyrics. But to understand them properly they should be studied with a critical focus on the features of performance, shifting our attention from texts to acts, from products to processes, and from codes and structures to modes and dynamic strategies (see Carlson 2004). In fact, such a shift has been a major project in recent Cultural Studies as a whole, now trying to analyse societies and cultures not just like texts, as in interpretive ethnology (see 2.2.1), but as performative interactions. For instance, we could analyse the issues of hybridity, changing ethnic identities and cross-cultural consumption that arise when Chinese immigrants set up their fast food business in 1960s England – issues at the centre of Timothy Mo's novel *Sour Sweet* (1982) – as a matter of performance: for the sake and for the audience of English customers, the restaurant owners establish a public stage where they market and sell food as "Chinese" which they, in their own back-stage domain of family life, despise as "*lupsup*" fit only for foreign palates. The notion of cultural authenticity in this case is best regarded as a matter of cultural performance.

However, the most immediate case where matters of performance arise is theatre and drama. For Postcolonial Studies this is crucial because, unlike the novel which depends on literacy, on print and on a middle-class readership, theatre is a cultural medium at work and at home in nearly all societies. With its roots in ritual and religious practice, the theatrical offers central ways for communities to interact, to debate or educate, in short, to rehearse their tenets of belonging and make sense of life. The work of many postcolonial dramatists, like Wole Soyinka in Nigeria, Derek Walcott in Trinidad or Jack Davis in Australia, draws on this ritual heritage and reworks it for the modern stage. But it has only been in relatively recent times that academic studies have turned to these issues and have given comprehensive critical accounts of the particular aesthetic challenges posed by postcolonial drama. In their pioneering study, Helen Gilbert and Joanne Tompkins suggest that "most post-colonial criticism overlooks drama, perhaps because of its apparently impure form: playscripts are only a part of a theatre experience, and performance is therefore difficult to document" (1996: 8). This is clearly plausible, but it also makes quite clear why theatre and drama should, on the contrary, be absolutely central for all Postcolonial Studies: precisely because of their evidently

Theatre and drama are a challenge for postcolonial analysis

"impure" form – exploring the creative tensions between texts and bodies, words and action, voice and movement and whatever other codes and levels matter in performance – theatrical projects are especially apt for the hybrid forms of postcolonial culture.

Theatrical syncretism: decolonizing the stage

In a wide-ranging and theory-based study of this issue, Christopher Balme therefore suggests to speak of "theatrical syncretism" to analyse the process whereby culturally heterogeneous signs and codes are merged together on the postcolonial stage, often as part of a political strategy: "Syncretic theatre is one of the most effective means of decolonizing the stage, because it utilizes the performances of both European and indigenous cultures in a creative recombination of their respective elements, without slavish adherence to one tradition or the other." (1999: 2). Syncretism is a term borrowed from the discipline of comparative religion, used here to describe a postcolonial strategy of cultural recombination and resistance, closely related to what is also described as creolization (see 3.5) or hybridity (see 1.2.6). But it is important to note that, basically, such a creative strategy is central to *all* theatre performance and always at work whenever actors deliver a text an author scripted before them: "What appear on the printed page of the dramatic text to be stable, even relatively incontrovertible, meanings accumulate in the act of enunciation on stage a range of additional signifiers." (Balme 1999: 106) These additional meanings can help to destabilize what has been set down and so contribute to subvert written authority. Always working with excess and difference, performance therefore is a strategy of cultural redress.

Postcolonial Shakespeares: performance as resistance

This is especially relevant for postcolonial performances of scripts which are traditionally invested with major cultural authority, above all the works of William Shakespeare. As noted earlier (2.4.4), Shakespearean re-enactments have a long history of cross-cultural appropriation, syncretic staging, parody and critical rewriting (see Loomba/Orkin 1998, Massai 2005), many of them questioning the canonical status of Shakespearean drama even while reminding us of it. For to subvert a monument means also to pay tribute to it. In the same way as argued at the outset with reference to the term *postcolonial* (1.2.1), all such projects show a contradictory dependence on and independence from what they attack and, literally, what makes them possible. So the issue where authority lies in performance, and whose authority postcolonial Shakespeare performances ultimately confirm or contest, remains a vexed question.

But there are other postcolonial fields where this issue comes up, most notably the Caribbean carnival tradition. Carnival is a popular mass performance with an ambivalent relation to authority. Originating in the festive calendar of the Catholic church, where the period before Lent is set aside for feasting, masking, entertainment and all forms of physical excess, carnival breaks major social taboos and prohibitions and yet it is licensed by authority to do so. Carnival presents the world turned upside down, with social hierarchies reversed and kings of misrule crowned in mockery or even in defiance of the powers that be. And yet, as the exception to the rule, carnival rather helps to confirm this rule by allowing social pressure, popular unrest or dissatisfaction to find an outlet for some time, strictly limited and tightly controlled, like a safety-valve mechanism. On the other hand, the transgressive energies of the people released in carnival festivities are not easily contained and may well erupt in real violence and actual rebellion.

Carnival performances: safety-valve or popular transgression?

These general points have special relevance for colonial societies, such as eighteenth-century Trinidad, where French settler families and planters first celebrated carnival as part of their fashionable season entertainment. Though initially restricted to the white élite, this introduced an element of transgressive performance into the strictly compartmentalized world of the plantations, a practice which was quickly taken up by slaves. For the African majority, carnival offered a prime opportunity to engage in mimicry and the "arts of resistance", as discussed earlier (2.3.3 and 1.2.3). As part of the masquerades, for instance, the fashion included whites in blackface; so conversely, blacks responded to this role change by taking on the guise and status of their masters, soon infusing the entire celebrations with many elements from African culture, especially music, masks and dance, and so asserting their own presence. This trend was strongly emphasized with slave emancipation in the 1830s. By this time, Trinidad had become a British colony. Yet the local carnival tradition has continued and gained ever more political and cultural prominence as a central contact zone for the various traditions that have settled on the island to clash and mingle, mix and grapple with each other in a powerful syncretic performance. To this day, carnival is a major cultural (and commercial) operation in Trinidad, with strong implications for the postcolonial quest for national identity (see Hill 1972, Koningsbruggen 1997, Riggio 2004). And to this day, carnival is referred to in Trinidad as "Play Mas", which means both 'play mask' and 'play master',

The origins and relevance of Carnival in Trinidad

thus recalling the heritage of plantation history even while re-dressing it.

Carnivalization in Caribbean literature, in cultural theory and contemporary media

Carnival has strong repercussions in a lot of Caribbean literature, as novels by Earl Lovelace (1979) or Robert Antoni (2005) exemplify (see 3.5.2). It also has social and political consequences for diasporic communities where carnival celebrations have long been a central forum of creativity and conflict in multicultural societies, most prominently in London's district Notting Hill (see 3.6.1). In cultural theory, discussions of carnival and its social significance tend to rely on the work of Mikhail Bakhtin, the twentieth-century Russian critic whose focus was on early modern European culture and who championed carnival performances as "a second life of the people", establishing for a time "the utopian realm of community, freedom, equality and abundance" (Bakhtin 1994: 199). We need not share Bakhtin's utopian emphasis to appreciate the uncanny power of carnivalesque acts, potentially subversive though always ambivalent. This is manifest even in contemporary media shows on British television and their ethnic masquerades, such as *Goodness Gracious Me*, the Asian British comedy series with Meera Syal, or in AliG., the outrageously funny and offensive TV character impersonated by Sacha Baron Cohen. Both these examples work by means of masking and stereotyping, and both raise the urgent question of whether they expose the ethnic clichés or exploit them. Especially AliG., a sexist and rude interviewer who poses as black even though his impersonator is evidently white, shows with breathtaking virtuosity how performance is a cultural strategy that may not just constitute and complicate gender identity (see 4.1) but also ethnic identity.

SUMMARY

This chapter has

▶ emphasized the need for wider critical perspectives beyond texts
▶ pointed out the difficulties of analysing theatrical syncretism and postcolonial performances on the stage
▶ introduced carnival as a performance licensed by authority which it may still subvert
▶ looked at the historical developments of Caribbean carnival and its contemporary consequences for literature, society and theory

3 Books That Matter

This book has been written for students of English, yet its aim has been to offer reasons for rethinking the study of English in some fundamental ways. Discussing "Postcolonial Literatures in English", as the title of this introduction has it, has led us to consider several points which question the cultural understanding of what "English" is or means and which therefore challenge the assumptions that have traditionally shaped our academic discipline. What then, after all, does "English" signify? How can or should we define "Englishness" today? In 1697, Daniel Defoe wrote a satirical poem to ridicule claims to English purity, emphasizing the many different elements which went into its making; "From this amphibious ill-born mob began/That vain ill-natured thing, an Englishman" (1889: 190). So what do we do when we, in the twenty-first century, study English literature? Pursuing such questions and their implications, this final section would like to suggest some crucial differences and differentiations within our defining term.

What is "English" literature?

In a way, this is exactly what the current understanding of Postcolonial Studies, as described at the outset, comes down to: no longer take defining terms for granted but begin to think about what they imply, entail or hide. Above all, we should realize that we are now challenged to rethink a most familiar concept. We began with the question of what "African" might mean and considered how its meaning has completely changed with postcolonial developments (1.1). We now end up wondering what "English" is and how it should be reconceptualized to acknowledge these developments. In the larger field of theory, especially in theories of gender and of ethnic difference, just the same move has been going on in recent years. Initially, critical interests were focussed on efforts to define and describe the position of the dominated, i.e. "womanhood" or "blackness", and to debate what sort of identities such categories would support or impose. More recently, debates have moved to consider "masculinity" or, indeed, "whiteness" as the really problematic categories that need to be theorized – all the more urgently because, as majority positions, the identities they support are socially unmarked and so remain largely invisible. Thus, masculinity, whiteness and Englishness all used to go without saying. The point of Postcolonial Studies lies in finding a language to speak – and to speak differently – about them.

How to think about what remains socially invisible

The rise of English in the university

Historically, English was introduced as an academic subject to give a modern alternative to Classics (i.e. Greek and Latin) and so to offer something for prospective students, especially girls or lower class boys, who were thought incapable of dealing with the rigors of genuine philology. The earliest academic instruction in English literature was provided in the 1820s at University College, London, i.e. not in Oxford or Cambridge or any of the old, traditional institutions (see Doyle 1982: 26). In the twentieth century the study of English, especially of the English novel, eventually gained enormous cultural prestige when it was championed by the Cambridge critic F.R. Leavis in *The Great Tradition* (1948) as a way to cope with the divisive and corrosive tendencies of modern life; in postwar England, literature was read by him as the central medium to communicate and reinforce the sense of organic community and an essential English past evidently under threat in contemporary culture. So it is important to realize that such definitions of Englishness and English literature, responding to a feeling of alarm, are also symptoms of a cultural crisis.

The intricate colonial connections within English culture

This crisis has colonial dimensions. In 1891, Rudyard Kipling (see 3.3.2) published a patriotic poem entitled "The English Flag". It celebrates the naval power and world-wide connections represented by this flag and heaps scorn on what it calls "the poor little street-bred people", i.e. petty Little-Englanders who have never been to sea and in the world and thus resent England's imperial mission. Erasing the difference between England and Britain (what it calls "The English Flag" is *not* the flag of England, but the Union Jack), the poem contains the much-cited line: "And what should they know of England who only England know?" (1992: 95) On the one hand, this line suggests that we can only begin to understand our own country when we see it from outside by travelling to other places. On the other hand, given England's colonial connections celebrated here, the line makes the far more radical suggestion that "England" can never be known through and by itself, but is essentially constituted through these other places, cultural elements and foreign forces which colonial ventures necessarily involve – just as it needs the force of the wind to make the English flag fly. In line with this reading of Kipling's question we should ask: what do they know of English literature who only England know?

The establishment of English as an academic subject had important forerunners in Victorian school reforms trying to secularize education and so diminish the influence of the church. In fact, as the research and argument by Viswanathan suggest (see 3.3), these reforms introduced literary studies with a canon of English that had initially been defined and used for colonial education in India and was then, in a significant shift, re-imported for domestic purposes. If we accept this argument, we can see how literary models of Englishness first constructed to teach colonial subjects who "we" are, have become models of cultural self-identification. Simply put, the notion of the self is discovered by means of the colonial other. This also points to the construction or invention of tradition (see Hobsbawm/Ranger 1983), no longer taking what is said to be "traditional" as old and given, but as modern and purposefully produced. At the same time, the example illustrates rather well what Simon Gikandi has called "the extent to which colonialism had shaped the character of the domestic space" in England (1996: xi) and it gives power to his crucial claim in *Maps of Englishness* that we should think about "the ways in which Englishness was itself a product of the colonial culture that it seemed to have created elsewhere" (1996: x). As a result of such displacements, boundaries between inside and outside have become blurred – and necessarily so, moving towards different definitions. In the words of Black British writer Andrea Levy, "if Englishness doesn't define me, then redefine Englishness" (Jaggi 1996: 64).

All this is to argue that Postcolonial Studies is not just about *adding* something to English Studies or *expanding* its domain, *widening* its focus and *extending* the reading lists so as to include more authors from "outside". Important as additions clearly are, the real point lies in changes *from within*, transforming and reversing the critical focus in the first place, not just widening it. Postcolonial issues emerge from within English literature and put pressure on the standard repertoires of textual analysis to take their cultural contingencies into account. Postcolonial Studies, then, is not so much defined through a specific number of texts from a particular range of places, than through certain strategies of reading and of reading differently. This is why they concern *all* students of English, even if their interest is in Shakespeare and Jane Austen only. (In fact, these two authors, long thought to represent the traditional canon of English, have received very interesting postcolonial readings: see Cartelli 1999, Park/Rajan 2000). Few of the books mentioned in this introduction could be classified as "English" literature. In fact, any such description is likely to be

Inventing traditions, redefining Englishness

Changing English studies from within

resented because postcolonial authors would rightly insist on having their work treated as "African" or "Australian", or perhaps "Nigerian" and "Aboriginal" literature. So one might think that the best way to deal with them is to leave their books to specialists in institutes for African Studies or Australian Studies. No doubt, such specialists are needed and such institutions valuable. And yet to delegate all postcolonial books entirely to their expertise would mean to relegate postcolonial issues, in the desperate hope that English Studies would remain untroubled.

Texts are wordly events

Trouble, however, is productive – politically and intellectually. This is why postcolonial books matter and why they should matter to us: they introduce different ways of seeing, describing and debating the world. As a consequence, English literature can no longer proceed in the paradigm of national philology, on which it used to be founded. As illustrated with Wordsworth's daffodil poem when read in the tropics (see 1.1), our texts have principally become different when they are part of transcultural reading and writing. This is, at heart, what Edward Said's major challenge to literary studies has been: to deal with texts as "worldly", i.e. to acknowledge what difference books can make. To some degree, he argues, texts "are *events*, and, even when they appear to deny it, they are nevertheless a part of the social world, of human life, and of course the historical moments in which they are located and interpreted" (Said 1983: 4). These moments and locations, however, undergo continual change. The interpretations of texts in the social world, therefore, change accordingly and so change human life.

Identities are multiple, changing and interconnected

In this view, postcolonial literatures are not something exotic that helps us escape from the drab realities of Western life and offer us more colourful reading matter (even though they may be marketed as such). They rather draw connections to the different realities and other experiences that we are anyway and always part of. Again, this point has best been argued by Said (1993: 407–8): "No one today is purely *one* thing. Labels like Indian, or woman, or Muslim, or American are no more than starting-points, which if followed into actual experience for only a moment are quickly left behind. Imperialism consolidated the mixture of cultures and identities on a global scale. But its worst and most paradoxical gift was to allow people to believe that they were only, mainly, exclusively, white, or black, or Western, or Oriental. Yet just as human beings make their own history, they also make their cultures and ethnic identities. No one can deny the persisting continuities of long traditions, sustained habitations, national languages, and cultural geographies, but there seems no reason except fear and prejudice to keep insisting on their separation and distinctiveness, as if that was all human life was about. Survival in fact is about the connections between things." This book concludes in the hope of having mapped out such connections for readers to pursue them further by themselves.

Appendix

Recommended Reading

DÖRING, TOBIAS, ed., 2007. *A History of Postcolonial Literature in 12½ Books*. Trier: WVT. – A series of critical chapters each of which looks in more detail at one central novel in the light of larger postcolonial issues: Achebe, *Things Fall Apart*; Dangarembga, *Nervous Conditions*; Ihimaera, *The Uncle's Story*; Carey, *True History of the Kelly Gang*; Kunzru, *The Impressionist*; Rushdie, *The Moor's Last Sigh*; Selvon, *The Lonely Londoners*; Kureishi, *The Buddha of Suburbia*; Levy, *Small Island*; Kay, *Trumpet*; Atwood, *The Robber Bride*; Ondaatje, *The English Patient*.

CHILDS, PETER, JEAN JACQUES WEBER, PATRICK WILLIAMS, 2006. *Post-Colonial Theory and Literatures: African, Caribbean and South-Asian*. Trier: WVT. – A student-friendly handbook which gives an introduction to some basics of postcolonial theory as well as a regional and thematic survey of relevant fiction, drama and poetry.

ECKSTEIN, LARS, ed., 2007. *English Literatures Across the Globe: A Companion*. Paderborn: Fink. – A new approach to cover the global field of anglophone writing with a short chapter on each region and its history, including a concise outline of transcultural perspectives beyond postcolonialism.

BENSON, EUGENE, L.W. CONOLLY, eds, 2005. *Encyclopedia of Post-Colonial Literatures in English*. 3 vols. London, New York: Routledge. – A comprehensive reference work, including entries on authors, regions, countries, genres and historical developments.

CHRISMAN, LAURA, PATRICK WILLIAMS, eds, 1993. *Colonial Discourse and Post-Colonial Theory: A Reader*. New York, etc: Harvester Wheatsheaf. – Highly recommended reader, offering substantial excerpts from some thirty critics and their contributions to the field, with useful introductions.

ASHCROFT, BILL, GARETH GRIFFITHS, HELEN TIFFIN, eds, 2005. *The Post-Colonial Studies Reader*. London, New York: Routledge. – Compared with the previous entry, this reader is more up to date and includes more texts, but all of them only in very short excerpts.

BRYDON, DIANA, ed., 2000. *Postcolonialism: Critical Concepts in Literary and Cultural Studies*. 5 vols. London, New York: Routledge. – A broad collection of previously published theoretical essays, documenting crucial debates and critical developments.

Among the many introductory text-books available, the following five are recommended:

LOOMBA, ANIA, 2005. *Colonialism/Postcolonialism*. London, New York: Routledge. – Especially useful for its sharp theoretical focus, including issues of gender, sexuality and globalization.

BOEHMER, ELLEKE, 2005. *Colonial and Postcolonial Literature: Migrant Metaphors*. Oxford: Oxford UP. – Especially useful for its combination of theoretical with literary material for discussion.

INNES, C.L., 2007. *The Cambridge Introduction to Postcolonial Literatures in English*. Cambridge: Cambridge UP. – Especially useful for its emphasis on literary texts and thematic approaches.

YOUNG, ROBERT J.C., 2001. *Postcolonialism: An Historical Introduction*. Oxford: Blackwell. – Especially useful for its focus on the politics of third world liberation movements.

LAZARUS, NEIL, ed., 2004. *The Cambridge Companion to Postcolonial Literary Studies*. Cambridge: Cambridge UP. – Especially useful for its multi-authored spectrum of social, historical, theoretical and institutional topics discussed.

For more detailed literary and cultural histories of the various regions discussed in this introduction, the following titles are also recommended (in addition to the sources cited in the respective chapters):

KELLEHER, MARGARET, PHILIP O'LEARY, eds, 2006. *The Cambridge History of Irish Literature*. 2 vols. Cambridge: Cambridge UP.

IRELE, F. ABIOLA, SIMON GIKANDI, eds, 2004. *The Cambridge History of African and Caribbean Literature*. 2 vols. Cambridge: Cambridge UP.

ARNOLD, A. JAMES, ed., 1994–1997. *History of Literature in the Caribbean*. 3 vols. Amsterdam: John Benjamins.

MEHROTRA, ARVIND KRISHNA, ed., 2003. *A History of Indian Literature in English.* New York: Columbia UP.

WEBBY, ELIZABETH, 2000. *The Cambridge Companion to Australian Literature.* Cambridge: Cambridge UP.

HUGGAN, GRAHAM, 2007. *Australian Literature: Postcolonialism, Racism, Transnationalism.* Oxford: Oxford UP.

Works Cited

ACHEBE, CHINUA, 1988. "An Image of Africa: Racism in Conrad's *Heart of Darkness*", in *Joseph Conrad: Heart of Darkness*, ed. Robert Kimbrough. New York: Norton, pp. 251–262.

AHMAD, AIJAZ, 1992. *In Theory: Classes, Nations, Literatures.* London: Verso.

ANDERSON, BENEDICT, 1991 (1983). *Imagined Communities. Reflections on the Origins and Spread of Nationalism.* 2nd Ed. London: Verso.

ARISTOTLE, 1995. *Poetics.* Edited and translated by Stephen Halliwell. Cambridge MA: Harvard UP.

ASHCROFT, BILL, GARETH GRIFFITH, HELEN TIFFIN, 1989. The Empire *Writes Back: Theory and Practice in Post-Colonial Literatures.* London, New York: Routledge.

ASSMANN, JAN 1997 (1992). *Das kulturelle Gedächtnis: Schrift, Erinnerung und politische Identität in frühen Hochkulturen.* München: Beck.

BAKHTIN, MIKHAIL M., 1994. *The Bakhtin Reader.* Ed. Pam Morris. London: Edward Arnold.

BALME, CHRISTOPHER, 1999. *Decolonizing the Stage: Theatrical Syncretism and Post-Colonial Drama.* Oxford: Clarendon.

BARKER, FRANCIS, PETER HULME, MARGRET IVERSON, eds, 1994. *Colonial Discourse/Post-Colonial Theory.* Manchester: Manchester UP.

BENNETT, LOUISE, 1982. *Selected Poems.* Ed. Mervin Morris. Kingston: Sangster's.

BHABHA, HOMI K., 1994. *The Location of Culture.* London, New York: Routledge.

BRANTLINGER, PATRICK 1988. *Rule of Darkness: British Literature and Imperialism, 1880–1920.* Ithaca: Cornell UP.

BRATHWAITE, EDWARD KAMAU, 1984. *A History of the Voice: The Development of Nation Language in Anglophone Caribbean Poetry.* London, Port of Spain: New Beacon Books.

BROSCH, RENATE, 2007. "Peter Carey, *True History of the Kelly Gang*: Narrative Failure and the Mock-Resurrection of an Australian Legend", in *A History of Postcolonial Literature in 12½ Books*, ed. Tobias Döring. Trier: WVT, pp. 71–87.

BURMUA, IAN, AVISHAI MARGALIT, 2004. *Occidentalism: A Short History of Anti-Westernism.* London: Atlantic.

BUTLER, JUDITH, 1990. *Gender Trouble: Feminism and the Subversion of Identity.* New York, London: Routledge.

BUTLER, JUDITH, 1993. *Bodies That Matter: On the Discursive Limits of "Sex".* New York, London: Routledge.

CARETTA, VINCENT, 1999. "Olaudah Equiano or Gustavus Vassa? New Light on an Eighteenth-Century Question of Identity", *Slavery and Abolition* 20: 3, 96–105.

CARLSON, MARVIN, 2004. *Performance: A Critical Introduction.* New York, London: Routledge.

CARTELLI, THOMAS, 1999. *Repositioning Shakespeare: National Formations, Postcolonial Appropriations.* London, New York: Routledge.

CARTER, PAUL, 1987. *The Road to Botany Bay: An Essay in Spatial History.* London: Faber.

CARY, JOYCE, 1962. *The Case for African Freedom and other writings on Africa.* Austin: University of Texas Press.

CHATWIN, BRUCE, 2005 (1987). *The Songlines.* London: Vintage.

CHEW, SHIRLEY, ANNA RUTHERFORD, eds, 1993. *Unbecoming Daughters of the Empire.* Aarhus: Dangaroo.

CHILDS, PETER, ed., 1999. *Post-Colonial Theory and English Literature: A Reader.* Edinburgh: Edinburgh UP.

CLIFFORD, JAMES, GEORGE E. MARCUS, eds, 1986. *Writing Culture: The Poetics and Politics of Ethnography.* Berkeley: University of California Press.

CONRAD, JOSEPH, 1988 (1899). *Heart of Darkness.* Ed. Robert Kimbrough. New York: Norton.

CURTIUS, ERNST ROBERT, 1948. *Europäische Literatur und Lateinisches Mittelalter.* Bern: Francke.

DABYDEEN, DAVID, 1985. *Hogarth's Blacks: Images of Blacks in Eighteenth-Century English Art.* Mundelstrup: Dangaroo.

DABYDEEN, DAVID, JOHN GILMORE, CECILY JONES, eds, 2007. *The Oxford Companion to Black British History.* Oxford: Oxford UP.

DANGAREMBGA, TSITSI, 1988. *Nervous Conditions.* London: The Women's Press.

DEANE, SEAMUS, 1986. *A Short History of Irish Literature.* London etc: Hutchinson.

DEANE, SEAMUS, ed., 1991. *The Field Day Anthology of Irish Writing*, vols 1–3. Derry: Field Day. Vols. 4–5 *Irish Women's Writing and Traditions*, ed. Angela Bourke. Cork: Corke UP, 2002.

DEFOE, DANIEL, 1889. *The Earlier Life and the Chief Works of Daniel Defoe*, ed. Henry Morley. London: George Routledge.

DÖRING, TOBIAS, 1996. *Chinua Achebe und Joyce Cary: Ein postkoloniales Rewriting englischer Afrika-Fiktionen*. Pfaffenweiler: Centaurus.

DÖRING, TOBIAS, 2002. *Caribbean-English Passages: Intertextuality in a Postcolonial Tradition*. London, New York: Routledge.

DÖRING, TOBIAS, ed., 2007. *A History of Postcolonial Literature in 12½ Books*. Trier: WVT.

DOYLE, BRIAN, 1982. "The hidden history of English studies", in *Re-Reading English*, ed. Peter Widdowson. London, New York: Methuen, pp. 17–31.

DUERDEN, DENNIS, COSMO PIETERSE, eds, 1972. *African Writers Talking*. London: Heinemann.

EQUIANO, OLAUDAH, 2001 (1789). *The Interesting Narrative of the Life of Olaudah Equiano, or Gustavus Vassa, The African, Written by Himself*. Ed. Werner Sollors. New York: Norton.

FAIRCLOUGH, NORMAN, 1992. *Discourse and Social Power*. Cambridge: Polity Press.

FANON, FRANTZ, 1965 (1961). *The Wretched of the Earth*. Preface Jean-Paul Sartre. Trans.Constance Farrington. London: Macgibbon & Kee.

FANON, FRANTZ, 1986 (1952). *Black Skin, White Masks*. Foreword Homi K. Bhabha. Trans. Charles Lam Markmann. London: Pluto Press.

FOUCAULT, MICHEL, 1981 (1976). *The History of Sexuality*. Vol. I *An Introduction*. Trans. Robert Hurley. Harmondsworth: Penguin.

FRIEL, BRIAN, 1989. *Making History*. London: Faber.

FRYER, PETER, 1984. *Staying Power: The History of Black People in Britain*. London: Pluto Press.

FUCHS, ANNE and DAVID J. BARKER, eds, 2004. *Postcolonialism and the Past*. Special Issue *Modern Language Quarterly* 65: 3.

GANDHI, 1997. *Hind Swaraj and Other Writings*. Ed. Anthony J. Parel. Cambridge: Cambridge UP.

GEERTZ, CLIFFORD, 2000 (1973). *The Interpretation of Culture*. New York: Basic Books.

GIKANDI, SIMON, 1996. *Maps of Englishness: Writing Identity in the Culture of Colonialism*. New York: Columbia UP.

GILBERT, HELEN, JOANNE TOMPKINS, 1996. *Post-colonial Drama: Theory, Practice, Politics*. London, New York: Routledge.

GILBERT, SANDRA M., SUSAN GUBAR, 1979. *The Madwoman in the Attic: The Woman Writer and the Nineteenth-Century Literary Imagination*. New Haven: Yale UP.

GILROY, PAUL, 1987. *"There Ain't No Black in the Union Jack": The Cultural Politics of Race and Nation*. London: Hutchinson.

GILROY, PAUL, 1993. *The Black Atlantic: Modernity and Double Consciousness*. London, New York: Verso.

GLISSANT, EDOUARD, 1989. *Caribbean Discourse: Selected Essays*. Trans. J. Michael Dash. Charlottesville: University of Virginia Press.

GOLAN, DAPHNE, 1994. *Inventing Shaka. Using History in the Construction of Zulu Nationalism*. Bolder, London: Lynne Rienner Publishers.

GOLDIE, TERRY, 1989. *Fear and Temptation: The Image of the Indigene in Canadian, Australian, and New Zealand Literatures*. Kingston, Montreal, London: McGill-Queen's University Press.

GRIEM, JULIKA, 2007. "Hari Kunzru, *The Impressionist*: Intertextuality in a Postcolonial Context", in *A History of Postcolonial Literature in 12½ Books*, ed. Tobias Döring. Trier: WVT, pp. 89–103.

GUNNER, LIZ, 2004. "Africa and Orality", in *The Cambridge History of African and Caribbean Literature*, eds F. Abiola Irele, Simon Gikandi. Cambridge: Cambridge UP, pp. 1–18.

HABEKOST, CHRISTIAN, 1993. *Verbal Riddim: The Politics and Aesthetics of African-Caribbean Dub Poetry*. Amsterdam, Atlanta: Rodopi.

HALL, STUART, 1988. "New Ethnicities", in *Black Film, British Cinema: ICA Documents 7*, ed. Kobena Mercer. London: Institute of Contemporary Arts, pp. 27–31.

HALL, STUART, 1993 (1990). "Cultural Identity and Diaspora", in *Colonial Discourse and Post-Colonial Theory*, eds Laura Chrisman, Patrick Williams. New York, London: Harvester Wheatsheaf, pp. 392–403.

HALL, STUART, 1991. "Old and New Identities, Old and New Ethnicities", in *Culture, Globalization and the World-System: Contemporary Conditions for the Representation of Identity*, ed. Anthony D. King. London: Macmillan, pp. 41–68.

HASELSTEIN, ULLA, 2000. *Die Gabe der Zivilisation*. München: Fink.

HILL, EROL, 1972. *The Trinidad Carnival. Mandate for a National Theatre.* Austin: University of Texas Press.

HOBSBAWM, ERIC, TERENCE RANGER, eds, 1983. *The Invention of Tradition.* Cambridge: Cambridge UP.

HOF, RENATE, Hg., 1995. *Genus: Zur Geschlechterdifferenz in den Kulturwissenschaften.* Stuttgart: Kröner.

HUGGAN, GRAHAM, 2001. *The Postcolonial Exotic: Marketing the Margins.* London, New York: Routledge.

HULME, PETER, 1986. *Colonial Encounters: Europe and the Native Caribbean 1492–1797.* London, New York: Methuen.

HUTCHEON, LINDA, 1988. *A Poetics of Postmodernism: History, Theory, Fiction.* New York, London: Routledge.

INNES, C.L., 1993. *Woman and Nation in Irish Literature and Society, 1880–1935.* New York etc: Harvester Wheatsheaf.

INNES, C.L., 2002. *A History of Black and Asian Writing in Britain, 1700–2000.* Cambridge: Cambridge UP.

INNES, C.L., 2007. "Chinua Achebe, *Things Fall Apart*: Telling the History of African Colonization from the Inside", in *A History of Postcolonial Literature in 12½ Books*, ed. Tobias Döring. Trier: WVT, pp. 17–31.

IRELE, F. ABIOLA, SIMON GIKANDI, eds, 2004. *The Cambridge History of African and Caribbean Literature.* 2 vols. Cambridge: Cambridge UP.

JACOBS, HARRIET, 1987 (1861). *Incidents in the Life of a Slave Girl.* Ed. Jean Fagan Yellin. Cambridge MA: Harvard UP.

JAGGI, MAYA, 1996. "Redefining Englishness", *Waterstone's Magazine* 6: 62–69.

JAMES C.L.R., 1963. *Beyond a Boundary.* London: Hutchinson.

JAMESON, FREDRIC, 1988. *Modernism and Imperialism.* Field Day Pamphlet No 14. Derry: Field Day.

JANMOHAMED, ABDUL R., 1983. *Manichean Aesthetics: The Politics of Literature in Colonial Africa.* Amherst: University of Massachusetts Press.

JOYCE, JAMES, 1988 (1916). *A Portrait of the Artist as a Young Man.* London: Paladin.

KIBERD, DECLAN, 1989. "Irish Literature and Irish History", in *The Oxford History of Ireland*, ed. R.F. Foster. Oxford: Oxford UP, pp. 230–281.

KIBERD, DECLAN, 1995. *Inventing Ireland: The Literature of the Modern Nation.* London: Cape.

KINGSLEY, CHARLES, 1901. *The Life and Works of Charles Kingsley, edited by his wife.* London: Macmillan.

KIPLING, RUDYARD, 1992. *Selected Poetry.* Ed. Craig Raine. Harmondsworth: Penguin.

KI-ZERBO, JOSEPH, 1990. *Die Geschichte Schwarz-Afrikas.* Frankfurt a.M.: Fischer.

KLEIN, BERNHARD, JÜRGEN KRAMER, eds, 2001. *Common Ground? Crossovers between Cultural Studies and Postcolonial Studies.* Trier: WVT.

KONINGSBRUGGEN, PETER VAN, 1997. *Trinidad Carnival: A Quest for National Identity.* Basingstoke: Macmillan.

KUREISHI, HANIF, 1990. *The Buddha of Suburbia.* London: Faber.

LAKOFF, GEORGE, MARK JOHNSON, 1980. *Metaphors We Live By.* Chicago, London: University of Chicago Press.

LAMMING, GEORGE, 1991 (1953). *In the Castle of My Skin.* Foreword Sandra Pouchet Paquet. Ann Arbor: University of Michigan Press.

LEAVIS, F. R., 1948. *The Great Tradition.* London: Chatto & Windus.

LEMKE, CORDULA, 2007. "Margaret Atwood, *The Robber Bride*: Welcoming the Vampire", in *A History of Postcolonial Literature in 12½ Books*, ed. Tobias Döring. Trier: WVT, pp. 181–194.

LOOMBA, ANIA, MARTIN ORKIN, eds, 1998 *Post-Colonial Shakespeares.* London, New York: Routledge.

MACAULY, THOMAS BABINGTON, 1972. *Selected Writings*, ed. John Clive. Chicago: University of Chicago Press.

MALOUF, DAVID, 1984 (1975). *Johnno.* Harmondsworth: Penguin.

MASSAI, SONIA, 2005. *World-wide Shakespeares: Local Appropriations in Film and Performance.* London, New York: Routledge.

MATZKE, CHRISTINE, SUSANNE MÜHLEISEN, eds, 2006. *Postcolonial Postmortems: Crime Fiction from a Transcultural Perspective.* Amsterdam, New York: Rodopi.

MATZKE, CHRISTINE, 2007. "Tsitsi Dangarembga, *Nervous Conditions*: Food for Thought in Zimbabwean Writing", in *A History of Postcolonial Literature in 12½ Books*, ed. Tobias Döring. Trier: WVT, pp. 33–50.

Appendix

MINTZ, SIDNEY, 1985. *Sweetness and Power: The Place of Sugar in Modern History.* New York: Viking Penguin.

MOHANTY, CHANDRA TALPADE, 1991 (1984). "Under Western Eyes: Feminist Scholarship and Colonial Discourses", in *Third World Women and the Politics of Feminism*, eds. Chandra Talpade Mohanty, Ann Russo, Lourdes Torres. Bloomington: Indiana UP, pp. 51–80.

MORGAN, SALLY, 1987. *My Place.* Fremantle: Fremantle Arts Centre Press.

MUDROOROO, 1983. *Doctor Wooreddy's Prescription for Enduring the Ending of the World.* Melbourne: Hyland House.

MUDROOROO, 1997. *The Indigenous Literature of Australia: Milli Milli Wangka.* Melbourne: Highland House.

MÜHLEISEN, SUSANNE, 2002. *Creole Discourse: Exploring Prestige Formation and Change across Caribbean English-lexicon Creoles.* Amsterdam: John Benjamins.

MÜHLEISEN, SUSANNE, 2007. "Samuel Selvon, *The Lonely Londoners*: The Emergence of Migrant Voices", in *A History of Postcolonial Literature in 12½ Books*, ed. Tobias Döring. Trier: WVT, pp. 123–137.

MUKHERJEE, MEENAKSHI, 1971. *The Twice-Born Fiction.* New Delhi: Heinemann.

NAIPAUL, V. S., 1976. *The Overcrowded Baracoon and Other Articles.* Harmondsworth: Penguin.

NAIPAUL, V.S., 1985. *Finding the Centre: Two Narratives.* Harmondsworth: Penguin.

NAMJOSHI, SUNITI, 1985. *The Conversations of a Cow.* London: The Women's Press.

NEHRU, JAWAHRALAL, 1959 (1945). *The Discovery of India.* New York: Double Day.

NEHRU, JAWAHARLAL, 1989 (1936). *An Auto biography.* Centenary Edition. Delhi: Oxford UP.

NGŪGĪ WA THIONG'O, 1986. *Decolonising the Mind: The Politics of Language in African Literature.* London: Currey.

NICHOLS, GRACE, 1989. *Lazy Thoughts of a Lazy Woman and other poems.* London: Virago.

ONG, WALTER J., 1984. "Orality, Literacy, and Medieval Textualization", *New Literary History* 16, 1–11.

OSTERHAMMEL, JÜRGEN, 1997. *Colonialism: A Theoretical Overview.* Trans. Shelley L. Frisch. Princeton: Randle Publishers.

PARK, YOU-ME, RAJESWARI SUNDER RAJAN, eds, 2000. *The Postcolonial Janes Austen.* London, New York: Routledge.

PARRY, BENITA, 2004 (1987). "Problems in Current Theories of Colonial Discourse", in Parry, *Postcolonial Studies: A Materialist Critique.* London, New York: Routledge, pp. 13–36.

PRATT, MARY LOUISE, 1992. *Imperial Eyes: Travel Writing and Transculturation.* London, New York: Routledge.

QUINT, DAVID, 1993. *Epic and Empire. Politics and Generic Form from Virgil to Milton.* Princeton: Princeton UP.

RALEGH, WALTER, 1997 (1596). "From *The Discovery of the Large, Rich and Bewtiful Empire of Guiana*" in *The English Literatures of America: 1500–1800*, eds Myra Jehlen, Michael Warner. London, New York: Routledge, pp. 91–94.

RAO, RAJA, 1989 (1938). *Kanthapura.* Delhi: Oxford UP.

REICHL, SUSANNE, 2002. *Cultures in the Contact Zone: Ethnic Semiosis in Black British Literature.* Trier: WVT.

REICHL, SUSANNE, 2007. "Hanif Kureishi, *The Buddha of Suburbia*: Performing Identity in Postcolonial London", in *A History of Postcolonial Literature in 12½ Books*, ed. Tobias Döring. Trier: WVT, pp. 139–154.

RICHTARIK, MARILYNN J., 1994. *Acting Between the Lines: The Field Day Theatre Company and Irish Cultural Politics.* Oxford: Clarendon Press.

RICHTER, VIRGINIA, 2007. "Andrea Levy, *Small Island*: Imagining Multiracial Conviviality in British Postwar Literature", in *A History of Post-colonial Literature in 12½ Books*, ed. Tobias Döring. Trier: WVT, pp. 155–168.

RIEMENSCHNEIDER, DIETER, Hg., 1983. *Grundlagen zur Literatur in englischer Sprache: West- und Ostafrika.* München: Fink.

RIGGIO, MILLA COZART, ed., 2004. *Carnival: Culture in Action – the Trinidad Experience.* London, New York: Routledge.

RUSHDIE, SALMAN, 1982 (1981). *Midnight's Children.* London: Picador.

RUSHDIE, SALMAN, 1991. *Imaginary Homelands: Essays and Criticism 1981–1991.* London: Granta.

RUSHDIE, SALMAN, 1995. *The Moor's Last Sigh.* London: Cape.

SAID, EDWARD W., 1983. *The World, the Text and the Critic.* Cambridge MA: Harvard UP.

SAID, EDWARD W., 1985 (1978). *Orientalism.* Harmondsworth: Penguin.

SAID, EDWARD W., 1988. *Yeats and Decoloniza-tion*. Field Day Pamphlet No 15. Derry: Foyle Arts Centre.

SAID, EDWARD W., 1993. *Culture and Imperialism*. London: Chatto & Windus.

SAID, EDWARD W., 1997 (1975). *Beginnings: Intention and Method*. London: Granta.

SAID, EDWARD W., 1999. *Out of Place. A Memoir*. New York: Knopf.

SCHREINER, OLIVE, 1987 (1883). *The Story of an African Farm*. Harmondsworth: Penguin.

SCHÜLTING, SABINE, 1997. *Wilde Frauen, fremde Welten: Kolonisierungsgeschichten aus Amerika*. Reinbek: Rowohlt.

SCHÜLTING, SABINE, 2007. "Salman Rushdie, *The Moor's Last Sigh*: Remaking the Past and the Future", in *A History of Postcolonial Literature in 12½ Books*, ed. Tobias Döring. Trier: WVT, pp. 105–121.

SCHULZE-ENGLER, FRANK, 2007. "Witi Ihimaera, *The Uncle's Story*: Indigenous Literatures in a Globalized World", in *A History of Post-colonial Literature in 12½ Books*, ed. Tobias Döring. Trier: WVT, pp. 51–69.

SCOTT, JAMES C., 1990. *Domination and the Arts of Resistance: Hidden Transcripts*. New Haven: Yale UP.

SEBBA, MARK, 1993. *London Jamaican*. London, New York: Longman.

SEBBA, MARK, 1997. *Contact Languages: Pidgins and Creoles*. Basingstoke: Macmillan.

SINGH, JYOTSNA G., 1996. *Colonial Narratives/ Cultural Dialogues: "Discoveries" of India in the Language of Colonialism*. London, New York: Routledge.

SPIVAK, GAYATRI C., 1985. "Three Women's Texts and a Critique of Imperialism", *Critical Inquiry* 12, 243–261.

SPIVAK, GAYATRI C. 1993 (1988). "Can the Subaltern Speak?", in *Colonial Discourse and Post-Colonial Theory*, eds Laura Chrisman, Patrick Williams. New York, London: Harvester Wheatsheaf, pp. 66–111.

SPIVAK, GAYATRI C., 1999. *A Critique of Post-colonial Reason*. Cambridge MA: Harvard UP.

SPURR, DAVID, 1993. *The Rhetoric of Empire: Colonial Discourse in Journalism, Travel Writing and Imperial Administration*. Durham: Duke UP.

STEIN, MARK, 2004. *Black British Literature: Novels of Transformation*. Columbus: Ohio State UP.

STEIN, MARK, 2007. "Jackie Kay, *Trumpet*: Life Border Writing", in *A History of Postcolonial Literature in 12½ Books*, ed. Tobias Döring. Trier: WVT, pp. 169–180.

STOCKHAMMER, ROBERT, 2005. *Ruanda. Über einen anderen Genozid schreiben*. Frankfurt a.M.: Suhrkamp.

SULERI, SARA, 1992. *The Rhetoric of English India*. Chicago, London: University of Chicago Press.

SWINDELLS, JULIA, ed., 1995. *The Uses of Autobiography*. London: Taylor & Francis.

SYNGE, JOHN M., 1958. *Plays, Poems and Prose*. London: Dent.

TERADA, REI, 1992. *Derek Walcott's Poetry: American Mimicry*. Boston: Northeastern University Press.

TERDIMAN, RICHARD, 1985. *Discourse/Counter-Discourse: The Theory and Practice of Symbolic Resistance in Nineteenth-Century France*. Ithaca, London: Cornell UP.

TODOROV, TZVETAN, 1984 (1982). *The Conquest of America: The Question of the Other*. Trans. Richard Howard. New York: Harper & Row.

TORRES-SAILLANT, SILVIO, 1997. *Caribbean Poetics: Towards an Aesthetic of West Indian Literature*. Cambridge: Cambridge UP.

TORRES-SAILLANT, SILVIO, 2006. *An Intellectual History of the Caribbean*. London, New York: Palgrave.

TRINH T. MINH-HA, 1989. *Woman, Native, Other: Writing Postcoloniality and Feminism*. Bloomington: Indiana UP.

VENUTI, LAWRENCE, 1995. *The Translator's Invisibility: A History of Translation*. London, New York: Routledge.

VISWANATHAN, GAURI, 1989. *Masks of Conquest: Literary Study and British Rule in India*. London: Faber.

WAGNER-EGELHAAF, MARTINA, 2000. *Autobiographie*. Stuttgart: Metzler.

WALCOTT, DEREK, 1990. *Omeros*. London: Faber.

WALCOTT, DEREK, 1992. *Collected Poems: 1948–1984*. London: Faber.

WHITE, HAYDEN, 1973. *Metahistory: The Historical Imagination in Nineteenth-Century Europe*. Baltimore, London: Johns Hopkins UP.

WHITE, PATRICK, 1960 (1957). *Voss*. Harmondsworth: Penguin.

WOLF, ERIC R., 1982. *Europe and the People Without History*. Berkeley: University of California Press.

Appendix

WRIGHT, JUDITH, 1994. *Collected Poems, 1942–1985*. Manchester: Carcanet.

ZABUS, CHANTAL, 1991. *The African Palimpsest: Indigenization of Language in the West African Europhone Novel*. Amsterdam, Atlanta: Rodopi.

ZABUS, CHANTAL, 2002. *Tempests after Shakespeare*. London, New York: Palgrave, Macmillan.

Index

Abbey Theatre
(Irish National Theatre)   76, 84, 101, 104
abolitionism   67, 112, 165, 166
aborigine   71–72, 98, 135–140, 142–143, 145
Achebe, Chinua   9, 78, 84, 111, 116–118
    No Longer At Ease   116
    Things Fall Apart   9, 78, 116
Act of Union   101–102, 175
Adebayo, Diran   170
Adichie, Chimamanda Ngozi   118
Adrian IV, Pope   100
Aeschylus   53
aesthetics   20–22
African (meaning of)   7–9, 14, 18, 108, 183
    (*see also* pan-African)
African National Congress   24
African-American Studies   41
Agard, John   170
Agbabi, Patience   89
Ahmad, Aijaz   54
Aidoo, Ama Ata   118
aisling   103, 175
Algeria   52
Ali, Monica   169–170
Amin, Idi   114
Anand, Mulk Raj   130–132
Anderson, Benedict   58, 95
anthologies   8, 108, 110
anthropology   27, 34, 46–47
Antoni, Robert   155–156, 182
Anzac Day   138–139
Aristotle   68, 75
Armah, Ayi Kwei   118
Ashcroft, Bill   16–18, 20, 81, 97, 134–135, 142
Assmann, Jan   49
Atwood, Margaret   172
Austen, Jane   23, 185
Austin, John L.   68
Australia   16, 71–73, 75, 134–145
autobiography (life writing)   65–69, 71, 82, 168

Bacon, Francis   39
Bakhtin, Mikhail   182
Balme, Christopher   180
Barker, David J.   44
Barker, Frances   23
Beckett, Samuel   99, 106
Behan, Brendan   106
Beier, Ulli   110
Bennett, Louise   155, 157
Berlin conference   113–114
Bhabha, Homi K.   36, 53, 55–58, 64, 74
    The Location of Culture   36, 56–57
    Nation and Narration   58
Bible   25–26, 35, 113, 116, 122, 151, 153
Bildungsroman   117, 168
Black British   61–62, 74, 94, 158–168, 185
Blake, William   104
Bligh, Governor   137, 139
Bloody Sunday (Derry)   102–103
Bowen, Elizabeth   106
Boyd, William   128
Brantlinger, Patrick   91, 112
Brathwaite, Edward Kamau   17, 28, 73, 148, 155–157, 167
    The Arrivants   155
Breeze, Jean 'Binta'   169–170
Brodber, Erna   154, 157
Brontë, Charlotte   83, 86–87, 168
    Jane Eyre   64, 83, 86–87, 119, 168
Brosch, Renate   141
Buruma, Ian   39
Butler, Judith   173, 177

canon   32, 41, 63, 82, 122, 167, 180, 185
Caretta, Vincent   43
Carey, Peter   84, 141, 144
    Jack Maggs   84
Caribbean (history, culture)   17–18, 21, 31, 62, 145–158, 181–182
Carlson, Marvin   179
carnival/carnivalization   154–156, 164–165, 178, 181–182
Carr, Marina   106
Cartelli, Thomas   185
Carter, Paul   72, 75, 135
Cary, Joyce   8–9, 84, 167
    Mister Johnson   9, 84
Castro, Fidel   152
Césaire, Aimé   8, 32–33, 61, 86, 108, 146
    Une Tempête   86
Chandra, Vikram   132
Chatwin, Bruce   72–73
    The Songlines   72–73

Chaudhuri, Amit 132
Chaudhuri, Nirad 92
Chekhov, Anton 85
Childs, Peter 81, 83
Chomsky, Noam 41
city writing 74, 168
Cliff, Michelle 156, 157
Clifford, James 47–48
Clive, Robert 124
Clune, Frank 92
Coetzee, J.M. 83, 118
  Foe 83
Cohen, Sacha Baron 182
Collingwood, Captain 165
colonialism 6, 17–18, 20, 24, 26–27, 31, 33, 52, 57, 65–66, 78, 110, 113, 174, 177
Columbus, Christopher 72, 145, 149, 152
Commonwealth 93, 138, 145
Commonwealth literature 20, 93
Congress Party (India) 24, 124–127
Connolly, James 101
Conrad, Joseph 79, 83–84, 94–95, 128
  Heart of Darkness 79, 83–84, 94–95
contact zone 29, 30
contrapuntal reading 55
Cook, James, Captain 136, 139
Cook, Robin 166
counter-discourse 25
creol/creolization 21, 48, 146–149, 153, 155–156, 164, 168–169, 180
cricket 93
crime fiction 90, 91
Cromwell, Oliver 100
Cultural Studies 45, 61, 159, 179
culture (definitions and debates) 45–48
curriculum 12, 22, 56, 122
Curtin, Prime Minister 138
Curtius, Ernst Robert 28
Curzon, George Nathaniel, Lord 126

Dabydeen, David 84, 86, 89, 157, 163–164, 169–170
  The Intended 84
  Turner 169
D'Aguiar, Fred 169
Dangarembga, Tsitsi 117–119
  Nervous Conditions 117, 119
Darwin, Charles/Darwinism 12, 34, 79, 98
Davis, Jack 144, 179
Deane, Seamus 107, 108
decolonization 18, 42, 79, 115–116, 158
deconstruction 13

Defoe, Daniel 68, 83, 115, 156, 183
  Robinson Crusoe 68, 83–84, 87, 115, 156
Dennis, Ferdinand 160
Derozio, Henry 130
Derrida, Jacques 49, 56, 61
Desai, Anita 132, 133
Desai, Kiran 132
Deshpande, Shashi 132–133
Devi, Mahasweta 61
Devlin, Anne 106
Dhondy, Farrukh 170
diaspora 7, 30–34, 61–62, 66, 128, 153, 156, 167, 182
Dickens, Charles 23, 80, 84, 140, 154, 168
difference 12–13, 17, 29, 36, 57, 59, 62, 172–173, 180, 183, 186
diglossia 27–28, 50, 147
discourse 23–24, 26, 35, 41, 43–44, 55, 83, 109, 174
Disraeli, Benjamin 40, 124–125
Donohoe, Jack 141
Döring, Tobias 81, 90, 93, 158
Doyle, Arthur Conan 79, 90–91
  The Lost World 79
Doyle, Brian 184
DuBois, W.E.B. 114

Easter Rising 101–102
education 11, 26, 42, 56–57, 113, 117, 120, 122–125, 184–185
Eliot, T.S. 116
Elizabeth I, Queen 100, 123, 165
Emecheta, Buchi 117–118, 158, 168
empire 6, 11–12, 16, 18, 28, 40, 49, 53, 72, 78, 82–83, 93, 97, 113, 123–126, 128, 136, 138, 158, 162, 164–165
English 28–29, 48, 94, 107, 120–122, 153, 183–185
English literature 10–11, 14, 17, 28, 122, 123, 167, 183–185
English Studies 7, 10, 87, 183–186
Englishness 11–12, 14, 57, 62, 163, 183
epic 89, 103, 158
Equiano, Olaudah (Gustavus Vassa) 42–43, 67, 129, 165–166, 170
Ethiopia 110, 151–152
Ethiopianism 25
eurocentric 21
Evaristo, Bernadine 170
Ezekiel, Nissim 132

Fairclough, Norman 22, 23
famine, Irish 101–102

Appendix

Fanon, Frantz — 51–54, 67
   Black Skin, White Masks — 51–52, 67
   The Wretched of the Earth — 52
Farah, Nuruddin — 118
feminism — 59–60, 86, 172–177
Field Day — 107
Figueroa, John — 167
Flannagan, Richard — 144
Forster, E. M. — 129
Foucault, Michel — 22–23, 26, 38, 41, 67
Franklin, Miles — 144
Freud, Sigmund — 15, 56–57
Friel, Brian — 76, 106–107
   Translations — 107
Froude, J. A. — 152
Fryer, Peter — 162–163
Fuchs, Anne — 44
Fugard, Athol — 118

Gandhi, 'Mahatma' — 121–124, 126–127, 131
Gandhi, Indira — 124, 133
Gandhi, Rajiv — 124
Garrick, David — 167
Garvey, Marcus — 146, 151
gaze (controlling eye) — 27, 52–53, 57, 67
Geertz, Clifford — 45–47
gender — 59–60, 86, 117, 156, 172–178, 182
genocide — 31, 73, 114–115, 147
genre — 88, 178
genre writing — 88–91
Ghana — 69
Ghosh, Amitav — 132
Gikandi, Simon — 109, 185
Gilbert, Helen — 179, 180
Gilbert, Kevin — 73, 143
Gilbert, Sandra M. — 64, 86–87
Gilroy, Beryl — 168, 170
Gilroy, Paul — 161
Glissant, Edouard — 146
Goethe, Johann Wolfgang — 38
Golan, Daphne — 77
Goldie, Terry — 142
Golding, William — 167
Gordimer, Nadine — 118
Gordon, Adam Lindsay — 144
Grainger, James — 153
Gramsci, Antonio — 60
Great Trek — 112
Greene, Graham — 128
Gregory, Lady Augusta — 104, 106
Griem, Julika — 82
Griffith, Arthur — 102
Griffiths, Gareth — 16–18, 81, 97, 134–135, 142

Gubar, Susan — 64, 86–87
Guha, Ranajit — 60
Gunesekera, Romesh — 132
Gunner, Liz — 109
Gurnah, Abdulrazak — 84, 118
   Paradise — 84
Gwala, Mafika — 118–119

Habekost, Christian — 155
Hailee Selassie — 151–152, 153
Haiti — 24, 76, 151–152
Hall, Stuart — 61–63, 159–160, 163
Hammer, Josef von — 38
Hammet, Dashiel — 91
Hammond, David — 107
Harris, Wilson — 84, 154, 157, 167
   Palace of the Peacock — 84, 154
Hartog, Dirk — 139
Haselstein, Ulla — 69
Hastings, Warren — 123
Hawkins, John — 152
Head, Bessie — 118
Heaney, Seamus — 89, 106–107, 175
Hegel, Georg Wilhelm Friedrich — 78
Henry II, King — 100
Henry VIII, King — 100
Herero war — 114
Hewett, Dorothy — 144
Hill, Erol — 181
history writing (historiography) — 75–80, 82, 131
Hobsbawm, Eric — 44, 185
Hof, Renate — 172
Hogarth, William — 163
Hoggart, Richard — 61
home rule (Irish) — 101–102
Homer — 43, 44, 140, 158
Hope, A. D. — 144
Huggan, Graham — 134
Hulme, Peter — 23, 145
Humboldt, Wilhelm von — 38
Humphries, Barry (Dame Edna Everage) — 177
Hutcheon, Linda — 19, 80
hybrid/hybridity — 21, 34–36, 56, 64, 146, 149, 156, 179–180
Hyde, Douglas — 102

identity — 31–32, 51, 54, 57, 61–62, 95, 136, 141, 156, 166, 168, 182, 185
Ihimaera, Witi — 177
indenture — 151–152
India — 26, 56, 59, 60, 69, 79, 119, 120–133, 175
Innes, C.L. — 160, 162, 167, 175
intertextuality — 82–83, 87, 90

Ireland 74, 76, 97–108, 175
Irele, F. Abiola 109
Irish Renaissance 101–103
Irish Republican Army 102
Ishiguro, Kazuo 91
   When We Were Orphans 91
Iverson, Margret 23

Jacobs, Harriet 69–70
Jagan, Cheddi 152
Jaggi, Maya 185
Jahn, Janheinz 110
Jamaica 31, 61, 151–153, 155
James II, King 100
James, C.L.R. 93, 154, 157, 167
Jameson, Fredric 74
JanMohamed, Abdul 52–53
Jewish history 30–34
Jinnah, Muhammad Ali 126
Johnson, Amryl 92, 171
   Sequins for a Ragged Hem 92
Johnson, Lemuel 86
Johnson, Linton Kwesi 169–170
Johnson, Mark 13
Jones, William 125
Joyce, James 74, 99, 105–107, 175
   Portrait of the Artist as a Young Man 105, 107
   Ulysses 74, 107

Kavanagh, Patrick 106
Kay, Jackie 170, 177
Kelly, Ned 139, 141
Keneally, Thomas 144
Kenya 11, 113–114
Kenyatta, Jomo 114
Kiberd, Declan 99, 108
Kincaid, Jamaica 156–157
Kingsley, Charles 98
Kingsley, Henry 140
Kipling, Rudyard 129, 184
   Kim 129
Ki-Zerbo, Joseph 111
Klein, Bernhard 45
Koningsbruggen, Peter van 181
Kramer, Jürgen 45
Kristeva, Julia 176
Kunene, Daniel 77
Kunene, Mazisi 77
   Emperor Shaka the Great 77
Kunzru, Hari 82
   The Impressionist 82
Kureishi, Hanif 168–170
   The Buddha of Suburbia 168–169

L'Ouverture, Touissant 24, 151
Lacan, Jacques 56
Lahiri, Jhumpa 132
Lakoff, George 13
Lamming, George 65–66, 86, 157, 167, 170
   In the Castle of My Skin 65–66, 167
   The Pleasures of Exile 86
   Water With Berries 86
Las Casas, Bartolomé de 149
Laurence, Margaret 86
   The Diviners 86
Lawrence, Stephen 165–166
Lawson, Henry 141, 144
Leavis, F.R. 184
Lemke, Cordula 172
Levy, Andrea 169–170, 185
Lewis, Bernard 53
literacy 48–50, 109
Loomba, Ania 180
Lovelace, Earl 154, 157, 182
   The Dragon Can't Dance 154

Macaulay, Thomas B. 56, 122–124
Macpherson, James 43–44
Mahomet, S.D. 129–130, 167
Malcom X 156
Malouf, David 143–144
   Johnno 143
Malthus, Thomas 12
Mandela, Nelson 114
Manichean 52, 54
Manley, Michael 152
map/mapping 25, 54, 72–73, 94–95, 97, 107, 174, 185
Mapanje, Jack 118
Marechera, Dambudzo 89, 118
Margalit, Avishai 39
Markandaya, Kamala 132–133
Marley, Bob 152
maroons 150, 152
Marson, Una 155, 167
Martinique 8, 33, 52
Martyn, Edward 104
Marx, Karl/Marxism 40–41, 54, 59, 177
masks/masking/masquerade 22–23, 26, 51–53, 57, 156, 178, 181
Massai, Sonia 180
Matura, Mustapha 84–85, 156–157
   Play Mas 156
   The Playboy of the West Indies 84, 156
   Trinidad Sisters 85, 156
Matzke, Christine 90, 117
McCall Smith, Alexander 90

Appendix

McGuckian, Medbh 106
McGuiness, Frank 106
McGuiness, Martin 102
metaphor 11–13
migration 7, 31, 64, 73, 94
Milton, John 44
mimicry 56, 57
Mintz, Sidney 163
missionaries 25–26, 35, 70, 110, 112–114, 116, 122, 123–125
Mistry, Rohinton 132
Mo, Timothy 170, 179
  Sour Sweet 179
Mofolo, Thomas 77–78, 116
  Chaka 77, 116
Mohanty, Chandra T. 176–177
Molina, Tirso de 85
Moody, Ronald 165
Morgan, Sally 71–72, 144–145
  My Place 71, 145
mother country 16–17, 134, 136, 162
Mountbatten, Lord 127
Mudrooroo (Colin Johnson) 73, 85, 98, 140, 142–144
  Doctor Woodreddy's Prescription 143
Mugabe, Robert 114
Mühleisen, Susanne 90, 147, 168
Mukasa, Ham 92
Mukherjee, Bharati 132–133
Mukherjee, Meenakshi 130
Müller, Heiner 85
Müller, Max 38
Murray, Les 73, 89, 143–144
  Fredy Neptune 89
Mutiny (Indian) 24, 124–125

Naipaul, V.S. 92, 153–154, 156–158, 167
  A House for Mr Biswas 154
  The Middle Passage 92
  The Mimic Men 158
naming 15, 72, 107, 159
Namjoshi, Suniti 177
Napoleon 39, 77, 151
Narayan, R.K. 130–132
  The Guide 131
nationalism 17, 24, 58, 69, 74, 79, 95, 104, 110, 121, 130, 161, 175
négritude 32–33, 61, 77, 110, 155
Nehru, Jawaharlal 69, 80, 120, 124, 127, 133, 175
Neruda, Pablo 108
New English Literatures 20
Newland, Courttia 170

Ngũgĩ wa Thiong'o 11, 86, 117–118
  A Grain of Wheat 86
Nichols, Grace 170–171
Nigeria 9, 25, 78, 95, 113, 115–116
Nightingale, Florence 167
Nkrumah, Kwame 69, 79, 114
Noonuccal, Oodgeroo (Kath Walker) 73, 143–144
Northern Ireland 99, 101–103
Nowra, Louis 144
Nwankwo, Nkem 86
Nwapa, Flora 117–118
Nyabongo, Akiki 116

O'Brian, Flan 106
O'Casey, Sean 105–106
occidentalism 39
O'Connell, Daniel 101–102
Okara, Gabriel 50, 118
Okri, Ben 118
Ondaatje, Michael 91
  Anil's Ghost 91
O'Neill, Hugh, Earl of Tyrone 76, 100
Ong, Walter J. 49–50
orality 18, 32, 48–50, 109, 115, 140, 154, 178
orientalism 38–40, 64, 109, 120, 125
Orkin, Martin 180
Ortiz, Fernando 154
Ossian 43–44

Paisley, Ian 102
Palestine 55
palimpsest 50, 116
Pan-Africanism 8, 69, 111, 114, 151, 167
Park, You-me 185
Parnell, Charles Stewart 101–104
Parry, Benita 57, 60
Paulin, Tom 107
Pearse, Patrick 101
penal laws 100
performance 27, 105, 155, 172, 177–182
Phillips, Caryl 68, 157, 170
  Cambridge 68
Phillips, Mike 91
pidgin 148
Pinnock, Winsom 170
Pitt, David 165
Plaatje, Sol 42, 115–116
  Mhudi 42, 115–116
place writing 70–73, 82, 168
plantations 7, 17, 21, 68, 89, 100, 111, 146–150, 154, 181–182
Plato 49

postcolonial (definitions and debates)   6–7, 10, 12, 16–20, 24, 36, 38, 42–43, 51, 81–83, 134, 173, 180

Postcolonial Studies (field or discipline)   6–7, 9, 13, 16, 22, 24, 27–28, 31, 34, 38–39, 41–42, 45–46, 51, 55, 58, 61, 81, 93, 97, 167, 173–174, 176, 179, 183, 185

postcolonialism (or post-colonialism)   5–6, 14–15, 44, 65, 98, 134

postmodernism   5, 19, 131, 141

post-structuralism   5, 19, 58

Powell, Enoch   165

Powell, Patricia   156

power   9, 15, 20–27, 29, 35, 41, 51, 57, 62, 92, 159, 174, 176

Pratt, Mary Louise   30, 91

protestant ascendancy   100

psychoanalysis   52, 56, 58

Quint, David   89, 158

racism   34–35, 57, 164–165

Raj   26, 123–125, 127–129

Rajan, Rajeswari Sunder   185

Ralegh, Walter   152, 174

Randhawa, Ravinder   169–170

Ranger, Terence   44, 185

Rao, Raja   42, 121, 130, 132

   Kanthapura   42, 121, 130, 133

Rastafarianism   31, 146, 151, 153

Ray, Satyajit   91

Rea, Stephen   107

Reichl, Susanne   160, 168

Renan, Ernest   58

representation   40, 46, 62, 76, 78, 92

rereading   13

resistance   24–27, 181

rewriting   81–86, 90

rhetoric   23–24, 28, 53, 92, 99, 113

Rhys, Jean   64, 87, 157

   Wide Sargasso Sea   87

Richtarik, Marilynn   107

Richter, Virginia   169

Riemenschneider, Dieter   110–111

Riggio, Mila Cozart   181

Riley, Joan   156–157, 170

Rodo, J. E.   86

romanticism   10–11, 13, 20, 104

Roy, Arundhati   132–134

   The God of Small Things   133

Roy, Rammohan   120, 122

Rushdie, Salman   18, 32, 57, 58, 64, 74, 79–80, 131–133, 165, 169, 175

   Midnight's Children   79–80, 131, 133

The Moor's Last Sigh   131, 175

The Satanic Verses   64, 165

Ruskin, John   127

Sahgal, Nayantara   132–133

Said, Edward W.   38–41, 47, 53–56, 58, 73–74, 76, 108, 142, 174, 177, 186, 187

   Beginnings   41

   Culture and Imperialism   54–55, 73, 186–187

   Orientalism   38–41, 47, 53–54, 76, 142, 174, 177

   Out of Place   55

   The World, the Text, and the Critic   55, 186

Salkey, Andrew   167

Sancho, Ignatius   166–167, 170

Sanskrit   120–122

Saro-Wiwa, Ken   114, 118

Sartre, Jean-Paul   8, 110

sati   60, 125

satyagraha   60, 124, 126

Savery, Henry   140

Schreiner, Olive   70–72

   The Story of an African Farm   70–71

Schülting, Sabine   131, 174

Schulze-Engler, Frank   177

Scotland   43–44, 97–98, 161

Scott, James D.   27

Scott, Lawrence   156–157, 177

Seacole, Mary   167, 170

Sebba, Mark   147, 164

Selvon, Samuel   157, 167–168, 170

   The Lonely Londoners   168

Senghor, Léopold Sédar   8, 32–33, 61, 77, 108, 110

   Ethiopiques   77

Seth, Vikram   131–132

sexuality   22, 34, 172–174

Shaka Zulu   77, 112

Shakespeare, William   44, 76, 83, 85–86, 89, 116, 125, 134, 162, 180, 185

   The Tempest   83, 85–86, 107

Sidhwa, Bapsi   132

Singh, Jyotsna G.   175

Sinn Feín   101, 102, 104

slave narratives   67, 70

slavery/slave trade   7, 18, 31, 42, 62, 78, 111–112, 114–115, 146, 150–152, 163

Smith, Zadie   169–170

sonnet   89

South Africa   70–71, 77, 112, 114–116, 119

Soyinka, Wole   33, 77, 118, 179

   Ogun Abibimañ   77

Spence, Catherine Helen   140

Appendix

Spivak, Gayatri C.   58–61, 87, 125, 176
   A Critique of Postcolonial Reason   60
Spurr, David   23, 53, 91
Stead, Christina   144
Stein, Mark   168, 177
Sterne, Lawrence   167
Stockhammer, Robert   115
Stow, Randolph   144
structuralism   49
subaltern   59–60
subversion   18–19, 57
sugar   62, 89, 149–150, 152, 154, 163
Suleri, Sara   129
Swift, Jonathan   99
Swindells, Julia   66–67
Syal, Meera   170, 182
Sydney, Lord   135
syncretism   35, 138, 153, 180
Synge, John M.   84, 104–106, 116, 131, 175
   The Playboy of the Western World
   84, 104–105, 131

Tagore, Rabindranath   124, 132
Terada, Rei   158
Terdiman, Richard   26
Tharoor, Shashi   131–132
Thatcher, Margret   64, 165
theatre   27, 85, 105, 178–180
theory, role and function of   5, 14–15, 55,
   63–64, 183
third space   30, 35, 54, 74
Tiffin, Helen   16–18, 81, 97, 134–135, 142
Tiolkas, Christon   144
Todorov, Tzvetan   72
Tompkins, Joanne   179–180
Tone, Wolfe   101
Torres-Saillant, Silvio   146
transcultural   30, 117, 154
translation   27–30, 44, 50, 61, 107, 117
transnational   30
travel writing   18, 46–47, 53, 79, 91
Trinh T. Minh-ha   174, 176
Trinidad   8, 156, 181
Trinidad Theatre Workshop   156
Trollope, Anthony   131
Turner Hospital, Jeanette   144
Turner, J. M. W.   169
Tutuola, Amos   50, 116, 118

Union Jack   161, 184
United Irishmen   101
Uys, Pieter-Dirk   177

Valera, Eamon de   102
Venuti, Lawrence   28
Vera, Yvonne   118
Vespucci, Amerigo   152, 174
Victoria, Queen   40, 124–125
Viswanathan, Gauri   122–123, 185

Wagner-Egelhaaf, Martina   65
Walcott, Derek   34, 73, 76, 83–85, 89,
   155–158, 167, 179
   Another Life   155
   Dream on Monkey Mountain   156
   Henri Christophe   76
   The Joker of Seville   85, 156
   Omeros   89, 158
   Pantomime   83, 156
Waldseemüller, Martin   152
Warner, Marina   86
   Indigo   86
Warner, Thomas   149, 152
White, Hayden   75, 80
White, Patrick   139, 141, 144
   Voss   141–142
Wilde, Oscar   99, 106
William III, King   100
Williams, Eric   112, 153
Williams, Henry Sylvester   8
Williamson, David   144
Windrush   61, 152, 162, 164–165, 167
Wolf, Eric   78, 111
Women's Studies   41
Wordsworth, William   10–14, 186
   "The Daffodils"   10–13, 153, 186
world war   10, 13, 115, 126, 138
Wright, Judith   73, 143–144
writing   47–50, 110, 155, 178
writing back   18–20

Yeats, William Butler   73–74, 98, 101,
   104–106, 108, 116, 175

Zabus, Chantal   50, 86, 116
Zephaniah, Benjamin   169–170